STRIKE:

A Firsthand Account of the Largest Operation of the Afghan War

By
Stephen G. Hummel

Disclaimer

This is the story of the 2nd Brigade (STRIKE), 101st Airborne (Air Assault) Division's deployment to Afghanistan in 2010 - 2011 as seen from my perspective. I acknowledge and understand that this account as it is written is not encompassing of all events, daily acts of courage, and stories of STRIKE's deployment. It is, however, derived from my own daily notes as a mentor to the Afghan Army and a planner for the Brigade as well as from the STRIKE Book of Valor. To borrow the words of Ambrose Bierce in *What I Saw of Shiloh*, "This is a simple story of a battle, such as tale as may be told by a Soldier who is no writer to a reader who is no Soldier." The views expressed in this book are my own and do not necessarily reflect those of the 2nd Brigade, the 101st Airborne Division, the United States Army, or the United States Government.

Acknowledgements

To the Soldiers of the STRIKE Brigade, past, present, and future, thank you for your service. Your sacrifice makes the Army, the 101st Airborne Division, and the STRIKE Brigade the best organization in the world. What you do day in and day out makes a difference. As a member of STRIKE, I truly worked with the best and always remember, "I am a STRIKE Soldier! I fight where I am told and win where I fight!"

Thank you to the Army Public Affairs Office and the 101st Airborne Division Public Affairs Office for allowing me to tell this story and your support.

I would also like to thank my friend Darryl Pottorf for the wonderful cover. And to the efforts of Mark Pace and Andrew Corke who brought Darryl's vision to life. I appreciate your time and effort.

To Randy Wayne White, I have always been a fan. Thank you for your encouragement and your support throughout the process. You had your own deadlines but took the time to advise and mentor me. Your timely thoughts and criticisms helped this lefty tremendously.

To Colonels Myron Reineke, Antonio Aguto, George Shaplinkov, and Drew Meyerowich, thank you for your professional mentorship and development over the years. You taught me so much about what it means to be an Officer in the United States Army.

To Colonel Arthur Kandarian, you are a great warrior and leader. Your tireless efforts in Afghanistan are the reason for STRIKE's overall success. You will always be STRIKE 6.

To Command Sergeant Major John White, you were instrumental in teaching me about caring for Soldiers and completing the mission. No one is more professional than you.

To my family, Brian, Kristin, Christian, Maggie, Sydney, and Jordan, thank you for always being there when I was not. I hope this book sheds light on some of my overseas adventures. More specifically, Christian, thank you for your comments and feedback, and to Maggie, thank you for allowing me to borrow your husband, Jon, for advice. And to my mom, Katy, thank you for giving me direction in life.

To my son, Asher, my daughter, Hannah, and my wife, Krissy, thank you most of all for your support while deployed. Krissy, you were the brave soul who bore the brunt of reading my unpolished, freshly written manuscript. Your comments, thoughts, and questions will hopefully let the world know and understand better what the STRIKE Brigade did.

For the brave 65 who made the ultimate sacrifice while serving with the 2nd Brigade (STRIKE), 101st Airborne (Air Assault) Division during Operation Enduring Freedom 10 - 11.

HHC BDE
SSG James P. Hunter

526 BSB
SPC Matthew C. Powell

2 BSTB
SPC Andrew J. Castro
SGT Michael J. Beckerman

1-75 Cavalry
SPC Deangelo B. Snow
SGT Justin A. Officer
SGT Karl A. Campbell
SSG David J. Weigle
SPC David A. Hess
CPL Loren M. Buffalo

1-320 FAR
PFC Brandon M. King
SPC Michael L. Stansbery, Jr.
SGT Kyle B. Stout
SGT Patrick K. Durham
1LT Todd W. Weaver

1-502 Infantry
PFC Benjamin J. Park
PFC David A. Jefferson
SFC John H. Jarrell
SSG Leston M. Winters
SSG Jaime C. Newman
1LT Eric D. Yates
SPC Pedro A. Maldonado
PFC Andrew N. Meari

1-502 Infantry (continued)
SPC Jonathon M. Curtis

2-502 Infantry
SGT Aaron K. Kramer
SSG Adam L. Dickmyer
CPL Brett W. Land
CPL Jacob R. Carver
SSG Jaun L. Rivadeneira
SPC Jacob C. Carroll
SSG Sean M. Flannery
CPL William K. Middleton
CPL Patrick D. Deans
SGT Willie A. McLawhorn, Jr.
CPL Derek E. Simonetta
CPL Kenneth E. Necochea, Jr.
SGT Sean M. Collins
CPL Jorge E. Villacis
CPL Brandon M. Kirton

3/2 SCR
PFC John E. Andrade, Sr.
PFC Paul D. Cuzzupe II
SPC Steven L. Dupont
SPC Joseph T. Prentler
SPC Kelly J. Mixon
SGT James A. Ayube II
PFC Conrado D. Javier, Jr.
1LT Darren M. Hidalgo

2-508 Infantry
SPC Clayton D. McCarrah
SPC Christopher J. Moon
SGT Christopher N. Karch
SSG Brian F. Piercy

4 BSB
SSG Jesse Infante

4 BSB (continued)
SPC Chad D. Clements
SSG Kevin J. Kessler
CPL Timothy L. Johnson

1-66 Armor
CPT Dale A. Goetz
SPC Pedro A. Millet Meletiche IV

1-187 Infantry
SGT Justin E. Culbreth

1BSTB
SPC Gerald R. Jenkins

71 EOD
SSG Matthew J. West

212 MP
SGT Zainah C. Creamer

723 EOD
SPC Joshua T. Lancaster

2 Engineer
CPL Nathan B. Carse

863 Engineer
CPL Justin D. Hoss

AWG
MSG(R) Robert W. Pittman, Jr.

Prologue

I have been at this, and a lot of us have been doing this, nonstop since 2001, and this is one of the most significant combat operation I have seen during that time. That includes the fight to Baghdad, every one of the others, Fallujah, Sadr City, Baqubah, Ramadi, and all the rest of this stuff. This is really impressive.[1]

General David Petraeus,
ISAF Commander
October 7, 2010

I am one of the few. Roughly two million people including active duty and reserve components serve in the United States Military. There are, however, nearly 120 million Americans considered fit for service out of a population of over 325 million. So by my rough calculations that is less than 0.1% of Americans who are currently serving and that number is shrinking under the drawdown and tightening budget.

Being a Soldier, Sailor, Airman, or Marine is not for everyone, and I am proud of what I do and whom I serve. Like all of those who serve I took an oath "to support and defend the constitution of the United States against all enemies; foreign and domestic. And to obey the orders of the President of the United States and the Officers appointed over me."

When I meet people for the first time they are generally shocked to learn that I am in the Army. I don't exactly look the part. I do not resemble anything close to a recruiting poster and my hair is often too long despite regulations telling me otherwise. "Really, you're in the Army?" is often what I hear which is quickly followed by "have you ever deployed?" "Yes," I respond, knowing the next question is, "What was it like?"

This is a difficult question for me. There is no civilian equivalent to a deployment, of course. Moreover to me a deployment is not a single

---

[1] Petraeus, D. (2010, October 7). *Speech to STRIKE Brigade.* Speech delivered at FOB Wilson, Zharay District, Kandahar, Afghanistan.

moment of intense fighting, though those happen; rather it is a montage of events all built around people, whether fellow Soldiers, local nationals, or the enemy. They are good times and bad times. They are laughs with a fellow Soldier, a conversation with a local about governance, and ramp ceremonies loading the dead onto helicopters. These moments are filled with joy, frustration, jokes, and tears. They are moments watching young men and women do extraordinary things in difficult conditions because it is just what needs to be done.

I have served all over the world. I've been stationed in Europe and saw combat in Iraq early in my career. In the summer of 2010, I deployed with the 2nd Infantry Brigade Combat Team from the 101st Airborne (Air Assault) Division, commonly known as the STRIKE Brigade, to Kandahar Province, Afghanistan.

As a surge brigade in Afghanistan, the STRIKE Brigade was charged with clearing the Taliban from the contentious environs around Kandahar City to include the districts of Arghandab, Zharay, Maiwand, and part of Panjwa'i. Prior to deploying to Afghanistan I had never heard of these districts and yet to my ignorance their importance has been noted throughout history. It was here the Pashtun tribes fought against, and later with, Alexander The Great. It was where the Mujahedeen fought the Russians in massive ambushes along Highway One, and it was where Mullah Muhammed Omar and a group of religious students formed what the world now knows as the "Taliban." It is there that in the summer of 2010, the STRIKE Brigade would make its stand against the Taliban. It would be there in the heavily vegetative green zone that we would lose 66 Americans while nearly 600 others were wounded, some multiple times earning multiple Purple Hearts.

Using a combination of heavy-handed military tactics and non-kinetic nation-building skills in what is commonly referred to as counterinsurgency (COIN) operations, the STRIKE Brigade changed the landscape of southern Afghanistan. STRIKE's operations - Economic Corridors, Dragon STRIKE, and Dragon Wrath - cleared the Taliban from their historic home and set conditions for the Government of the Islamic Republic of Afghanistan to not only have a presence but also the ability to communicate and connect with the local population through *shuras*, which is a council of elders, and providing other basic services such as education. Operation Dragon STRIKE is the largest combined operation in Afghanistan to date.

The roughly 3,500 Soldiers that make up the STRIKE Brigade represent America and all walks of life. Soldiers come from red and blue states, trailer homes, mansions, rural countryside, inner cities and sometimes broken homes. Some Soldiers are college graduates, some are doctors, and some barely passed high school. Some Soldiers were born in the United States and some immigrated and became citizens. Together this group sought to make a difference in a place 7,000 miles from home.

STRIKE accomplished what had previously never been achieved against the Taliban. Together, those 3,500 Americans orchestrated, launched, and led through a million moving parts, the largest combined operation in Afghanistan to date. Joined by nearly 8,000 Soldiers, Airmen, Marines, and Afghan Army partners, this coalition worked in concert to destroy the enemy in the very place where they began. The Soldiers of STRIKE cleared the Taliban from their strongholds in southern Afghanistan and then showed the local population what an alternative to the Taliban could be. Working to support the government of Afghanistan, we helped deliver governance and economic growth to a part of Afghanistan that had known nothing but the Taliban since the collapse of the Soviet Union. It was, in a word, a success.

During a visit to Forward Operating Base Wilson on October 7, 2010, to recognize the heroic actions of many STRIKE Soldiers, the Commander of the International Security and Assistance Force (ISAF), General David Petraeus, gave a short speech lauding our achievements. His words put perspective to the day-to-day actions of our brigade. It was standing there during that speech that I realized the scope of what the STRIKE Brigade had not only sought to achieve but was achieving. We were still in the fight and the Taliban had not surrendered, but we were on the verge of breaking their backs in their historic home. If the Taliban ever had some something worth fighting for, it would be their home, the place where they remained undefeated.

For its actions, the STRIKE Brigade would later be awarded both a Valorous Unit Citation and a Presidential Unit Citation, the highest honor an American unit can receive. Most importantly, by the time that the STRIKE Brigade left Afghanistan for Fort Campbell, Kentucky, we left southern Afghanistan a better place than we found it.

This is the story of STRIKE in Afghanistan told from my perspective. It is the only one I know. During the deployment, I was the Assistant Planner for the STRIKE Brigade and the lead mentor to our Afghan Army partners. Nearly everyday, I traversed the battlefield and saw, met, and worked with many of the STRIKE heroes directly. I hope that the reader may gain here an appreciation for the hardships and the losses that all endured and the individuals who in horrific and devastating times rose to the threat and defeated the enemy, sometimes making the ultimate sacrifice for their comrades and their nation. I also hope that readers can gain a perspective of how the STRIKE Brigade operated and conducted counterinsurgency operations at all levels. The STRIKE Brigade fought hard and left Kandahar and Afghanistan with a chance for rebuilding.

28 Articles of Counterinsurgency[2]

These articles were instrumental in how I thought, planned, and provided guidance for the execution of complex operations as well as guided many on the Brigade staff through our partnered work with the Afghan army, police, and government.

1. Know your turf.
2. Diagnose the problem.
3. Organize for intelligence.
4. Organize for inter-agency operations.
5. Travel light and harden your CSS.
6. Find a political/cultural advisor.
7. Train the squad leaders – then trust them.
8. Rank is nothing; talent is everything.
9. Have a game plan.
10. Be there.
11. Avoid knee jerk responses to first impressions.
12. Prepare to handover from Day One.
13. Build trusted networks.
14. Start easy.
15. Seek early victories.
16. Practice deterrent patrolling.
17. Be prepared for setbacks.
18. Remember the global audience.
19. Engage the women, beware of the children.
20. Take stock regularly.
21. Exploit a "single narrative."
22. Local forces should mirror the enemy, not ourselves.
23. Practice armed civil affairs.
24. Small is beautiful.
25. Fight the enemy's strategy; not his forces.

---

[2] Kilcullen, D. (2006, March). Twenty-Eight Articles: Fundamentals of Company-level Counterinsurgency. *Small Wars Journal*. Edition 1.

26. Build your own solution; only attack the enemy when he gets in the way.
27. Keep your extraction plan secret.
28. Whatever else you do, keep the initiative.

Speech by General David Petraeus, ISAF Commander, to the Soldiers of STRIKE on October 7, 2010, at Forward Operating Base Wilson in Central Zharay District, Kandahar, Afghanistan:[3]

"It is extremely important what you are doing together with our Afghan partners, and it is an honor to have the Afghan Brigade Commander as well as the STRIKE Brigade Commander here. What you are doing is historic; it is extraordinary. There are some folks back there [the United States], every now and then, that say that our Army doesn't know how to fight anymore because Petraeus has us doing nation building or something like that, and I would love for them all to come out here and see how you have used combined arms against a very resilient enemy, who is adaptive and smart, who owns and knows the terrain, and is determined to hang onto it, until confronted with the kind of power you represent.

What you have done again is absolutely extraordinary. You don't realize it because you are living it. Even with all the adventure, excitement, the moments of fear, as well as the moments of everything else, it is still a 'Groundhog Day' experience.

You have forgotten how much that the eyes of the world are on you. Kandahar is enormously important to this effort. Now, the truth is we have not yet unveiled it to the press. We truly want to under-promise and over-deliver. We are not out to beat our chests in advance of anything, but as this continues and as you close in on the final areas in the Horn of Panjwa'i, and as you establish the hold force, we have got to get them [the press] in here to understand what you have done, the skill with which you have done it,

---

[3] Petraeus, D. (2010, October 7). *Speech to STRIKE Brigade.* Speech delivered at FOB Wilson, Zharay District, Kandahar, Afghanistan.

the valor that has been demonstrated along the way, and the tremendous leadership by our commissioned, warrant, and non-commissioned Officers.

Now, there is another reason I am very pleased to recognize some individuals here. That is because I don't think we have done it adequately. This has not to do with the whole deal with how many Medals of Honor are coming out of Iraq and Afghanistan. This is about day-to-day valor that is extraordinary, and yet we have gotten used to it...

You don't realize the significance of this and, again, what it is you are doing and how courageous this stuff is, and you are taking this for granted. Look, I have been at this, and a lot of us have been doing this, nonstop since 2001, and this is one of the most significant combat operation I have seen during that time. That includes the fight to Baghdad, every one of the others, Fallujah, Sadr City, Baqubah, Ramadi, and all the rest of this stuff. This is really impressive.

What is most impressive, as we have had some tough, tough losses, is they have not been frankly what a lot of feared they would be because of the skill and the will of all of you and the way you have brought together combined arms. We got Brits out here with Pythons, we got Marines helping with dogs, and obviously all of our Afghan, Canadian, and British partners. And, so again what I want to stress to you is the significance of this endeavor, how important it is, why I have directed a historian team to come out here, and why I want to do more of this [awarding medals]. I want to make sure the bureaucracy doesn't keep us from recognizing those who have demonstrated valor on the battlefield.

There is no medal that any of you who have a V on a medal who will ever think more of than that one. You can have a chest full of stuff, but I will tell you it is the one that has the V on it, that is the one that will make you the most proud. And, again, today it is a privilege to pin those on some of these heroes and recognize others who have shed blood in the service of our Nation."

Chapter 1
The Road to Nowhere that Leads to War

Experience and Skill in the various particulars is thought to be a species of Courage: whence Socrates also thought Courage was Knowledge.

Aristotle,
Nicomachean Ethics

The opening salvo was ferocious and appeared out of nowhere. Rocket-propelled grenades (RPGs) screamed out of the green zone and slammed into the sides of the mine resistant armored vehicles. The RPGs disabled two vehicles preventing the convoy from pushing through the kill zone. An RPG pierced the armor and entered the vehicle's cabin, exploding under the seat of Command Sergeant Major (CSM) Alonzo Smith, the senior enlisted Soldier in the 2nd Brigade "STRIKE," 101st Airborne Division. The explosion shredded his lower legs and left him withering in pain.

The Soldiers in the convoy had had a long day. They were sweaty and exhausted from maintaining their vigilance in the June heat and humidity of southern Afghanistan. This fatigue instantly vanished as the rounds from Taliban's AK-47s zipped past them. Reacting to contact is drilled into every Soldier, and these Soldiers were professionals despite being in country for only a couple of weeks. The RPGs had sent shrapnel into the legs of Specialist Stephen Hochstetler as well as giving him a concussion. Applying tourniquets to his legs to stanch the bleeding, SPC Hochstetler remounted his vehicle's turret to get into the fight and provide suppressive fire on the enemy south of Highway One.

Suddenly emerging from the thick vegetation a Taliban fighter raced toward the disabled convoy. The Soldiers on the convoy quickly took notice and engaged the fighter with their M-4 rifles and the vehicle-mounted automatic weapons. The fighter unbeknownst to the American Soldiers had been wearing a suicide vest and their gunfire caused him to explode safely away from the Soldiers on the ground.

Once able, Private First Class (PFC) Andrew Maxwell raced over 50 meters across open terrain, exposing himself to Taliban fire in order to treat the wounded Soldiers including CSM Smith, Lieutenant Colonel (LTC) Johnny Davis, and CSM Brandon Haywood, who together were the command team for the 1st Battalion, 502nd Infantry Regiment. PFC Maxwell remained with the wounded Soldiers and the STRIKE leaders, shielding their bodies with his own from sporadic fire, until all were loaded onto a medical evacuation helicopter that transported them to the hospital at Kandahar Airfield.

The fire quickly died out and the Taliban retreated into the canals and lush vegetation from which they had so suddenly emerged. The Soldiers took stock of the situation and awaited a quick reaction force to assist with the recovery efforts of the disabled vehicles. Both SPC Hochstetler and PFC Maxwell received the Army Commendation Medal with Valor for their actions along Highway One; additionally a total of eight Soldiers earned the Purple Heart for wounds sustained during the attack, including SPC Hochstetler.

Both the Taliban and the STRIKE Brigade had been very lucky that day. It is not likely that the Taliban knew a contingent of the Brigade's leadership was in the vehicles, but virtually like all attacks along Highway One, it had served its purpose. The brigade lost a leader in CSM Smith who was evacuated from southern Afghanistan to Lundstuhl Regional Medical Center in Germany and ultimately to Walter Reed Medical Center for several surgeries and months of physical therapy. The Taliban also demonstrated to the locals that they still controlled Highway One, the lifeline for the people in Arghandab, Zharay, and Maiwand districts in Kandahar Provence.

Highway One is certainly not the autobahn of Germany nor is it like the multilane highways connecting cities and towns across the United States. It is essentially a two-lane rural road, roughly 2,200 kilometers in length. (By comparison Interstate 95 along the eastern United States is nearly 3,100 kilometers in length.) It forms a ring connecting the major cities in Afghanistan: Kabul, Ghazni, Kandahar, and Herat. The highway is often referred to locally as the 'ring route' but is in reality a road to nowhere.

In a 2007 *New York Times* article C.J. Chivers described the route between Kabul and Kandahar as a "vehicle graveyard." The route "lies atop an ancient trade route that, in theory, could connect Central Asia and Afghanistan with ports in Pakistan, restoring Afghanistan's place as a transit hub for something besides heroin."[4] In 2003, the United Nations published an estimate that only 10 kilometers of the Afghan Highway was paved. The United States and Saudi Arabia subsequently funded a $250 million paving project.[5] Today, the road is completely paved with the exception of sections that have been decimated by roadside bombs.

In southern Afghanistan, the highway abuts the green zone to the south. The small green strip of land is fed from the Arghandab River, whose water provides life to the locals through a convoluted maze of overgrown irrigation canals to small farms and plots of land to grow grapes, pomegranates, and hashish, which is the real cash crop. The Highway, on the other hand, is their means of travel and commerce.

Forward Operating Base (FOB) Wilson is positioned in central Zharay reportedly near the spot where Mullah Omar led the first Taliban attack in 1996. Following the Soviet Union's withdrawal, local warlords emerged and controlled parts of the country. It is reported that Mullah Omar led a group of Afghans against the local warlords checkpoint on Highway One and strung their dead bodies from barrels of nearby tanks abandoned by the Soviet Union.

At the time of Mullah Omar's rise to power, Zharay did not exist. Prior to 2006, the district that is now Zharay had been part of Panjwa'i District. The small base sits on the north side of Highway One, encapsulates the small district center, and faces south toward the thick green zone.

Forward Operating Base Wilson would be STRIKE Brigade's home throughout its 2010-2011 deployment. Its most notable feature was not its plethora of amenities but rather its sparseness. FOB Wilson was not like the super-FOBs of Iraq, where Soldiers were photographed sipping Starbucks coffee and eating Burger King, much to the chagrin of the American taxpayer. A few weeks prior to our arrival, FOB Wilson held

---

[4] Chivers, C.J. (2007, December 3). Danger rules lawless Highway 1 in Afghanistan. *The New York Times*. Retrieved from http://www.nytimes.com
[5] United Nations. (2003, December). *Asian Highway Handbook*. United Nations Report. Retrieved from http://www.unescap.org/resources/asian-highway-handbook

barely a single company of Canadian Soldiers. After late May 2010, however, it rapidly became our home. We could not successfully wage a counterinsurgency campaign from the confines of Kandahar Airfield. Our Brigade Commander, Colonel Arthur Kandarian, had sent a request to International Security Assistance Force (ISAF) that our Brigade live in Zharay with the people. FOB Wilson was the ideal place to house the brigade. It was centrally located in our area of operations, abutting the district center and along Highway One.

I first saw FOB Wilson for myself in mid-June 2010. My journey began at KAF where I stared out into the darkness at the helicopter landing zone at Kandahar Airfield, listening and collecting my thoughts. I could hear the distant cacophony of combat: the screaming jet engines on the nearby runway, large armored vehicles lumbering on potholed roads, Soldiers talking and sharing stories. I strained to pick through the sounds, waiting to hear the telltale *whomp, whomp, whomp* of the large CH-47 Chinook helicopter that would carry me and my fellow Soldiers to our new home. We were loaded down with all we could carry and all that we would own for the next year. We carried assault packs, duffle bags, large rucksacks, weapons, radios, laptops, and pretty much anything else that could fit onto the bird.

The heat and humidity of the June night was overwhelming. I dripped with sweat. My uniform hung on me like a wet rag, absorbing the dust that whipped through the air. My feet swished with each step as my green issue wool socks tried to wick the sweat off my feet.

After what seemed like an eternity of waiting and sweating in the starless night, the time near one in the morning, I finally heard the familiar *whomp, whomp, whomp* growing louder.

Reaching down I grabbed my advanced combat helmet placed it on my head, adjusted the retention system and prepared for whatever destiny that lay ahead. I wondered briefly if I would survive the next year, the next month, the next week, or even the next day. Through the heat dual rotator wash and the smell of high-octane aviation fuel we moved with a sense of purpose. Deliberately and swiftly we loaded gear, personnel, and then more gear as the Soldiers began taking their seats, packing in a tightly as possible.

As one of the last Soldiers on the bird, I managed a seat near the gunner on the rear ramp. As we sped northwest away from Kandahar Airfield, commonly referred to as KAF, I stared across the ramp and into the opaque void that was southern Afghanistan. I thought about the journey that brought America to this place, this isolated country, thousands of miles away. My fellow Soldiers and I were the tip of the spear in the surge to regain control in Afghanistan and to finally defeat the Taliban. In a way, it was a fight nine years in the making.

That fateful Tuesday morning in September 2001 had changed everything. Just as an earlier generation had learned suddenly about the empire of the rising sun in December 1941, Americans, in a violent instant, learned about a new enemy, one steeped not on nationalism but in a religious fundamentalism. It was an empire built of young men who did not heed the call to support their nation but the transnational call of jihad.

September 11, 2001, changed the United States' assumptions. The concept of terrorism was no longer some distant notion. Terrorism was no longer a paltry threat made by bearded men in faraway caves. It had reached America's soil. Few Americans had any concept of jihad. Americans, for generations, had resided peacefully in the belief that such horrors could not happen here.

Seemingly overnight, heroes were no longer just the athlete who hit brilliant home runs or scored game-winning touchdowns. Heroes took the form of New York City police Officers, firemen, paramedics, and Soldiers, the men and women who selflessly raced against the crowd into the burning World Trade Center towers to rescue the injured.

Heroes were men like Rick Rescorla, who had served brilliantly in Vietnam, notably under LTC Hal Moore in the Ia Drang Valley, which earned him the Silver Star. It is Rick Rescorla's image immortalized on the cover of *We Were Soldiers, Once...and Young*. In his final act, Rescorla evacuated nearly 2,700 workers at the World Trade Center.

Heroes were those like Todd Beamer whose unforgettable "let's roll" command rallied a group of utterly selfless passengers to retake control of Flight 93 from the terrorists and relinquish it to a Pennsylvania farm field.

That morning changed America's perception of itself and of the world. Afghanistan was no longer the Soviet Union's folly or the distant land that had vanquished over the British Empire in the 1800s. It instantly became the world's epicenter. Americans pondered the poor, war-torn, land-locked country surrounded by such dubious partners as Pakistan, Iran, and former Soviet states. Was this country hiding

Osama bin Laden? And who were the Taliban that protected him? Americans watched the twenty-four hour news cycle of coverage from Afghanistan. Citizens such as myself watched in awe as CIA operatives and Army Special Forces teams worked with the North Alliance. In a matter of weeks these units, along with Air Force support, toppled the Taliban government and its army.

Afghanistan was not destined to remain the world's and America's focus for long, however. New words emerged: weapons of mass destruction, Anthrax, poison gas, Iraq, Saddam Hussein. Victory, it was presumed, had been achieved in Afghanistan with the initial defeat of the Taliban and with al-Qaeda fleeing into the Pakistani tribal regions.

In spite of the general global consensus that the Taliban's withdrawal from Afghanistan equated to its defeat, the Taliban were busy reorganizing and regrouping. Afghanistan was their birthplace and home. Their retreat from it would only be temporary. In the isolated southern village of Sangsar in the then-district of Panjwa'i in 1994, fed-up farmers had met with their religious leader and fellow former Mujahideen fighter, Mullah Mohammed Omar, to demand justice for their children. The children, they explained, had been raped by the local warlord's fighters who ran the checkpoints along Highway One. It was in the Sangsar mosque that the Taliban movement was born and Mullah Omar became its leader.

Notwithstanding the rapid fall of the Taliban in October 2001, the Taliban were not defeated. They had merely left the battlefield temporarily for Pakistan. The misconception of victory that followed allowed America to turn its attention elsewhere.

By 2003, America was suddenly split between two wars: the quest for weapons of mass destruction in Iraq and the forgotten war in Afghanistan. The heroes who signed up to serve after September 11th were now met with questions of why they wanted to fight in the Iraq quagmire. As the world argued about just and unjust wars, Soldiers were dying. Technology and techniques were transferred from one battlefield to another. The Taliban learned how to build and implant the devastating improvised explosive devices (IEDs) that were crippling coalition units in Iraq. America's sons and daughters were dying in droves and a solution against the enemy was found in the resurrection of an old concept: counterinsurgency.

With the bloodshed growing in both Iraq and Afghanistan changes were needed to tilt the scales back in favor of the coalition's units. Iraq was the first to undergo a "surge" of troops in the summer of 2007 and to employ the concepts of counterinsurgency (COIN). The growth in governance and economic development was the result of the increased security, which was deemed achievable only through the presence of additional troops and through increased interaction with the people. As stability took hold in Iraq and the Iraqi government improved its capability to protect its people, the world's attention once again returned to "the forgotten war."

Stories of heroic action and valor against a numerically superior enemy by such men as Staff Sergeant Jared Monti, Staff Sergeant Sal Giunta, Sergeant Dakota Meyer, Staff Sergeant Robert Miller, Lieutenant Michael Murphy, Staff Sergeant Leroy Petry, and Staff Sergeant Clinton Romesha helped turn the American public's attention on the war in Afghanistan. All of these men received the Medal of Honor for their actions but they were not and are not alone in their heroism.

In the summer of 2010 it was Afghanistan's turn for a coalition surge. A final push of troops and political support would mean a conclusive defeat of the Taliban and a real chance for the government of Afghanistan to govern its own people.

The first units selected for the surge by President Barack Obama were those from the 101st Airborne Division, and unlike the other Brigade Combat Teams within the Division that were going to the mountains of eastern Afghanistan, my Brigade, 2nd Brigade, was destined for the south. We were to clear, hold, and build in the highly contested districts west and north of Kandahar City, including the Taliban's hometown.

The 2nd Brigade, 101st Airborne Division, commonly referred to as the "STRIKE" Brigade, is the 502nd Parachute Infantry Regiment, and has a long history of heroes and leaders since its formation during World War II. The Soldiers of the STRIKE Brigade are immortalized in the picture of General Dwight D. Eisenhower talking to First Lieutenant Wallace Strobel and the men of Company E with the distinctive hearts emblazoned on their helmets prior to the jump into Normandy, France, in 1944. It was Lieutenant Colonel Robert Cole who, while leading the 3rd Battalion, 502nd Infantry Regiment during the invasion that would earn the Division's first Medal of Honor, lead a charge through open terrain to take out German artillery that was massacring Soldiers coming ashore on the beaches. The Brigade fought through World War II, Vietnam, the first Gulf War, and Operation Iraqi Freedom. The Brigade had been led by great military leaders along the way including Colin Powell, who later served as the Chairman of the Joint Chiefs of Staff and Secretary of State. The Brigade has earned four Presidential Unit Citations and four Valorous Unit Citations.

Afghanistan would prove very different than STRIKE's previous fights, however. The Taliban were not the anti-Iraqi fighters that the STRIKE Brigade had fought. The STRIKE Brigade had orders to fight in the heart of the Taliban's base and not only purge the enemy from it but prevent them from returning. Previous units, such as 5th Brigade, 2nd Infantry Division as well as the Canadian Army, had tried over the previous decade to do as much but had failed. The success of the surge and of the war in Afghanistan as a whole hinged on our success. Opportunities for success in Afghanistan were limited. Failure was not an option.

As the CH-47 Chinook banked hard and rapidly descended onto the open gravel-laden field that was FOB Wilson's helicopter landing zone, I caught a quick glimpse of my new home. Through the opaque shadows created by the moon and sporadic lights dimly flickering on the black-out operating base, I could see a few tents and port-a-potties lining the barriers. The potent mixture of fear, adrenaline, and anticipation at being on the tip of the spear of the surge in Afghanistan was all consuming. Knowing that we would be wheels down in a matter of seconds, we gripped our gear a little tighter and prepared ourselves, like runners waiting for the sound of the starting pistol, in order to get off and unload the bird as rapidly as possible.

The walls of Wilson, a previous company-sized outpost, had been expanded to support our brigade and our mission. This expansion provided us with a landing zone roughly the size of four football fields and a small landing strip to launch and recover unmanned aerial vehicles. HESCO barriers for the expanded outpost were being filled by Soldiers in armored bucket loaders, the Navy sent a detachment of engineers, commonly known as SeaBees, were constructing a few hard standing structures including the tactical operations center (TOC).

Ultimately FOB Wilson would house our Brigade Headquarters and parts of four of our subordinate Battalions as well as our Afghan Army Partners from the 3rd Brigade, 205th Corps ANA.

STRIKE's immersion into the green zone forced us to learn how the Taliban operated and how they used the green zone as cover to launch attacks against coalition forces, Afghan security forces, and the local population that used Highway One. We were far from the first unit to have learned this deadly lesson. Previous ISAF units as well as the Soviet Union during the 1980s in the Soviet-Afghan War had also learned the dangers of Highway One in southern Afghanistan with the abutting green zone. Mujahideen commander Mulla Malang described the ambushes along Highway One in Vignette 11 of *The Other Side of the Mountain: Mujahideen Tactics in the Soviet-Afghan War*:

> "We planned to position several interconnected ambushes, manned by small groups of Mujahideen, to surprise and take the entire length of the column under simultaneous fire. This required selection of a favorable stretch of the road that could accommodate all the ambushes required to attack the entire column. We selected a stretch of nearly seven kilometers between a point at the end of Sanjari (the beginning of Ashoqa villages) and a point immediately to the east of Pashmol as the killing zone for the enemy column ...
> At that time, most of the local population still lived in their homes along the road. Few had migrated to Pakistan since no major Soviet military actions had taken place there. The Mujahideen groups coming from Malajat and other neighboring bases moved during the night to their designated ambush sites."[6]

The most important aspect of an effective insurgency is the will of the people to support your agenda. Whether in Afghanistan or anywhere else in the world, the insurgent needs the support of the local

---

[6] Jalali, A. A., & Grau, L. (1995). *The Other Side of the Mountain: Mujahideen Tactics in the Soviet-Afghan War*. Military Bookshop, page 44.

population for both his own survival and the survival of his cause. Support gained with a weapon is short-lived and can quickly alienate the people. The support must also come to either the insurgent or counterinsurgent because they offer a better alternative. If the Mujahideen had not had the support of the locals who lived along the road the locals could have easily informed the Soviets of the Mujahideen's plans.

As STRIKE continued to settle into FOB Wilson and the surround outposts, the attacks along the road continued. We quickly realized that if a heavily armored ISAF convoy could not move freely along Highway One, how could we expect the Afghan population to? Colonel Arthur Kandarian, the STRIKE Brigade's Commander, was told by Zharay's district governor, Karim Jan, that Mullah Omar, the founder of the Taliban, was able to come to power because he secured Highway One and in turn provided security to the local population. The locals traveled to and along Highway One for the bazaars to buy and sell goods. This point of security along Highway One was further explained in the foreword to *My Life with the Taliban* by Felix Kuehn and Alex van Linschoten:

> "The major difference between Kandahar in 2009 and early 1994: in 1994 you knew – at least to some extent – where the danger was coming from. In 2009, hazards can emerge and disappear out of nowhere without explanation. Assassinations, beheadings, suicide bombers, IED attacks, aerial bombing, large scale infantry attacks, or just crime-with-a-gun remain actual and present threats to ordinary residents of Kandahar province ... Insecurity on the road has made it increasingly difficult to find drivers willing to transport goods the 136 kilometers to Lashkar Gah. One construction company owner said that shifting materials from Kandahar City to Lashkar Gah costs him several times more than getting the same material from Lahore to Kandahar."[7]

---

[7] Zaeef, A. S. (2010). *My Life With The Taliban*. Hurst Publishing. Page xi.

When we analyzed the movement of people, we saw they did indeed come to the road for economic purposes. The approximately 40,000 residents were scattered across an area the size of Rhode Island, the biggest population in our area of operation being the village of Sanjaray, which is situated at a crossroads. The village sits along Highway One at the shared edge of both Arghandab and Zharay districts next to the bridge that crosses the Arghandab River into Kandahar City. The rest of the population was scattered in tiny villages south of Highway One while Combined Task Force STRIKE sat within three outposts along Highway One and a few smaller ones that were a few hundred meters further south. If the district was viewed as a human body, then the highway was its main artery and the people its blood, which was under constant attack by the parasitic Taliban.

In my first few weeks in Afghanistan I came to understand a few truths about the area. Chief among them that Afghanistan was not Iraq in terms of people, terrain, or enemy. To say because a strategy or tactic worked in Iraq it would translate to success in Afghanistan was a misconception. Both countries had or were engulfed in an insurgency but not all insurgencies are built the same. In fact, there are significant differences even within a country due to the difference in people and terrain.

In Afghanistan the insurgency we faced in the south was different from the one fighting in the mountains of eastern Afghanistan. What was universal, however, throughout the Afghan insurgency was we were fighting the Taliban in their homeland, which they would not give up easily, and on a terrain that favored them greatly.

Counterinsurgency operations by doctrine are about securing the people but the environs surrounding Kandahar City were not sprawling cities or suburbs. Clear, hold, and build are the common terms military personnel use when discussing, planning, or conducting COIN, but their application takes on an entirely different meaning in this environment. The concepts are fairly simple: clear an area of insurgents, hold the area to prevent the insurgents from returning, and ultimately build the local security forces and government to keep the insurgents out. Counterinsurgency focuses on the population because it is the currency of any insurgency. Thus the key, we determined, to securing the people was securing Highway One.

Protecting the people on Highway One would mean not driving our bulky military vehicles along the small two lane road 24 hours a day. In fact we, as coalition forces, sought to be off the actual highway as much as possible. Yes, we needed Highway One but so did the people. As such, our large convoys traveled late at night and patrols were instructed to use restraint whenever on the highway. We realized that every time we forced a cart of the road, cut off an Afghan car, or caused an accident, we drove a wedge deeper between ourselves and the people. Their resentment toward us could and at times did push local support towards the Taliban.

Most importantly, we needed to take the fight to the Taliban, away from the population along Highway One.

Prior to our arrival in Afghanistan, the headquarters at Regional Command South had also recognized the significance of Highway One and charged the 5th Brigade, 2nd Infantry Division, from Joint Base Lewis-McCord in Washington, with securing Highway One from Lashkar Gah to Spin Boldak in the Zabul Provence, east of Kandahar along the Pakistan border. This brigade operates with the Stryker Combat Vehicle to move its Soldiers around the battlefield.

The 5th Brigade and its commander, Colonel Harry Tunnell, did not, however, see securing the population along Highway One as a counterinsurgency operation. In fact, Colonel Tunnell instructed his subordinate units to follow the Army's counter-guerilla manual, which focuses on using small unit tactics/guerrilla tactics such as small team ambushes to counter the guerrillas or in this case the Taliban's movement. The main difference between COIN and counter-guerrilla tactics is the role of the people.

The concepts of COIN, which had been drilled into leaders and Soldiers at all levels in recent years, focuses on the population and ensuring that leaders at all levels understand that any negative actions have lasting consequences in the hearts and minds of the locals.

The paradox of counterinsurgency as highlighted in the success in Iraq is the more exposed a unit becomes by interacting and living with the people, the more secure they become.

Living among the people builds a mutual trust and hopefully an allegiance. The people see the threat from the Taliban against both coalition forces and themselves as equal. Hiding behind walls, in compounds, and in huge, several-ton armored vehicles does little to develop a bond.

Security on Highway One required the trust of the people but when we arrived this trust did not exist. The trust the previous unit had gained early in their deployment was lost through the detrimental acts of some individual Soldiers, including those in the infamous "Kill Squad." These few Soldiers murdered innocent civilians, mutilated their bodies, and ultimately marred the reputation of 5th Brigade, pushing the support of the population to the Taliban.

The concept of COIN and protecting the people along Highway One never had traction within the 5th Brigade, 2nd Infantry Division as their Brigade Commander did not believe in the mission. In August 2010, Colonel Harry Tunnell sent a letter to the Secretary of the Army stating as much:

> "COIN has become such a restrictive dogma that it cannot be questioned; any professional discussion about its strengths and weaknesses is discouraged. It has reached such a crisis that those who employ other Army doctrinal concepts do so at their own professional peril because they will be subject to censure for not adhering to COIN … The population-centric approach which places the population as the center of gravity is applied to the point of absurdity. The enemy is entrenching himself among the civilian population as we cede to him territory and lines of communication."[8]

COIN focuses on the population and provides guidelines and a foundation of what could be done. The manual provides historical examples of both successes and failures, highlighting the intrinsic necessity for adaptation. But a unit cannot apply the concepts of COIN if it does not understand the local environment. Particularly in STRIKE's area of operation, the people did not necessarily live along

---

[8] Tunnell, H. (2010, August 20). *Open Door Policy – Report from a Tactical Commander*. Letter to Secretary of the Army.

Highway One; rather they used the highway to travel and transport goods to market. No COIN scenario is the same and what works in one place may not work in another as the people, terrain, tribal influences, and society in general are different.

We as a Brigade were learning some hard lessons and making difficult choices in the first few weeks upon arriving in Zharay. We needed to devise our own plan for success. It is always easy to avoid casualties if you sit on a protected base all day and don't interact with the people, but to be successful not only in Afghanistan but in any counterinsurgency operation you must to step outside the wire.

In contrast to Colonel Tunnell's pro-counter-guerrilla belief, David Galula, a former French military Officer and influential military scholar renowned for his theory and practice of counterinsurgency, highlights that,

> "Insurgency warfare is specifically designed to allow the camp afflicted with congenital weakness to acquire strength progressively while fighting. The counterinsurgent is endowed with congenital strength; for him to adopt the insurgent's warfare would be the same as for a giant to try to fit into a dwarf's clothing. How, against whom, for instance, could he use his enemy's tactics? He alone offers targets for guerrilla operations. Were he to operate as a guerrilla, he would have to have the effective support of the population guaranteed by his own political organization among the masses; if so, then the insurgent would not have and consequently could not co-exist; there would be no need for the counterinsurgent's guerrilla operations."[9]

David Galula emphasizes the critical role of the population. Anyone can operate with counter-guerrilla tactics, but it is such tactics that alienate the people. The counterinsurgent, on the other hand, operates

---

[9] Gaula, D. (2006, August). *Counterinsurgency Warfare: Theory and Practice.* Praeger Publishing. Page 51.

with the support of the people by building a relationship with the local population, wrestling momentum away from the insurgent.

As an infantry brigade in the 101st Airborne Division we knew we were easily one of the most lethal units in the world. We were capable of out shooting and outmaneuvering any force. We were capable of traversing the battlefield and air assaulting objectives while massing intense artillery and air support but for what? We could undoubtedly kill and destroy all that stood in our way, but this would have instantly alienated the population. So we choose a different route.

We chose to understand the people and to attempt to provide them with what they needed, not what we thought they needed. At times we were lethal, conducting the largest combined military operation of the war, and at other times, we spent days talking and drinking chia with mullahs and village elders. We sought that most delicate balance of lethal actions and nation-building.

We chose to remove the wedge between ourselves and the people. We sought to highlight the differences between living under Taliban rule and living under the government of Afghanistan. For the remainder of the deployment we devised new ways to secure the people and drive the Taliban out of Zharay while assisting the local government in connecting with the people, bringing sustainable economic growth, and developing our Afghan security force partners. Everything we sought to do was with the intention of handing the district over so we would never have to come back.

Chapter 2
Descent into History

Sometimes you have to be really high to see how small you really are.

Felix Baumgartner,
Seconds before skydiving from 124,000 feet

There is no Hindu Kush in Zharay. There is no pass that travelers have used over the centuries. There are no looming mountain peaks that reach through the clouds and into the heavens. In fact, both Zharay and Maiwand districts are remarkably flat. With their proximity to the Arghandab River, their fertile soil, and their overall flatness, the districts are a breadbasket for Afghanistan. But it was the maze of canals, lack of roads through the fields, and lush dense vegetation that hindered ISAF's ability to clear the Taliban. Highway One and the Arghandab River to the south are perhaps the only pieces of key terrain in the area, other than Ghundy Ghar.

Most of Maiwand and Zharay are endlessly flat, easily making Ghundy Ghar, at 900 feet, the region's highest point. In an area remarkably void of strategic terrain, however, the elevation (*ghar*, in Pasthu, means "mountain") was a veritable giant. It is rumored to have been built by Alexander the Great's soldiers so that they could watch over the local tribes.

I had seen Ghundy Ghar for months before I finally had an opportunity to climb it. We had a tiny outpost at its top that was initially manned by STRIKE Soldiers until we had trained our Afghan partners enough and they were comfortable supporting themselves on the peak outpost.

Body armor, weapons, ammunition, and water were just a few of the things we carried on daily patrols, which is difficult enough when walking through the flat fields of Zharay in the heat and humidity of the summer. Making the steep climb up the dusty road on Ghundy Ghar, the gear felt like an 800-pound gorilla on our backs.

Despite fatigue from climbing, you couldn't help but feel connected to the history and legacy of Afghanistan when you stood at the top. For better or worse the Brigade's presence would be known for decades to come. We had scarred the terrain through daily firefights, indirect fire, and the destruction of homes and compounds that the Taliban had used to make IEDs. Being atop Ghundy Ghar revealed a more distant history. When I shuffled my feet even slightly, I turned up parts of ancient earthen works.

Around 330 B.C., Alexander the Great began his quest to expand his empire starting his 22,000-mile, 13-year trek east from Mesopotamia through the Hindu Kush to India. It took Alexander and his army only six months to conquer Persia (present-day Iran) but a full three years to subjugate Afghanistan. His difficulties were due to fierce tribal resistance. Even then, the people of Afghanistan believed in a hierarchy of allegiance, with family and tribe at its pinnacle. Even then, it was evident that the people of Afghanistan would not roll over in the face of foreign aggression.

Alexander eventually managed to capture what is now Kandahar, Herat, and Kabul. Prior to his expansion into India, Alexander met the daughter of a local tribal chief whom he married. It was only through this familial relationship with the tribes of Afghanistan that he was able to move forward with his expansion. While fighting in India, Alexander was injured and forced to travel back to Baluchistan in Afghanistan, where he died in 323 B.C.

Alexander the Great may have died during his quest to expand his empire but the physical evidence of his legacy lives on at the small combat outpost on Ghundy Ghar and in the faces of many Afghan people, distant relatives of Alexander and his family. Kandahar is, in fact, the Pashtu name for Alexander.

The dusty outpost, as in ancient times, still provided a look-out over the local population, like a sentry in a prison tower. Moreover, it enabled us to observe Highway One to the north and south down to the Arghandab River. Even the Taliban understood its strategic importance. A few years prior to our arrival, the Afghan National Police (ANP) ran the outpost; it was thought they would do a better job of managing it than ISAF personnel due to their connections with the locals. Unlike the Soldiers in the Afghan Army who come from various regions of the country and the foreign ISAF troops, the generally indigenous forces of the ANP tended to connect better with the locals. Late one night, however, the Taliban overran the ANP at Ghundy Ghar. It's speculated that the ANP merely handed the post over and never actually fought, but regardless of any speculation, the end state was the same. The Taliban reportedly occupied Ghundy Ghar for several days until ISAF units from KAF were able to conduct an offensive operation to reclaim the outpost. It proved a simple operation, but then again, it was not the Taliban's tactics to occupy infrastructure for a long period of time, if ever. Moreover, they had established a defense using IEDs on the road leading to Ghundy Ghar thus leaving themselves a means of escape back into the protectively lush green zone.

During our deployment, the STRIKE Brigade and the Afghan National Army ran the outpost. We did very little if anything by ourselves. We sought Afghan solutions to Afghan problems. As Colonel Kandarian said to Kevin Sites of *Global Post* in July 2010, "We need to have our Afghan army out here with us. And once that's out here, I think it's irreversible because it's all about the Afghan perception of them seeing their Afghan Army out there."[10]

Each and every day we fought both the Taliban and history. History tends to repeat itself and quests into Afghanistan had not stopped with Alexander the Great. Beginning in the early 1800s, Great Britain and Russia fought several wars over control of Afghanistan. The British had colonialist ties to India, and security in Afghanistan provided them an overland route back to Europe following the ancient silk trade route.

By the late 1830s, Moscow's interest in Afghanistan was growing and a Persian force with Russian advisors and mercenaries attempted to seize the city of Herat in 1837. Herat at the time, however, was in the Indian city-state of Kandahar, thus causing a diplomatic uproar and military pressure from Britain as the incursion into Herat threatened its interests in India (controlled then by the British East India Company). This early fight in Afghanistan became known as the "Great Game," which aptly describes the British and Russian struggle for influence. Afghanistan was a land that stood directly in the path of both Britain and Russia's strategic interests.

---

[10] Sites, K. (2010, July 22). *Hot, Dirty, and Looking for a Fight*. Global Post. Retrieved from http://www.globalpost.com/dispatches/afghanistan/hot-dirty-and-looking-fight

At the end of the 1830s, the First Afghan-Anglo War[11] (1839 – 1842) began as British forces invaded Afghanistan in order to reestablish its economic interests. The hard-fought war ended in what is known as the Massacre of Elphinstone's Army. In January 1842, an Afghan force overran Major General William Elphinstone's Army of both British and Indian Soldiers from the British East India Trading Company. The Army, consisting of approximately 4,500 troops and 12,000 civilian workers and family members, had been garrisoned in Kabul when the uprising began. The Army left Kabul and attempted to reach Jalalabad, but few survived the 90-mile trip. Only one British Officer survived and made it to Jalalabad. All others were either dead or hostages.

For different reasons the British would invade Afghanistan two more times. It was during the Second Afghan-Anglo War that one of Afghanistan's most enduring legends was born. On July 27, 1880, as the Afghan Army fought the British in the Battle of Maiwand, a young Pashtun woman named Malalai was tending to the wounded and providing water and spare weapons to Soldiers when, despite its superior strength in numbers, the Afghan / Pashtun Army began to flounder. Legend has it that when the flag bearer was killed, Malalai rushed forward, picked up the flag, and rallied the Army to fight, shouting,

> "Young love! If you do not fall in the battle of Maiwand,
> By God, someone is saving you as a symbol of shame!
> With a drop of my sweetheart's blood,
> Shed in defense of the Motherland,
> Will I put a beauty spot on my forehead,
> Such as would put to shame the rose in the garden!"[12]

---

[11] Dalrymple, W. (2013). *Return of a King: The Battle for Afghanistan, 1839-42.* Alfred A. Knopf Publishing.

[12] Pashtun Culture and History. (2010, July). *Malali of Maiwand – Pashtun heroine of the Second Anglo-Afghan War.* Retrieved from http://pashtuncultureandhistory.blogspot.com/2010/07/malalai-of-maiwand-pashtun-heroine-of.html

Malalai's words and efforts so inspired the Pashtuns in the fight, it spurred them to victory and effectively ended the Second Afghan-Anglo War. Though Malalai was killed during the battle, her legacy lives on still today. She is considered the "Afghan Jeanne D'Arc" and the mother of Pashtun nationalism. Her actions and words united all the sub-Pashtun tribes to victory and became a rallying point of Pashtun ideology and effort.

It was during the third Afghan-Anglo War in 1919 that the Afghan government, after recognizing the Bolshevik government in the newly formed Soviet Union, asked the Soviets for military aid to defeat the British. The war ended before the Soviets sent aid, but this diplomatic warming led to the 1921 Afghan-Soviet Treaty, which brought both military and economic aid to Afghanistan from Russia. This treaty was the beginning of a complex give-and-take relationship between the Soviets and the Afghan government.

For example, in 1929, Amin Amanullah, the leader of Afghanistan and a Soviet ally, was overthrown, causing the Soviet government to send in a 1,000-man expeditionary force, all disguised as Afghans, to restore Amanullah to power. The Soviets eventually withdrew their force in the face of international condemnation, but the Soviets conducted an incursion into Afghanistan again the next year when they chased a group of border-crossing Muslim rebels 13 miles back into the Afghanistan.

Then in 1947 came the region's seismic shift: the British withdrawal from the newly independent states of India and Pakistan. Up to that point, the British, right or wrong, had served as a de facto stabilizer in the region, including in Afghanistan. In 1950, following the death of Soviet leader Joseph Stalin, the Soviets again demonstrated interest in the region and began selling weaponry to Afghanistan. The Soviets also increased their trade and economic aid to Afghanistan. They built hospitals, airfields, hydroelectric dams, and the Salang Pass highway tunnel in Parwan Provence, linking northern and southern Afghanistan. By the early 1960s some 4,000 Afghan Officers had been sent to the Soviet Union for military training, and Soviet military advisors were assigned to the Afghan Army's schools and units.

Ghundy Ghar is far from the highest point in Afghanistan, but standing atop it, you couldn't help but feel like a king looking out over his kingdom, albeit a helpless king. From Ghundy Ghar we watched ambushes along Highway One unfold. You felt impotent from this eagle's nest. All you could do was pick up the radio and report the attack. You could see the entire district yet you were utterly isolated from it. It was this isolation that made you vulnerable, too. If the Taliban were accurate with their mortars or rockets, it would have been devastating for the exposed troops. Instead they only faced sporadic small arms fire. The Taliban preferred IEDs, targeting the Soldiers as they came and went from Ghundy Ghar.

Watching Highway One the Soldiers could see vehicles, both military and civilian alike, travel through places where the Taliban enjoyed freedom of maneuver. These were known ambush locations, but you had no ability to circumvent the road unless you were lucky enough to be able to fly over it. The thick vegetation, intermixed with grape huts and walls, and the lack of roads provided the Taliban with cover and concealment. Seeing this, you couldn't help but feel sorry for the Soviet troops of the 1980s. Contrary to what I thought I knew of the Cold War, the Soviets were extremely reluctant to become engaged in Afghanistan.

It began in early 1978 when Mir Akbar Khyber, a popular political figure in Afghanistan, was assassinated outside of his home. The government of Afghanistan immediately denounced the murder, however, Mur Mohammad Taraki of the Communist People's Democratic Party of Afghanistan (PDPA) publicly accused the government of Khyber's murder. During the Islamic funeral ceremonies for Khyber, a protest against the government broke out, and shortly thereafter most of the PDPA leaders were placed under house arrest by government forces. Subsequently, Hafizullah Amin, a PDPA member, ordered an uprising, instructing a group of rebel Army Officers to overthrow the government.

On April 27, 1978, the Saur Revolution, which would lead to the formation of the Democratic Republic of Afghanistan, began. The Saur Revolution is named for the second month of the Dari calendar, when the PDPA's uprising and overthrow of the secular government of Afghanistan occurred.

This rebel faction of the Army Officers, referred to as the Khalqi, led military units loyal to them against President Daoud. The coup d'etat ended violently on the morning of April 28, 1978, when the PDPA stormed the presidential palace in Kabul and executed President

Daoud and his family. The coup was planned to begin on Thursday, April 27 and continue into Friday, the Muslim day of worship.

Once in power, the PDPA installed a socialist agenda and advocated equal rights for women, which angered conservatives who viewed this in particular as an attack on Islam. Anahita Ratebzad, a member of the Afghan Revolutionary Council and a Marxist leader, wrote in a May 28,1978, *New Kabul Times* editorial that, "Privileges which women, by right, must have are equal education, job security, health services, and free time to rear a healthy generation for building the future of the country...educating and enlightening women is now the subject of close government attention." [13] The PDPA further alienated the religious conservatives by promoting an atheist state and suppressing the expression of Islamic faith. Proposed land reform was resented by almost all Afghans and the PDPA changed the national flag from traditional Islamic green to a near copy of the Soviet Union's red and yellow banner.

The PDPA policies were brutal and anti-Islamic, rendering the group's control over Afghanistan tenuous at best. Their policies angered the majority of Afghans, and to maintain power, the PDPA imprisoned or murdered thousands of the traditional elite, the religious establishment, and the intelligentsia. The Taraki government sought to modernize Afghan society and uproot the feudalism associated with Islamic Afghan society. Any opposition to the reforms was met with government-sanctioned violence.

In December 1979, the Soviet Union feared that the PDPA government would soon be toppled by outside influences and so signed a "friendship" treaty with it. The intent of the treaty was to provide Afghanistan with military support against foreign aggressors. Afghanistan was primarily concerned about India, which had, in 1978, tested a nuclear weapon. Most of the PDPA's new policies, however, clashed directly with the traditional Afghan understanding of Islam, which was and remains one of the only issues capable of unifying the tribally and ethnically diverse population. An uprising in Herat led President Taraki to ask Alexei Kosygin, the chairman of the Soviet Council of Ministers, for "practical and technical assistance with men

---

[13] Ratebzad, A. (1978, May 28). *Editorial.* New Kabul Times.

and armament."[14] Both Kosygin and General Secretary Leonid Brezhnev denied his requests, despite the friendship treaty.

In 1979, law and order in Afghanistan began to deteriorate, leading to a serious diplomatic incident involving the United States and Soviet Union. U.S. Ambassador to Afghanistan Adolph "Spike" Dubs was kidnapped by four militants belonging to the radical communist faction Settam-e-Melli, literally meaning National Oppression. The National Oppression demanded the release of their communist leader Badruddin Bahes, whom the Afghan government denied holding. Moreover, the Afghan government refused to negotiate with the militants despite the U.S. government's demands to resolve the situation.

On February 14, 1979, Ambassador Dubs was killed by heavy crossfire as Afghan security forces, accompanied by Russian advisers, swarmed the hotel where he was being held. It is believed that KGB advisor on scene may have recommended the assault, which the Afghan government had clearly authorized.

Despite rebuffing initial requests from the communist government of Afghanistan for help, the Soviet Union could no longer ignore the growing insecurity along its southern border. The Soviet military began rolling into Afghanistan in December 1979, and as the Afghans refer to it, "the bear went over the mountain."[15] It was the "other side of the mountain"[16] that ensnared the Soviets. Aid to the Mujahideen from the American CIA, the Pakistani ISI, and other nations contributed heavily to the Soviet Union's failure in Afghanistan, which, in turn, contributed to its later collapse.

Standing on Ghundy Ghar, I couldn't help but wondered if we were going down the same path as the Soviets. Would we repeat their mistakes? Could we continue to survive against the Taliban in the

---

[14] Camp, D. (2012, January). *Boots on the Ground: The Fight to Liberate Afghanistan from Al-Qaeda and the Taliban*. Zenith Press. Page 8.

[15] Grau, L. (1996). *The Bear Went Over the Mountain: Soviet Combat Tactics in Afghanistan*. National Defense University Press.

[16] Jalali, A. A., & Grau, L. (1995). *The Other Side of the Mountain: Mujahideen Tactics in the Soviet-Afghan War*. Military Bookshop.

green zone? Could we outmaneuver the Taliban? Could we push into their strongholds?

Chapter 3
To The Surge

The war is brought to the Afghans; Afghans are not in favour to the war.

Abed Rahmani
Afghan poet

"As Commander-in-Chief, I have determined that it is vital in our national interests to send an additional 30,000 U.S. troops to Afghanistan," President Barack Obama said to 4,400 West Point Cadets at the United States Military Academy on December 1, 2009.[17] I was asleep thousands of miles away in Germany at the time those words were spoken on the heights along the Hudson River in New York. As President Obama had previously stated in his address, "Afghanistan is not lost, but for several years it has moved backwards." I had known a troop surge in Afghanistan was coming for some time but the question was how big? I knew it was necessary to meet the current needs of fighting but the war was nearly a decade old.

Thick, black smoke billowed up from the building. It was breaking news and I didn't know how I had missed it. I stared at the small television mounted on the wall in disbelief. It took me a few moments to process what was going on and to recognize the tower. It was one of the towers of the World Trade Center. It was Tuesday, September 11, 2001.

I was a couple of weeks into my senior year at Boston College and planning life after graduation. (I was leaning toward a career in medicine.) I liked to get up early on Tuesdays and Thursdays and grab coffee at a small shop on campus on my way to a political philosophy class on Kant and morality. The class seemed like a good idea to demonstrate my well-roundedness and more importantly it fit into my

---

[17] Obama, B. (2009, December 1). *Remarks by the President in Address to the Nation on the Way Forward in Afghanistan and Pakistan.* The White House – Office of the Press Secretary. Retrieved from https://www.whitehouse.gov/the-press-office/remarks-president-address-nation-way-forward-afghanistan-and-pakistan

schedule. I was watching the morning news in my apartment before I had left so that I could in class I could participate in our discussion of Kant and current events of the world but had caught none of those harrowing images.

I stood there with dozens of other students in disbelief. We watched a second plane suddenly race into view and an instant later the South tower erupted in a fireball. Panic enveloped the crowd in the coffee shop. No one knew what to make of the scene. There was speculation that the first plane was an accident, but the second plane confirmed our worst fears; this was no accident. I wondered about friends who had recently started their first jobs out of college at the World Trade Center. I wondered if they were at work. While I stared at the TV in disbelief, the news cut a live shot of Pentagon on fire and thick black smoke rising from its side.

The news was chaotic and speculative as reports came in about other planes and other targets. Reporters talked about a plane crashing in Pennsylvania that was headed for Washington. In shock I wandered to my class. I wasn't even sure if we were going to have class, but I couldn't sit there and watch. I was mad.

My class was canceled and I raced back to my apartment to wake up my roommates and to tell them what was happening.

In those next few days, I learned a lot. Names and countries that I had previously been ignorant about were coming to the forefront of my vocabulary. I learned about Afghanistan. I remembered the place only slightly from my childhood, through pictures and videos of Dan Rather in Pakistan with the Mujahideen but I understood very little. I had heard of al-Qaeda and Osama bin Laden that day but my knowledge ended with his involvement in the USS Cole bombing in Yemen and a couple of embassy bombings in Africa. Those were distant places and events for me. I realized that I had led a sheltered life when it came to understanding the world. I also began to think about service.

After my sophomore year of college, I had enlisted in the Marines to attend Officer Candidate School. A close family friend from home who was a few years older than me had joined up and remarked that being a Marine and leading others was a life-changing experience. He seemed to love the Marines and it made me consider my options. I also wanted a plan, a path in life. I talked to a recruiter who really made it hard to say no.

At the time I had been thinking of medical school as well but was unsure if that was the right choice for me. I wanted to do more than to be a student for the next ten years. So without telling my parents, I signed up for the Marines. As I prepared to ship out to Quantico, Virginia, to begin the first of two summer sessions of the platoon leadership course, I received a phone call from my recruiter. Apparently my packet from the Medical Entrance Processing Station (MEPS) in Boston had was lost on its way to Quantico. Without my medical records and contract, I could not report. I needed to start the process over. I was disheartened and frustrated when my recruiter recommended I sign-up again for the ten-week course the following year. Instead of Marine OCS, I spent the summer doing medical research and waiting tables at home in Florida. I hadn't thought much about the Marines again until September 11th. The months immediately following the attack were a whirlwind education for me.

I watched the recovery efforts at the World Trade Center and tried for the first time to understand the world in which I lived. I learned more about Afghanistan. I searched the internet, read *National Geographic* magazines, and looked for books about the country. I came to understand these attacks were coordinated with the assassination of the Northern Alliance Commander, Ahmed Shah Massoud. I watched as President George W. Bush sought to calm the American public and demanded justice for these terrorist attacks.

In October my sense of tragedy transformed into rapt admiration. I watched news reports on what I perceived as the greatest adventure in the world unfold before my eyes, Special Forces teams and CIA Officers moving into a land 7,000 miles away. I watched footage of coordinated strategic bombings. I caught glimpse of Soldiers riding on horseback and working with the Northern Alliance in an effort to capture or kill Osama bin Laden and to destroy the Taliban regime. I constantly flipped through every news channel to try and see something different, even more footage.

I learned that the Taliban were led by Mullah Mohammed Omar and supported al-Qaeda by providing Osama bin Laden and his subordinates with sanctuary. I began to put the pieces together and to understand what my professors in my political science classes had been trying to teach me. Mullah Omar and the Taliban movement came to power in the political vacuum created when the Soviets withdrew from

Afghanistan. For many in my generation, the events of September 11th became a galvanizing moment.

Following the U.S.-led invasion, in December 2001 a group of Afghan dignitaries and tribal leaders agreed to a power-sharing interim government that would be headed by Hamid Karzai. In January, the first contingent of NATO-led forces began arriving in Afghanistan under the banner of the International Security Assistance Force (ISAF); marking the start of a protracted fight against the Taliban. A grand council, or Loya Jirga, months later elected Hamid Karazai interim head of state, allowing him to pick members of his administration while the council drafted a constitution with a presidential election slated for October 2004.

As Afghanistan seemed on its way to a better future, President Bush defined the "axis of evil," and Americans were exposed to a world we barely understood, if at all. Terrorism, roughly defined as the use of violence or intimidation in the pursuit of political aims, became part of Americans' everyday conversations. Previously I had perceived terrorism as some distant threat but now it was real and on our doorstep. It was no longer isolated incidents overseas but a threat in our everyday life.

I heard about weapons of mass destruction and learned through the news about biological agents sent to the Capitol building, to our elected leaders, and to members of the media. But time passed, our lives continued, and we began to lose sight of Afghanistan. Iraq came into our periphery. Pre-emptive war now seemed acceptable in order to prevent weapons of mass destruction from getting into the hands of terrorists.

I was in my second semester of graduate school at the University of Iowa when on March 20, 2003, a U.S.-led coalition invaded Iraq. I had watched Secretary of State Colin Powell present evidence to the United Nations about Iraq's weapons of mass destruction program. Afghanistan seemed like an even more distant memory as the United States now had a new threat to its security. Simultaneously in the halls of academia I saw anti-war protests and had lengthy discussions with my professors and friends over the merits of a war in Iraq. For the first time since September 11th, America was not united, and despite what other people thought, I still wanted to serve. I felt an obligation to protect the United States.

I listened to my professors and friends complain about the government and lack of funding for research. Some of my professors believed the money that was going to the Department of Defense should be allocated to them and their research. When I asked these professors if they themselves had served in the military, I invariably received answers that involved Vietnam. One professor had served, in fact. He had enlisted in the Air Force out of high school and served for a few years before using his GI Bill to attend college. Another professor questioned why he should serve for a government that he did not support. I was flabbergasted by his hypocrisy. He felt entitled to public funding from the U.S. government to support his research yet he did not support that same government. At that moment I realized that I did not want to look back on my life and be in their positions. Americans who were my age and younger were fighting and dying, serving their country, right or wrong. American Soldiers were fighting their way into Baghdad and within the mountains of Afghanistan, and there I was, a lifetime away in Middle America. So I did what I felt I had to do. I contacted the local Marine and Army recruiters. The Marines wanted nothing to do with me due to my previous knee surgery, but the Army was interested, assuming I could pass all of the physicals.

I entered into the Army's delayed entry training program; I would finish my master's degree and then attend basic training and Officer candidate school. While I waited to ship off to Basic Combat Training and then Officer Candidate School, I intently followed what was going on in the world. I followed as Iraq stagnated and devolved into civil war between Sunni and Shia Muslims.

While Iraq raged in the forefront of the media, I remained fascinated with Afghanistan. I read books about what the world was missing, such as Operation Anaconda, which saw nearly two hundred Soldiers enter Shahikot Valley in an effort to catch Osama bin Laden. Instead of the war ending in Afghanistan these Soldiers saw as, author Sean Naylor in *Not a Good Day to Die* described, "the fanaticism of their ferocious enemy."[18]

---

[18] Naylor, S. (2006). *Not A Good Day to Die*. Berkley Trade.

In military terms, Afghanistan had become an *economy of force* operation, where the minimal force required to maintain the status quo is utilized. The goal of this force was to help the Afghans help themselves through the development of governance and economic growth. The economy of force mission's efficacy can be measured by examining America's desire for news during the time of the operation. In 2006, the American Journalism Review highlighted the numbers from the 2005 Tyndall Report, which provides statistics on news stories. It revealed that in 2005 only 147 minutes of airtime in nightly U.S. newscasts of three major news networks was devoted to Afghanistan compared to 1,288 minutes on Afghanistan in 2001.[19] The perception based on troops on the ground and news coverage at the time was that the Taliban and al-Qaeda had been defeated. This was not the case. This small economy of force troops on the ground was too small to both build a nation and confront the Taliban. The Taliban grew strong and spread.

The Taliban actively recruited and worked to build their network. In *Koran, Kalashnikov, and Laptops: The Neo-Taliban Insurgency in Afghanistan,*[20] Antonio Giustozzi highlights that in early 2002 the Taliban leadership was safely inside Pakistan and reorganizing their network. As their numbers began to swell with recruits under the perception that infidels had invaded a Muslim country, the Taliban leadership began pushing back into Afghanistan, slowly at first, working around Zabul Province, which lies just east of Kandahar and along the Pakistan border. By 2004 new strongholds were emerging in parts of both Uruzgan and Kandahar Province and between 2005-06 the Taliban had well-established camps around Kandahar City and in the northern area of Helmand Province. At the same time the Taliban were pushing north along the Pakistan/Afghan border in the areas of Paktia and Khost.

As I continued my military training in 2006 and the world watched the Iraqi civil war erupt, the concept of counterinsurgency operations

---

[19] Ricchiardi, S. (2006, August/September). *The Forgotten War*. American Journalism Review.

[20] Giustozzi, A. (2008). *Koran, Kalashnikov, and Laptops: The Neo-Taliban Insurgency in Afghanistan*. Columbia University Press. Pages 1 – 5.

began to reemerge. Both military and civilian leaders saw that typical high intensity conflict operations were antiquated. Simultaneously in Afghanistan, NATO assumed responsibility for security across the whole of the country and opium production sets were at a record high, according to United Nations' reports. An April 2006 *Vanity Fair* article by Sebastian Junger eluded to the spillover of Iraq tactics to Afghanistan as the Taliban had adopted a strategy of "civil terror." Junger also summarized in an interview that if America prematurely withdrew from Afghanistan, it "would collapse back in on itself, and it would go very fast...Kandahar would fall immediately [to the Taliban], warlords would impose their will...a replay of all the things that brought us 9/11."[21]

In 2007, President George W. Bush, at the request by troop commanders on the ground in Iraq, pushed for a surge in troops. The goal was to restore order in Iraq, all while Afghanistan slipped further into the background. The COIN concepts of "clear, hold, and build" proved effective in Iraq, and Afghanistan reemerged on the world's political stage when the July 2007 bombing at the Indian Embassy in Kabul killed more that 50 people. An extra 4,500 troops were sent into Afghanistan two months later in what was called a "quiet surge," a minimalist effort to shift the tides in Afghanistan. It could be argued that the political fight of the upcoming elections and the strain of two wars left President Bush with few alternatives. With forces committed in Iraq, there were just so few options.

In early 2009, NATO countries pledged to increase military commitments in Afghanistan after newly elected President Barack Obama announced an extra 17,000 troops as well as an additional 4,000 U.S. personnel to train the Afghan Army and police. This troop increase was not seen as the answer to the failing security in Afghanistan but provided the administration with time to assess the situation. Overtime, competing options emerged on a prospective troop surge. Ambassador Karl Eickenberry wanted to focus American efforts on Pakistan and securing Afghanistan's borders. In a leaked diplomatic cable he wrote, "More troops won't end the insurgency as long as Pakistan sanctuaries remain. Pakistan will remain the single

---

[21] Junger, S. (2006, April). *America's Forgotten War*. Vanity Fair.

greatest source of Afghan instability so long as the border sanctuaries remain, and Pakistan views its strategic interests as best served by a weak neighbor." [22] Alternatively, VicePresident Biden called for expanded training and formation of Afghan forces in order to disrupt the Taliban and withdraw U.S. forces from nation-building and population protection of counterinsurgency operations.

Meanwhile, General Stanley McChrystal submitted an outline with three mission options and their required troop strengths. The first plan called for sending 80,000 additional troops to conduct a counterinsurgency campaign throughout the country. The second plan called for 40,000 troops to reinforce both the southern and eastern regions of the country where the Taliban was the strongest. And the third option relied on only 10,000 to 15,000 troops mainly to train Afghan forces.

Throughout the summer and fall of 2009, President Obama and his National Security Council debated the merits of each strategy. On December 1, President Obama traveled to the United States Military Academy at West Point, New York, to announce his surge plan to the Corps of Cadets and to the world. The plan, referred to as Option 2A and entitled "Max Leverage," called for an additional 30,000 troops and potentially 10,000 from NATO allies. [23] The plan outlined a rapid deployment and redeployment a year later for the surge troops. The aim was to get the majority of the proposed 30,000 troops into Afghanistan in the next six months so that the sudden jolt of forces could knock the Taliban on its heels long enough for Afghans to take over the fight.

Three weeks later, on December 22, 2009, the 2nd Brigade, 101st Airborne Division received its deployment orders. The Brigade would be the lead surge brigade into southern Afghanistan in support of Operation Enduring Freedom. As the Brigade began to do the million

---

[22] Schmitt, E. (2009, November 9). *Documents: Ambassador Eikenberry's Cables on U.S. Strategy in Afghanistan*. New York Times. Retrieved from http://documents.nytimes.com/eikenberry-s-memos-on-the-strategy-in-afghanistan

[23] Baker, P. (2009, December 5). *How Obama Came to Plan for 'Surge' in Afghanistan*. New York Times.

and one things that need to happen before a deployment, I was on leave for the holidays, having just reported to my Captain's Career Course. At the time, I had no idea that within the next few months I would become part of the surge and that I would be in Afghanistan for some of the worst fighting U.S. troops had seen in Afghanistan.

Chapter 4
Breaking the Iraq Mindset

Men of genius are admired, men of wealth are envied,
men of power are feared; but only men of character
are trusted.

Alfred Adler *(1870-1937)*

I was exhausted. The day had not been physically demanding but my mind was racing. It was the night before my scheduled flight to Afghanistan from Fort Campbell, Kentucky. *Did I have everything packed that I needed? Was I ready?* I thought of people I knew and people I had never met. I thought about Staff Sergeant James Hunter who recently had been killed in action. I had never known him but wondered if I would have liked him. Everyone I talked to had.

I thought about my family. Unsure of when I would speak to my son again, I called him. Only four years old, he was still the most reassuring thing in my life. I told him that I loved him very much and that I missed him.

I laid on the bed in the dark hotel room, thinking about everything. My mind raced from one topic to the next. I recalled assignments day three months prior when I had learned my fate at the Captain's Career Course.

One of the most important events at the Captain's Career Course is when your branch manager arrives. He weighs all the factors for everyone in the class and assigns people to their next duty station. It is a short visit, but it is the only opportunity you get to meet with him. Command is the key to promotion so everyone in the class hoped to get an assignment that would lead the to command quickly. But there were other considerations. Some Captains had families, special needs that must be considered, and dwell time, which is the required time spent at home before returning to another deployment. I had no family or special needs and little dwell time compared to others in the class. The process gets pretty contentious and political if individuals are hell-bent on specific assignments or duty stations.

It was Wednesday, March 17, 2010, when the branch manager arrived. He walked in into our classroom at the end of the day and wrote out the list of available assignments. When he finished he told us to discuss the options among ourselves, figure out what we wanted, and write down our top five choices. He would collect those choices the next morning, meet with us individually to determine our assignments, and then make the announcement to the class by lunchtime.

I remember the day the announcements were made well and not for good reasons. Not only did I not get the assignment I had wanted but like a good portion of my friends in the course we were nursing horrible hangovers, the result of St. Patrick's Day the day before. I am not Irish, but we had wanted to celebrate our pending assignments. The lure of cheap green beer at one of the bars on post was also too strong a call to resist.

I remember seeing my name next to the assignment "2nd Brigade, 101st Airborne Division" and I was far from happy. The previous day there had been an available assignment with one of the U.S. Army's Special Forces Groups, what I had truly desired. I relished how the Special Forces operate in small teams doing Foreign Internal Defense. I had worked with them before and believed that working with them I could make a difference.

I had previously begun the Special Forces selection process but was dropped during selection due to a shoulder injury. It seemed to me that the opportunity to work with the Green Berets even if in a more support role would be ideal. But when I looked on the board, that spot had been erased. I later learned about politics and the games that some branch managers play. The game had been played while I was out celebrating St. Patrick's Day with friends and I was the loser. That afternoon I had learned one of the others Captains in my class was friends with the branch manager and had taken him out to dinner the night before in order to lobby for his assignment choice.

In fact despite my disappointment over the now gone Special Forces slot I was excited about two facts: the tremendous heritage of the 101st Airborne Division and its imminent deployment to Afghanistan.

I remember arriving at Fort Campbell, Kentucky, on the night of June 9, 2010, after graduating from the Captain's Career Course earlier that morning. It had been a long drive from Missouri and as pulled through the main gate, I suddenly felt lost. My Google directions to Fort Campbell ended at the gate, and it was nearly 2300 as I struggled to read street signs and building numbers. In typically Army fashion, however, very few buildings are named let alone have large signs. The buildings are numbered so until you figure out how the buildings are numerically arrayed, you are lost.

I had wanted to arrive weeks earlier. Upon getting my assignment to a deploying unit, I petitioning the Brigade Commander via his personnel Officer, Major Darren Haas. But my request was denied. I was told that "Colonel Kandarian felt it was more important to stay at the career course until graduation." At the time I was frustrated. I wanted to get to the unit, to meet the people I would be deploying with and to learn how it operated and fought. But like my assignment to the Brigade itself, the decision was not mine to make.

In the darkness I spent nearly an hour or so trying to figure out where I needed to be. I drove back and forth between the base's hotel and the replacement company that manages the incoming personnel. I wanted to find the Brigade Headquarters and report directly to staff duty desk, which is manned constantly. Without a map and relying on others' directions and "I think you need to be here," I was lost.

Having been stationed overseas for almost four years prior to attending the Captain's Career Course, I had forgotten how to sign into a unit. In Germany I had been stationed with three different units in different parts of the country. There, I would report to the lodging office and then someone from the unit would meet me the next morning and show me where I needed to be. But Fort Campbell was a far cry from the tiny kasernes of Germany. Instead I drove around in circles, straining to read small signs and avoid going the wrong way down one-way streets. Eventually, I found the replacement company, which took my paperwork. The non-commissioned Officer on duty told me to go back to lodging and report back to the replacement company the next morning.

The next morning at nearly five minutes to six, I stood in a mass accountability formation at the replacement company. Once accountability was taken we were ushered into a small gym to receive the "dos and don'ts" briefing. Ten minutes later, I received my two-page in-processing checklist, which covered both Fort Campbell facilities and the 101st Airborne Division offices. I would still need a separate list from 2nd Brigade. It sounds redundant but the checklist from Brigade is more of a personnel in-processing to make sure our paperwork with the correct people there while the large one covers medical, dental, and equipment issue. In my impatience I wanted to be done in-processing already. There was a lot I felt I needed to do before I could deploy.

The concept of deploying is simple: get every trained person and every item needed to fight to the correct spot on time. The execution in an orderly fashion is obscenely difficult.

In the case of the 2nd Brigade "STRIKE," 101st Airborne Division, deployment was Kandahar Province, Afghanistan, which is part of Regional Command South while the rest of the Division was going to take over Regional Command East. The brigade and the division were going in different directions. STRIKE would be operating independently and could not rely on the Division headquarters so everything from Fort Campbell needed to be sent nearly 7,500 miles into a land-locked country. This includes close to 4,000 Soldiers and equipment including several tons of weapons, computers, uniforms, radios, batteries, cables, vehicles, light bulbs, pens, paper, staplers, chem-lites and just about anything a Soldier could need. In country we would draw our ammunition and our mine resistant armored vehicles.

Needless to say, deploying is a lengthy process. The equipment typically leaves some 90 days ahead of personnel, and personnel transport itself requires nearly an additional month to complete from start to finish. It is a detailed choreographed ballet. You can't just load 4,000 Soldiers on planes and expect them to be in the fight the next day. There are only so many beds in country, and everything must be built along the way. All I knew when I signed into the replacement company at Fort Campbell on the night of June 9 was that the Brigade was somewhere in the midst of this lengthy process. And if I didn't hurry through the process I would be stuck for a while.

Following the mandatory briefing at the replacement company, I found the Brigade Headquarters and reported to the Rear Detachment Commander, Major William Parker. I was saddened to learn that the Brigade was nearly completely gone. There were only a couple of main body flights remaining and if I missed those it could be months before there were enough replacements to warrant another flight.

I also knew that if I missed deploying with the main body, I would fall into the replacement category, which is not a bad thing except it meant I would be forced to attend Individual Readiness Training (IRT).

The IRT program was designed to prevent sending new Soldiers directly into combat. It is the train-up to and them more time to hone some basic Soldier skills such as first aid and marksmanship. The rule is simple: if you missed your unit's training at one of the national training centers then you were to attend IRT.

I had clearly missed the Brigade's train-up for the deployment, but I also understood that within the Army there is an exception to every rule. You just need to find the person who has the authority to grant that exception. So I pleaded my case to Major Parker.

I asked him to put me on one of the remaining main body flights, telling him I was ready to go since I had no family to settle into the area. I argued it would be easier to go sooner than later since I was staying in a local hotel which the Army only pays for up to 10 days. I also cited my recent deployment history to Iraq. During this conversation I found out that we had operated in the same area while in Baghdad. I had been deployed to Iraq during the surge there as well as completed an operational deployment while assigned to the United States Army Headquarters in Europe.

Despite being the Brigade's Rear-D Commander, Major Parker was not the approving authority. Due to events in the past where Soldiers had been killed going straight into combat, the approval authority to skip IRT was retained by the Division Commander.

I was initially concerned that I would have to finagle a way onto the Division Commander's schedule; it is never an easy task for an extremely junior Captain to secure a meeting with a two-star General. It is better not to be seen nor heard until you have things figured out. Such enlightenment generally occurs when a Captain is in their second year of command. Otherwise if the Commanding General knows who you, the junior Captain, are, you likely have done something wrong.

Luckily as part of the post in-processing requirements there was a scheduled briefing for all newly arriving personnel to Fort Campbell with the Division Commander. These took place a couple times per month and fortunately for me, one was scheduled the following day with the Division Commander and the Division Command Sergeant Major to introduce themselves to all of the newly arriving Soldiers and their families. But since the Division Headquarters was deployed, it would be the Division Rear Detachment Commander, in this case a Colonel.

I am generally not intimidated by of rank but was thankful it was not the actual Division Commander. It is simply easier to talk to a Colonel than a General, somewhat comparable to conversing with your local Mayor versus your U.S. Senator.

The next morning I used the same case I had pleaded to Major Park and got my approval. I am not sure why the Colonel approved my case but remain thankful nonetheless. I am not a war hawk or an adrenaline junkie who craves being in the action, but I am also not one to sit back and let someone else do the work I feel I should be doing. I would eventually be deployed with the unit to Afghanistan, so why shouldn't I go straight away? I could be an asset to the Brigade and would achieve nothing by remaining back at Fort Campbell. For me there was no point in waiting around.

I suspect the Colonel's approval was the result of other questions he was receiving that morning. Several of the non-commissioned Officers in the room were expressing concerns about having to deploy so soon upon their arrival to Fort Campbell. I, on the other hand, had displayed my willingness to deploy to the Colonel.

With the verbal approval from the Division Rear Detachment Commander, I raced back to the Brigade Headquarters and informed Major Parker of the news. I now needed the rear detachment of Soldiers in the personnel shop to begin working the temporary change of station orders (also referred to as deployment orders) and get me on the June 20 flight manifest. At the time I was perhaps the only happy person about to get deployment orders because while I struggled to go, the Battalions of the STRIKE Brigade were on the ground and in the fight. Soldiers I had never met were being killed.

I was nearly 48 hours out of the Career Course and in about a week I would begin my second combat deployment, my first deployment to Afghanistan. There was a lot to get done and reality was starting to set in. I was about to deploy with a unit in which I knew no one. Mere days ago, I had never even set foot on Fort Campbell, let alone worked with anyone from the STRIKE Brigade. Now I was going to war with these men and women.

I had missed the STRIKE's train-up and all other pre-deployment training events, but I was not the only one, in fact. As I sat and discussed what needed to happen with Major Parker, I was introduced to three other Majors who had arrived to the Brigade a couple weeks prior to me. They, too, were working on getting ready to deploy. For them things were more complicated. Each had families, so their time was divided between in-processing, settling their families into new homes, and readying to deploy. One of the Majors who had been hoping to make the flight was told that his deployment orders would not be approved by Division until he had completed IRT. He would miss the June 20 flight, delaying him. He would have to wait until there was enough replacements to fill a flight.

As I spent my last few nights in the United States in the safety of the my tiny hotel room on Fort Campbell, there were hundreds of other Soldiers within my Brigade already in harm's way and engaging the Taliban. Only in retrospect did I understand how the Brigade got to where it was.

The 101st Airborne Division is a mobile infantry unit. Soldiers carry a lot, but it is a lot less than armor and Stryker units, which require additional maintenance assets and supplies. Since the Division had returned from Iraq over a year prior and was easily deployable, it was the likely choice to meet President Obama's surge requirements. Not only did the Division need to get there, it needed to get there fast.

In terms of strategic necessity, Kandahar Province was crucial. The Taliban in recent years had gained a tremendous foothold in the environs surrounding Kandahar City. The 5th Brigade, 2nd Infantry Division was slated to leave in May 2010 and without the surge their battle space would have been left unoccupied. Other units would have been stretched extremely thin just to man and occupy the combat outpost; let alone patrol and train the Afghan national security forces. A lack of coverage meant the Taliban could gain more ground, not necessarily in terrain but in influence over the people.

So while I was at the Captain's Career Course, the 2nd Brigade, 101st Airborne Division had been selected to operate apart from the other organic Brigades of the Division and the Division's headquarters. The STRIKE Brigade would support ISAF's RC-South while the rest of the Division took control of RC-East.

Within the condensed timeline it was recognized there would be tremendous difficulty in getting the entire Brigade on the ground and operation in time to prevent a gap between the Stryker Brigade out of Fort Lewis and us on the ground. In anticipation of this shortfall, Secretary of Defense Robert Gates approved the early deployment of a single Battalion, 1st Battalion, 502nd Infantry Regiment, also known as "First Strike," from within the STRIKE Brigade. Its mission would be to hold critical infrastructure like the array of Combat Outposts (COPs) in the Zharay District until the rest of the Brigade could be operational.

Unbeknownst to me at the time, this accelerated timeline had a profound impact on the units' preparation for deployment. Training to deploy, like an actual deployment, is a tedious process that begins well over a year before the actual deployment. Each training phase builds upon the last and starts at the lowest level possible, the individual Soldier.

First, a unit inventories its personnel and equipment to ensure both are in good and working condition for combat. Then the individuals train in marksmanship and first aid. These develop into team and squad drills before moving to full platoon- and company-level operations and live fire exercises. Ultimately the entire unit, to include staffs at the Battalion and Brigade level, exercise at one of the national readiness training centers. There are two such training centers within the continental United States and one in Europe.

Prior to my deployment to Iraq, I went through the European Center, the Joint Multinational Training Center (JMTC) in Hohenfels, Germany, with the 2nd Squadron, 2nd Stryker Cavalry Regiment. I was new to the unit and still a young Second Lieutenant at the time when I was placed as a Battle Captain within the Squadron's Tactical Operations Center (TOC). I did not know any of the unit's tactical procedures and felt lost. I also did not understand it was game with a level of make-believe involved. So I didn't take it seriously. I did my job to the best of my abilities but couldn't understand why people began running around when a little message popped up on a screen telling us that our base was being attacked. My first instinct was to laugh and type back, "No, it's not!" but that would have been a colossal mistake as every movement and action is being judged and graded by an assigned army of observer controllers.

What I didn't fully understand at the time were the actions that were occurring on the ground in the training areas that surrounded our little base. These training exercises were realistic of what would be seen on the ground. The Soldiers, from the lowest Private to the Battalion Commander, were getting rapid lessons in asymmetric warfare, counterinsurgency operations, and current enemy tactics from Iraq.

The Army spends millions of dollars a year hiring people who come from places like Afghanistan and Iraq to act as tribesmen, villagers, sheiks, Imans, and the like in simulated training. Leaders will engage "local leaders" to simulate interactions that they could soon be having in the future. It's an intense process that is designed to go through hundreds of scenarios and Soldiers from all levels in order to replicate the "First 100 days" of a deployment. There is a rule in the military that most casualties occur within those "First 100 days" as units are being tested by the enemy while they are still learning the new environment.

Despite my inability to hide my humor at the situation on the first day, I was tired and deflated by the time the training exercise was over. The second morning was particular rough when a Major set off an artillery simulator next to my tent. I was the only one in the tent having just come off the night shift as Battle Captain. Having been up the previous twenty-fours, I was not in the mood for games. Deploying to the training area and established our tactical operations center is not a quick process but the training begins as soon as you arrive. I am pretty sure the Major thought the tent was empty when he set off the simulator since everyone else was working the day shift. After realizing what had happened he gave me a kill card, and I was taken to the aid station where I slept most of the day away. As much as I thought the training was a silly game, this preparation proved helpful. A few weeks later I would hear the real sound of incoming rockets and mortars that were constantly launched at us in FOB Falcon, Baghdad, Iraq.

But the reality is Iraq and Afghanistan are two completely different places, despite both being part of the war on terror these combat zones share very little in common. About the only two things Iraq and Afghanistan have in common is the presence of allied troops and the Islamic faith. Iraq has evolved with the times in terms of living conditions and technology. Despite being ruled by a dictator for decades at least Iraq had a functioning government at both local and national levels. People understood the role of civil servants and what public services provided, granted, it was not perfect, but it was better than the alternative, such as the stranglehold of the Taliban on the Afghan people.

To deal with Afghanistan, Soldiers and Officers across the Brigade needed to think, plan, and operate differently than they had on previous deployments. While in Iraq I often heard the saying, "Iraqi solutions to Iraqi problems." Now it would be "Afghan solutions to Afghan problems." The distinction would prove monumental.

Simply put, the counterinsurgency planning and tactics that were successful in Iraq were not working in Afghanistan. A December 2009 *Army Times* article by Sean Naylor highlighted the necessity of training toward Afghanistan versus Iraq as he embedded with our preceding unit in Afghanistan. The 5th Brigade, 2nd Infantry Division had "spent the previous two years training for combat, but preparing for the wrong theater – until February (2009), when it got orders for Afghanistan, it was scheduled to deploy to Iraq."[24] During the first part of the deployment 1-17 Infantry Regiment, which is part of 5th Stryker Brigade, 2nd Infantry Division was fighting in the Arghandab District and 21 Soldiers were killed in the fighting. As Staff Sergeant Jason Hughes from 1st Battalion, 17th Infantry Regiment pointed out in the article, "We trained for urban fighting in Iraq and then they give us Afghanistan. The principles are the same but the details are day and night different, and we've learned that the hard way over the last almost five months."[25]

The 5th Brigade motto of "Strike – Destroy" did not embrace General McChrystal's counterinsurgency plans for Afghanistan, where published guidance stated, "Protecting the people is the mission. The conflict will not be won by destroying the enemy."[26] Instead of incorporating the Army Field Manual 3-24.2 for counterinsurgency Operations, Colonel Tunnell had his Brigade focused on the Counterguerrilla Operations Manual (Army FM 90-8), which was last updated in 1986.

I had been pleasantly surprised to learn from Major Parker that many of the Soldiers within not only the Brigade but also the 101st Airborne Division had attended weeks of Pashto classes at Fort Campbell before deploying. I was excited because that to me indicated

---

[24] Naylor, S. (2009, December 21). *Stryker Soldiers Say Commanders Failed Them*. Army Times.

[25] *Ibid*.

[26] McChrystal, S., (2009). *ISAF Commander's Counterinsurgency Guidance*. ISAF Command. Page 1. Retrieved from http://www.nato.int/isaf/docu/official_texts/counterinsurgency_guidance.pdf

that the leadership within the Brigade understood the necessity of connecting with the people. It does little to no good to yell at an Afghan to do something if you are yelling at him in English. Knowing the language even if just a little bit goes a long way in terms of building good will.

T.E. Lawrence understood this concept in World War I as he led Arabs across the Middle East to attack German and Turkish troops along their supply lines. Many of our Afghan Army partners, however, did not speak Pashto. Our newly created Afghan Army counterparts were mostly from Northern Afghanistan. Ethnically, they were Tajiks and Hazaras. These groups primarily speak Dari. In short, translators became a prized commodity. Not only did we need translators that could talk to our Afghan counterparts (Dari) but we also need translators to help talk to the villagers (Pashto) in our area of operation. Ideally you found a translator who spoke both Dari and Pashto but these were few and far between, You took what you could get and hoped that the translations provided were accurate.

We often claim victory in a counterinsurgency when the local government provides a needed service for the people or when violence is down because of the cost of achieving the minimum is extremely high in terms of lives and money. In Iraq we would hire those who fought against us to guard roads and other pieces of infrastructure. This hiring was known as the "Sons of Iraq" and part of the "awakening" movement, but in reality we simple paid better than the bad guys. So Iraqis were eager to stand guard in their own towns and villages, but Afghanistan was different. We could not buy their loyalty; instead we had to prove to them that we cared.

As Albert Adler put it, "men of character are trusted," and despite the fact that we were going to be frustrated and losing great Soldiers, we still needed to be there. Only then would the Afghans begin to trust us. These were lessons and opportunities that were missed in the train-up as people talked about work programs and solacia payments.

The concept of counterinsurgency is recognizing that "all politics are local."[27] There is no cookie-cutter blue print or one-size-fits-all method for counterinsurgency operations. COIN, as it is referred to, is more a set of options to be applied in various situations. We had to think outside of the box and think of what the people in our area of operations needed. We also had to understand tribal dynamics and how the villages interacted with each other. More importantly we had to prove to the people that we were men of character and that we would be there when things went wrong because if we weren't there then the Taliban surely would be.

I did not know what Afghanistan would be like, but I knew it would not be Iraq. Some COIN concepts could be applied but the application would be different. I wondered how different and how they could be applied. I did not know much about the unit we were replacing, but I knew they had struggled. Stories of atrocities through the "kill squad" had already begun to appear in the media.

I thought of the Soldiers already over there and wondered what they were going through? How were they living? And what tomorrow would bring from them? The next 24 hours or so would be very different for the Soldiers already down range.

It was a restless night of sleep. I do not remember what I dreamt about or if I dreamt at all, but I was awake and ready before my alarm went off a few hours later.

---

[27] PBS. *Tip O'Neill Biography*. PBS.org. Retrieved from http://www.pbs.org/wgbh/americanexperience/features/biography/carter-oneill/

Chapter 5
Getting There

Time. Time. Time. When you fly from Fort Campbell, Kentucky, to Leipzeg, Germany to Manas, Kyrgyzstan, to Kandahar, Afghanistan, it feels like you are sitting on a plane for an eternity. The flight's length invariably leaves time for self-reflection. Even if you try to sleep, watch movies, read, and talk to others on the plane, there is still time to reflect. You cannot escape it.

The first two flights were on a chartered commercial aircraft, which provides a basic level of comfort but nothing extraordinary. I remember being one of the last Soldiers to board the aircraft and managed to get a seat right were the coach section would normally have ended and first class would begin. I say normally because despite the bulkhead separating first class from coach on a commercial aircraft, there is no difference in service; everyone is coach. I did not need all the extra legroom and nearly volunteered to head further back, but being the new guy I decided to keep my mouth shut. I also figured if the other Captain sitting in the center section with me didn't say anything then neither should I.

I remember sitting there bemusing myself with the concept of traveling to fight the Taliban. As American Soldiers, we were flying thousands of miles in several multi-million dollar aircraft while the Taliban typically walk—a handful if they are lucky ride on a moped or in a car—to battle us. The Taliban go to war with the clothes on their backs and the sandals on their feet while we go with an assortment of weapons, body armor, boots, flame retardant uniforms, quick dry shirts, radios and a whole assortment of other things.

While at the University of Iowa and right after I enlisted for the Army in 2005, I remember reading the book *The Things They Carried* by Tim O'Brien. Sitting on those flights the book drifted back to my mind. I don't remember caring about or thinking about the book on my previous deployment, but mentally Afghanistan was different. Its title reminded me of how much gear we lug around. Like Vietnam a generation before, this would be the defining conflict of the young men and women on that plane. Many were still in elementary school when al-Qaeda attacked the World Trade Center on September 11, 2001, and yet here were America's young men and women. These young Soldiers had grown up seeing the violence of combat in Iraq and Afghanistan on TV, and here they were on their way to Afghanistan, all having volunteered for their seat on that plane.

For some it was not their first deployment but for most it was. They chatted about killing the enemy and about how they want to help the people. Among the chatter was discussion about who the hottest model was and what the best video game was. Everyone had a different story and came from a different place. The 82nd Airborne Division was called the "All-American" Division when it was formed during World War II because it had a Soldier from every state of the union. And decades later sitting in a plane thirty-five thousand feet above the earth, going into a different war we represented that same tradition. These Soldiers were not concerned about being shot while jumping into France during D-day rather the contemporary fear was what laid buried in the ground in that distant place we were headed toward.

Looking around I knew some would walk away heroes perhaps trying to save the Soldiers sitting next to them right then. Others would not be so lucky. Tim O'Brien's novel outlines the fact that modern warfare no longer has front lines. You live with and around the enemy in Afghanistan. You are surrounded day in and day out by the enemy. You see them, you talk to them, you know them yet they are not known to you. The Taliban secretly plan attacks. The Taliban fire rockets at the bases and emplace IEDs on the roads and trails. So while the enemy plans we also plan. We planned to stay ahead of the Taliban and to counter their actions by removing the Taliban from the people.

Many veterans of Iraq and Afghanistan understood the asymmetric fight that awaited us when we landed. Many of the veterans did not talk about killing people rather they focused on their families and their Soldiers. Some were still working on homework for their continuing education classes in order to get their college degree. Many senior veterans preached to their junior Soldiers about taking classes and financial responsibility. Despite being thousands of miles from home, Soldiers understand that life continues. Bills still need to get paid, children still need to go to school, and spouses work to keep their home lives thriving while constantly wondering if their Soldiers are safe.

Before you deploy you often hear other Soldiers talking about getting their personal life in order. Each and every day you are deployed you live with the risk of dying in combat, but if your mind is not focused on the task at hand because of issues at home you can easily falter. Deployments are not constant action or firefights. Monotony is everywhere. Soldiers struggle to fight the doldrums of constant routines. Guard duty, patrolling, weapons maintenance, vehicle maintenance, and mission briefs all become monotonous. Soldiers seek an escape and let their minds wander to thoughts of home, of their wives, of their children, of bills and so forth. A Soldier's mind can easily drift to thoughts of a better life. When your mind wanders, you quit paying attention to your surroundings. When you are on patrol, you can let your mind wander off the path in front of you. Suddenly that misstep puts you on top of an improvised explosive device and your life changes instantly. Death lurks everywhere but you get up and carry on each and every day.

As we got closer to Afghanistan you could feel the tension and excitement build, tempered only by switching planes from a massive commercial airframe to a military one. Luxuries are stripped away and replaced with military utility, no frills. We landed in Manas, Kyrgyzstan, in late morning on a beautifully clear summer afternoon. In the distance I could see snow covered mountain peaks that to me had to be the top of the world in a country that is slightly smaller than South Dakota. I wondered to myself if these were mountains that Alexander the Great ran into, but I doubted it. At the time about all I knew was that I was in Kyrgyzstan, and according to the CIA fact book, Kyrgyzstan's tallest peak is roughly 7,400 meters, which is 24,000 feet.[28] The height is daunting even from miles away. For me, it was like staring up at the Empire State Building from the street below, and the high elevation of Kyrgyzstan overall made our flight descent seem non-existent.

Operations at Manas are like military operations everywhere else in the world: complicated. The mission is simple, though: move personnel and equipment in and out of Afghanistan. The complication comes from weather, mechanical issues, and every little thing that could prevent the operations from being a simple transfer from commercial

---

[28] CIA Fact Book. *Kyrgyzstan*. Retrieved from
https://www.cia.gov/library/publications/the-world-factbook/geos/kg.html

to military aircraft. The Air Force has the tremendous task of moving all the Soldiers, Sailors, Airmen, and Marines off the large commercial aircraft and into smaller military aircraft. For every arriving commercial flight you need at least two departing military aircraft to accommodate the load. This is assuming you are sending everyone on the commercial flight to the same location, but Soldiers are constantly going to different hubs—Kandahar, Kabul, Jalalabad, and Herat. Everyone hopes the transit through Manas is quick, but there is no guarantee.

Fortunately, I was lucky. I spent maybe a total of five hours on the ground in Manas. There was a flight to Kandahar in a few hours that was scheduled to take a group of Soldiers from the 2nd Stryker Cavalry Regiment, my old unit. I was happy to know some of these people and they told the group of Soldiers I was with about the flight. Upon talking to the personnel in flight operations we managed to secure about 25 seats for the group of Soldiers I was accompanying. There would be more flights later in the day, but we decided to take the first one we could get.

Once we had given our names, the last four of our social security numbers, and weapons' serial numbers for the flight manifest we secured our bags from the previous flight and then built a pallet of our bags to be loaded onto the C-130 "Hercules."

Unlike commercial aircraft where you ride on one level while your bags are in the storage hold below, everything on a large military transport plane is in the same open cave. Seats on a Hercules are suspended interwoven straps connected to metal poles. Seat belts are a luxury that I have never seen in the cargo section and I laugh at the idea of there ever being any. I have always been so slammed in with other passengers that seat belts seem absurd. Windows seats are available but do little good since your back is up against the bulk side of the aircraft and you can't look out. Soldiers sit facing each other so sometime you are fortunate just to catch a glimpse of sunlight as someone's head drops when they fall asleep.

Once all of the personnel are seated on the plane, the loadmaster oversees the placement of pallets carrying everyone's gear. During the flight while all of the Soldiers are crammed into what feel like the smallest airplane seats in the world, the Air Forces loadmasters move freely about the cabin. They often have little to do and you tend to see them sleeping on top of the palleted bags. I spent most of the time listening to music on my iPod and wishing that I did not have to pee so badly.

The flight lasted a few hours, and landing was completely uneventful. We were thankful to be on the ground at Kandahar Airfield (KAF), having spent the past few hours staring at the guy sitting across from each of us. As we taxied toward the terminal the plane's ramp was lowered slightly and the rush of humidity and heat was instantly stifling in the enclosed space. I stared out the back and thought to myself, "Here we go."

As soon as the pallets were removed we all grabbed our personal gear and weapons and filed like ants off the back of the plane and into the heat. We weaved around the tarmac single-file, some struggling under the weight of all their gear until we reached the passenger terminal. KAF was not our final destination, and at the time I didn't actually know where that would be. But for the next couple of days, this was our home. I knew the Brigade was setting up and taking over several small outposts. I hoped that I would be sent to one of them.

In the terminal, the group was met by a liaison from the unit who had a couple of trucks and a bus waiting to take us to the barracks. There are two different categories of barracks on KAF. One set is for those who are stationed there. The other set is for those passing through. Those passing through live in giant gymnasium-type structures with hundreds of other Soldiers. The communal latrines are constantly a mess and with so many people trying to take showers, shave, and use flushing toilets one last time, you often run out of water. In fact, I don't think I had water once in the building while I stayed there, which was nearly 48 hours while we went through a process called "Reception, Staging, and Onward Integration," or RSOI for short.

The process of RSOI is meant to give incoming Soldiers a quick run down of the latest tactics and techniques used by the enemy. In one such portion, we were taken out to a field, given a quick run-down of the latest IEDs in the area, and then told to walk around and find them. The counter-IED course is extremely discouraging. We often only found the IEDs when we were standing on top of them. The landscape hid them well. The instructors wanted us to leave discouraged and scared so that we remain vigilant when on patrol. We also receive courses about the local culture as well as more dos and don'ts from the KAF commanders.

Kandahar Airfield is a monstrosity that arose from the super-Forward Operating Base (FOB) mentality that makes many American taxpayers cringe. There is a story about General McChrystal chastising a Captain he had witnessed sitting for hours at a coffee shop on one of these FOBs in Afghanistan. As the legend goes, General McChrystal had walked by on his way to a meeting, and hours later when he walked back the same Captain was still sitting there. Enraged by the Captain's actions, General McChrystal sought to have all of the big vendors removed from the FOBs.

The main area on Kandahar Airfield is known as the boardwalk, which houses a variety of local vendors, two coffee shops, a military gear shop, and a T.G.I. Fridays. I personally did not mind the local vendors because through them I managed to pick up a few books that I felt were critical to my understanding of Afghanistan including an introduction to basic Pashto, *The Bear Went Over The Mountain* and *The Other Side of the Mountain*. These books depict both the Russian and Mujahideen sides of the Russian incursion into Afghanistan in the 1980s, a perspective I felt would be incredibly crucial to understanding my new home.

An interesting landmark on KAF is the "poo pond," which as the name suggests is a giant wastewater pond. It had originally been on the far end of the base but with the surge and the large influx of new Soldiers to KAF, the poo pond became an integral landmark when giving directions. Coincidently the RSOI barracks are next to the poo pond. As I would learn the next morning and virtually every morning thereafter you did not need an alarm to wake you; you just needed the wind to change slightly.

Still unsure of what I would be doing I decided to stick with one of the Majors that had been on my flight from Fort Campbell. Major Diogo Travares is an interesting man. He is an Armor Officer of Portuguese descent who had previously been a Company Commander in Ramadi, Iraq. Most recently he had completed a stint as an instructor at the engineer school at Fort Leonard Wood. He was excited to be joining the Brigade and to be deployed because, as he explained as soon as we landed, he was planning to grow a "deployment mustache." Another reason I would stick with him was that he knew what his job would be; he was slotted as the Brigade's Plans Officer before he could move down to a primary staff position at the battalion level.

In terms of organization, the plans group is part of the S3 or operations section. The operations section is responsible for not only coming up with future operations but for also monitoring and tracking current operations. Along with us were several other Captains who, like me, came from diverse backgrounds and were also newly assigned to the Brigade. One was an Air Defense Artillery Officer and the other was a Kiowa Pilot, Captain Meyers. Unlike the rest of us, Captain Meyers had previously deployed to Afghanistan and had been stationed in Jalalabad. He had flown numerous missions in support of the 173rd Airborne Brigade in the Korengal Valley. There were also two other Infantry Captains who, also like me, were fresh out of their respective Captains Career Courses. They knew they were going to have to cut their teeth on the Brigade staff for a few months until it was their turn to take Company Command.

Orientation is typically scheduled to last 96 hours from the time you land at KAF to moving out to your smaller FOB or outpost. We did not want to be there that long nor, as it turned out, did the Brigade. Kandahar Airfield can become a sand pit in which people get stuck. Being at KAF would not serve the Brigade's efforts, and personally I thought any place would be better than there. While we were at KAF that meant there were other people doing not only their jobs but ours as well. We eventually got word to the Brigade's executive Officer who was at FOB Wilson in the heart of Zharay. He told us to get on the first flight we could, which like most things in the Army, is easier said than done.

There was growing concern about us being able to leave right away. There were a lot of Soldiers from the Brigade who had completed orientation and had been stuck at KAF for weeks. We were supposed to be taking over security in the districts of Zharay, Maiwand, and the Arghandab, and yet were there was still a considerable number of Soldiers at KAF. The reason turned out to be infrastructure or rather the lack of latrines, cots, tents, food and so forth needed to support the number of Soldier. It is one thing to order a bunch of troops to an area, but it's another for sufficient resources to be there to support for them. The logistics needed to catch up.

The group of Captains I was with managed to get scheduled for a flight the next night. Despite leaving the relative safety, we were happy to be leaving KAF. We still had a couple briefings to sit through and being at KAF provided us one last opportunity to secure items such as toothpaste or socks that we had forgotten or things that we didn't even realize we needed until we were in country, namely sunscreen.

The next day we packed up, attended the final RSOI event, and were ready to move on. After dinner at one of the half dozen dining facilities we sat at the aviation terminal again, this time waiting for our ride. We double and triple checked our gear and hoped that we wouldn't lose anything along the way.

Following our manifesting, we learned that we were on the last flight of the night. There were three other chalks, or groups, ahead of us. All were headed to FOB Wilson and would begin flying in about an hour or so after sunset. We estimated that with the turnaround time and potential refuel stops, it would be close to midnight before we actually left.

Unlike flying in the large military airplanes, when you fly in a helicopter it's the passengers responsibility to load and unload all of the bags, tough boxes, and other equipment. In black out conditions under the roar of a CH-47 "Chinook" dual rotator, loading bags becomes orchestrated chaos. Having flown a few times in the back of a Chinook before, I knew where to sit. I preferred to sit in the back since the crew flies with the ramp partially open in order to have a rear gunner for security and at least for me it would be my first glimpse of Afghanistan.

When our chalk was given a 10-minute warning, we donned our body armor, our ACHs (Army Combat Helmets), and loaded our weapons. It was highly unlikely we would need to use our weapons but one never knew. About a minute out from loading we all grabbed a few bags and prepared to move to the helicopter. Once a few bags were loaded, a handful of people would assume their seats while the rest of the passengers continued to load behind them. This process continued until all the Soldiers and bags and equipment were loaded. Knowing how the timing and process worked, I managed to secure my desired spot: the last seat on the left side of the aircraft.

A few minutes after I sat down we rolled to the end of the runaway before suddenly lifting off. The lights of KAF quickly disappeared and we raced northwest away from the ISAF civilization and into the districts. It was now June 23rd and I was on the last leg of the journey to FOB Wilson. I was beginning my journey through southern Afghanistan.

Chapter 6
In Country

Nothing special. Standing on the dark helicopter landing zone, rank, size, race, stature, and social status mean nothing. In the Army you are nothing more than a Soldier. Regardless of rank there are still tasks that need to be completed, and whether Officer or enlisted these tasks need to be completed as fast as possible.

When our Chinook helicopter touched down on the gravel-laden helicopter landing zone (HLZ) at FOB Wilson, we were greeted with darkness. The rush of heat and wind from the rotator wash greeted us at our new home. In body armor, helmets, weapons in hand and without lights, we raced to off-load everything from the helicopter. We raced, each making multiple trips to get all equipment and bags to the edge of the landing zone. Each trip took us through the searing turbine heat and out of the rotator wash. Every passenger on the helicopter works. No rank is immune from the necessity to rapidly get every piece of gear and equipment off the Chinook.

We did not know where exactly the helicopter had dropped us on FOB Wilson. Prior to departing KAF, I was not able to find and look at any imagery of the forward operating base so I had no clue about its layout. I was not sure where we were in relation to anything else on the FOB due to the pitch darkness. I cannot recall if it was a moonless night but it wouldn't surprise me if it had been. There was little light on the FOB, due partly to the blackout conditions to impede the enemy and partly due to the sheer lack of lighting to illuminate the base.

Once cargo and passengers were off-loaded, which took little more than a minute, the two Chinooks roared off back into the dark sky, leaving us standing on the silent HLZ. We noticed a slightly lighter void in the darkness at the far side of the HLZ. Scanning the area, one of the passengers from the other Chinook over a hundred meters away yelled out. Piecing the tense night he called for us to join them. There First Sergeant (1SG) Morales, the senior non-commissioned Officer in the Brigade's Headquarters Company, introduced himself and gave some basic directions. Most of the passengers on the helicopters belonged to one of our subordinate Battalions while about fifteen of us were on the Brigade staff and fell under 1SG Morales' direction.   First

Sergeant Morales pulled us away from the main group and was extremely displeased at our presence. He informed us it was pointless for us to be there. There was no place for us to stay. I was initially perplexed by what he meant. Why else would we be there? I quickly came to understand the competing needs. LTC Matthew Stader, the Brigade Executive Officer, needed a staff. He needed a staff to plan and coordinate the logistics and operations for both current operations but also life support. First Sergeant Morales, as the FOB Mayor, was trying to build and distribute infrastructure to accommodate the Brigade Staff and Soldiers who coordinate the logistics and operations. FOB Wilson at the time was not prepared to accommodate the influx of personnel yet to coordinate with higher headquarters in order to get the materials and manpower to support the personnel there needed to be an operational staff present. The early days on FOB Wilson were a competition for assets. The situation that night left us in the lurch but it wasn't KAF. How bad could it be, I figured, and tried to make the best of the situation.

When STRIKE Brigade first received its mission to Kandahar Province, the Brigade sent a team of leaders from Fort Campbell to Kandahar to conduct a pre-deployment site survey (PDSS). The purpose of the PDSS is to get information about the area and learn from units that were already on the ground. One of the first problems seen by the PDSS regarding how our predecessor Brigade, 5-2 Infantry, operated was that its Headquarters and support were based out of KAF, which is no where near the fight. On a good day KAF is a solid two-hour convoy from Zharay or a twenty-minute helicopter flight. The staff of our predecessor unit at KAF had no first hand accounts about the conditions and problems that the Soldiers on the ground in Zharay and Arghandab faced. So with approval from ISAF, COL Kandarian had FOB Wilson expanded from a company-sized outpost that held a group of Canadian advisors to one capable of housing the bulk of a Brigade and our Afghan National Army partners.

Forward Operating Base Wilson's location in central Zharay was ideal for our mission. The base is not only centrally located in the district but also sits along Highway One and includes the district's government center. Within a few weeks of ISAF's approval Navy SeeBees began expanding the FOB's perimeters, enlarging the helicopter landing zone, and building operation centers for the Brigade headquarters and subordinate battalions that would be on the FOB. Additionally, local contractors were hired to build infrastructure such as latrines, shower trailers, living quarters, and dining facilities for our Afghan partners.

First Sergeant Morales' concern the night we landed had been the lack of a sufficient number of tents, let alone cots for all of us. There just had not been enough time to build the infrastructure necessary for the Brigade to live fully supported on FOB Wilson. Our presence was an additional strain to an already overloaded support system.

The first groups from the Brigade headquarters to arrive were not out fighting the Taliban rather they were setting up tents, connecting radios, and building tables and just about everything else imaginable in the excruciating June heat. With very few generators for power, these first Soldiers had no air conditioning or shade to provide relief. While Soldiers from the Brigade focused on FOB Wilson, Soldiers from the 1st Battalion, 502nd were on the ground and patrolling through the east and central portions of Zharay. Everyone felt a sense of urgency. Things needed to get done quickly and done correctly the first time. Soldiers were in harm's way and their efforts, in turn, deserved our best efforts back at the FOB. The night we came off the Chinook though, we had no sense of what needed to be done. So in true Army fashion, we would make due with what we had and what we could find.

We eventually managed to move our bags from the far side of the HLZ to a spot behind some HESCO barriers on the south side of the landing zone. HESCOs are simple yet durable, constructed of paper lining on the inside of a wire mess container. These barriers come in different heights and thickness and when opened and filled with sand, dirt, or gravel, these HESCOs become an expedient and rapidly deployable wall.

Here on the south side of the HLZ my chalk and I found mini-tent city. Most of the tents were up and overflowing with Soldiers. There is actually a military regulation that states each Soldiers is required to have 72 square feet of personal space to prevent transmission of diseases such as the flu and the deployment crud, which is slang for the malaise associated with the constant dust, heat, colds, and stress of being in combat. Despite the 72-square-foot requirement, there was no space to be found among the overflowing tents. Because of operational needs, Soldiers were crammed into every nook and cranny of the tents and many were thankful just to have a cot. I was not as fortunate. In addition to the tents that were set up we found a few tents folded up and ready to be put up in the days to come. These tents would become our cots as we figured it was better to sleep on rubber tents rather than on the ground. It was late and the morning light would soon be emerging over the HESCO barriers. With no protection from the sun it would be hot and unbearable. Sleeping beyond that point would be impossible so I figured I should get some while I could. I managed to find some bottles of water to drink and to use to brush my teeth in a far corner. Using my poncho liner as a blanket, I slept for, at best, four hours.

The next morning the bright light woke me early despite my best efforts to hide my face. The Soldiers I had flown in with were also beginning to stir under the increasing heat and under the anticipation of actually doing our jobs. I was excited to figure out where I needed to be and to see where exactly I was in relation to everything else. Using the leftover water bottles from the previous night we conducted personal hygiene, which is military speak for shaving and brushing our teeth. We then hid our bags under a collapsed tent and began wandering around the FOB. It was still too early to find our bosses so we decided to have a look around.

On the opposite side of the barriers we saw the massive HLZ where we were dropped off the night before. It was probably a football field in width and three fields in length with the north side lined with stacked HESCO barriers that were probably fifteen-feet high. In the distance to the east I could see large hills jutting out of the ground and hear helicopters racing through the sky but low to the ground and out of my sight. Further south from our location I could see the Brigade's Tactical Operations Center (TOC), which was pretty noticeable with all of its antennas.

We wandered around for about twenty minutes trying to get a layout of the FOB and to find the dining facility (DFAC). A few guys were grumbling about being hungry and wanting breakfast and more importantly for me, coffee.

As we waited to get into the DFAC we experienced another reminder of the sudden expansion of the FOB: the DFAC's horrifically long line. The facility had been set up to feed at most 600 Soldiers. But for the past few weeks the number of Soldiers on the FOB had nearly doubled as remnants of the Canadian Company moved out and the STRIKE Brigade descended on to FOB Wilson. The sheer numbers were more that the DFAC could physically handle. In those first few weeks the DFAC would routinely run out of food. Eventually, two of our Battalions set up their own DFACs in their living areas just to help easy the strain on the main dining facility. After eating, we headed toward the Brigade's TOC to learn where and how we could help out as well as figure out what our jobs would be.

The Combined Task Force - STRIKE Tactical Operations Center would eventually be a five-building complex that would accommodate both the STRIKE Brigade and our Afghan Army Partners, but on this day in June 2010, only two buildings were complete. In military terms when branches of the military such as the Army and Air Force operate together it is referred to as "joint," and "combined" refers to the United States' efforts with our international partners such as the Afghan Army.

The main building of the TOC complex was bursting at the seams with activity as Soldiers of all ranks scampered around trying to fix broken radios, establish internet connections on both the classified and non-classified systems, track on-going patrols, coordinate support for troops in contact, and prepare vehicles for future missions. While we waited for LTC Stader, the Brigade executive Officer, I wandered through the halls and met as many people as I could, figuring these were the people with whom I could be working and it would be best to introduce myself. My learning curve needed to be steep, and I hoped to gain some insight into how things worked and whom I would be working for and with, but, more importantly, I stayed out of the way and observed. I could easily do more harm than good and slow progress by wrongfully inserting myself.

After about thirty minutes or so of waiting we met LTC Matthew Stader who was clearly stressed. I am of average height, and I remember LTC Stader being a giant. LTC Stader easily had six inches on me, but his stature was more due to his personality. He was a man everyone respected and took orders from yet was approachable.

As the Brigade's executive Officer, he was in charge of getting everything up and running while supporting current operations. He clearly cared about the Soldiers of the Brigade. It was a stressful time and would not let up in the days and the months to come. We were quickly given our marching orders and assigned our immediate tasks.

CPT Meyers was put in charge of coordinating with flight operations at KAF to keep Soldiers and equipment moving. Having previously served with the aviation Brigade currently operating at KAF, CPT Meyers was ideally suited for the job. He knew a lot of members of the aviation unit and could get things accomplished by simply making phone calls to old friends. Two of the other Captains were assigned jobs as Battle Captains and would be over seeing the establishment of the TOC and coordinating all of the current operations. One would be a day battle captain and one would be the night battle captain, and their efforts were greatly appreciated by the "Battle Major" who oversaw both day and night operations. Prior to their arrival the Battle Major had been doing it all and needed to delegate responsibilities. Another Captain was sent to work at the District Center to help develop the local governance. Major Travares and I were assigned to the Operations section and to work for Major Clint Cox, the Brigade Operations Officer.

Major Travares and I would be the planning section. We were tasked with conceptualizing future operations, getting approval form the Brigade Commander for their execution, and then coordinating resources for them before passing them off to the current operations section, which would oversee their execution.

We were also in charge of writing the daily fragmentation order, commonly referred to as FRAGO, which would disseminate information and tasks to all subordinate units and staffs. The FRAGO is critical for ensuring that everyone knows what the Brigade is doing and when. Being the low man on the totem pole, I assumed this task would fall to me and was ready for it. As a planner and battle captain at a Battalion level in Iraq, I had written FRAGOs prior to becoming a platoon leader. I thought it was a pretty easy and straight forward.

You need two things to be successful with the task of writing FRAGOs: one, an internet connection to get Regional Command South's orders and two, a government computer to get on the network. I had neither. In fact, I did not have a place to sit. There was no room in a building already bursting at the seams.

Eventually the planning section would be moved into a separate building but that building would not be finished for some time. A specific transformer that was needed to provide power to the building from the generator had not be delivered to FOB Wilson despite having been ordered months ago. The transformer was on back order from the manufacture in Germany, and according to the SeeBees on the ground it had not yet been manufactured. American generators and transformers are generally designed to handle a 110-volt system, however the TOC buildings were designed to operate at 220 volts so that when ISAF's mission was complete the buildings could be transferred to the Afghans. The buildings needed to operable on their power system.

Major Travares and I managed to carve out a two-seat section on the top row of the auditorium-style main room of the TOC where we could interact with the liaisons from the subordinate unit versus sending an email via the usually spotty internet connection. It would also be the easiest way pass tasks and information to the subordinate unit. The Brigade's communication section managed to secure us a computer for us to share. We convinced ourselves a chair and a computer was progress.

According to Army doctrine, we should have had several more Captains and a couple non-commissioned Officers in our Brigade-level plans shop, however the Brigade as a whole was under-strengthed and the priority of support was to the Battalions. Our subordinate battalions were in the fight and needed the extra help more than we did; so the Brigade headquarters had to do more with less.

At some point that first morning, I met Colonel Arthur Kandarian, the STRIKE Brigade Commander whose call sign was "STRIKE 6." I don't exactly remember how the exchange went but I remembering snapping to attention and saying something along the lines of "I am new" and a lot of "Yes sirs" to his questions and comments. Colonel Kandarian is both a good Officer and leader yet a demanding man to work for. He is respected and feared at all levels and as I learned over the remainder of the deployment makes every decision with a great deal of forethought, drawn from research and personal experience. He stood few inches taller than me with a lean, athletic frame and a balding head with his remaining hair kept closely trimmed. I was nervous to say the least in our first encounter, mostly due to the fact I had not expected to see the Brigade Commander on my first morning down range.

Colonel Kandarian lives by the mantra of "leading from the front." He refused the luxuries normally enjoyed from high rank. He refused, for example, to use the shower tent or to have even his own shower, which is a privilege regularly enjoyed by senior leaders. Instead Colonel Kandarian showered with water bottles every day of the deployment behind his containerized housing unit. He figured if the young Soldiers in the field had to do this, then there was no reason for him not to as well. Over the subsequent weeks and months the Soldiers of the Brigade on the distant outposts would learn of his choices for hard living. We all grew to appreciate his character and respected him for it.

At the time I knew Colonel Kandarian had served a good portion of his career with the Ranger Regiment and then had been a Battalion Commander in Iraq within the STRIKE Brigade, commanding the 2nd Battalion, 502nd Infantry Battalion. He had deferred his slot at the War College in order to return to command the STRIKE Brigade in Afghanistan. At the end of our brief initial encounter, he told me that he would counsel me later. This sounded ominous. Brigade Commanders control the fates of Captains as they choose who will be one of their Company Commanders and when that coveted command occurs. So it is common to be immediately counseled on the Commander's philosophy and expectations of his subordinates.

I spent the next several hours wandering around the TOC, meeting more and more people and studying maps and imagery of the Brigade's area of operations. I had a lot to learn in a short period of time. I needed to learn our task organization, who was assigned to the Brigade and for whom the Brigade worked. I also needed to understand what and where the enemy was, which was information I learned by talking to the intelligence section. This day began my education into the Taliban and fighting in Afghanistan's "Green Zone," which earned its name from being a swath of dense farm land full of grapes, pomegranates, and trees on the north and south side of the Arghandab River.

I also began expressing an interest that I had kept to myself until I was at FOB Wilson with the Brigade staff since I did not know how people would react. I wanted to work with the Afghan Army. I had partnered and mentored Iraqi Police and Army personnel as a platoon leader in 2008 and wanted to do it again. As I expressed this desire to Majors Cox and Travares I got little to no resistance and was even encouraged to go that route as long as it did not interfere with my duties in the plans shop. Basically, if I did every thing that needed to get done, they did not care. I suspect that they expected me to struggle with my regular tasks and would not have time to devote to working with the ANA. They had little to no knowledge of my background.

Unique about our role with the 3rd Brigade, 205th Corps Afghan Army unit was that STRIKE Brigade was the first Infantry Brigade Combat Team in the war to be fully partnered. In the past ANA units had coalition mentors and trainers assigned to them but the 3-205th Brigade had neither. The ANA Brigade was newly formed. It was composed of basic training graduates and a smattering of Officers from the Afghan Army but had never worked together before. What I did not expect or know at the time was that each month I was required to accumulate a workbook of reports into what is referred to as the CUAT (the Commander's Update Assessment Tool) on the ANA's skills and capabilities from each *kandak* or battalion, and the Brigade staff as a whole.

Later that evening, I had my first introduction to the Taliban in what I'm sure they considered a welcoming present. As I walked back into the Brigade TOC from dinner at the DFAC, three rounds from an 82 recoilless rifle came toward the FOB. There was no early warning radar established in those early days and the sounds and flashes of the impacts were our only notice, so to speak. The closest impacted on the opposite side of a HESCO barrier about 50 feet away, sending sand high into the air. The other two rounds fell short and hit just on the outside of the wall and slightly east of the TOC. *Welcome to Afghanistan!*

No one was injured during the attack but this first attack would become the routine and brought to my mind flashes of my basic training days and Officer candidate schooling where we would conduct the time honored tradition of stand-to. The tradition dates back to the pre-night vision goggle days when the enemy would either attack at dawn or dusk, using the cover of darkness to either move into position or escape. In basic training, we would pull security in our little platoon patrol bases while our Drill Sergeants sat in the middle of our patrol base and on any given day we would be attacked by other Soldiers or Drill Sergeants who fired blank rounds and enjoyed throwing CS (tear) gas canisters to add to our misery. Here in Afghanistan, the Taliban used the same techniques and the concealment of darkness and of the foliage of the green zone to avoid the Brigade's surveillance and counter-attack capabilities.

In the dust of the incoming rounds we raced around to ensure no one was injured and to assess if any damage had been inflicted. Perhaps it was not the Taliban's intent to push and test the STRIKE Brigade but they did. The STRIKE Soldiers adapted quickly and learned from this attack and others that occurred in those early days. The operations center and intelligence section learned the Taliban's techniques and tactics. The Brigade honed its response capabilities and very soon our ability to clear airspace of all coalition aircraft and have eyes on the points of origin of the incoming became so fast that our fire support section could rain a barrage of precision counter-fire from our four M777 howitzers on to the Taliban firing points. We would STRIKE back at the Taliban and provide them with no means of escape.

Hours later I walked back to the tent area at the end of a long first day. I checked on my bags that I had stashed that morning and was thankful the few bags carrying my life for the next year remained unmolested. I found the shower tent but was frustrated to find there was no water. So I adapted. I took my first of many water bottle showers under the Afghan stars. Exhausted I wrapped myself in my trusty poncho liner and began to drift of to sleep and counted in my head: first day down, 364 to go. This would turn into a typical day when nothing special happened yet everything seemed to happen. Deployments are chaos, chaos that is repetitive and constant and almost predictable, almost.

Chapter 7
Shonna Ba Shonna

Do not try to do too much with your own hands. Better
the Arabs do it tolerably than that you do it perfectly.
It is their war, and you are to help them, not to win it
for them. Actually, also, under the very odd conditions
of Arabia, your practical work will not be as good as,
perhaps, you think it is.

T.E. Lawrence,
Twenty-Seven Articles, 1917

Partnership is tough to explain to an eighteen-year-old Soldier on his first deployment. Foreign internal defense, commonly seen as developing other nation's military capabilities, is a mission typically reserved for special operations Soldiers. But we weren't Special Forces and had no additional training. Our Soldiers had to work with and communicate our skills and knowledge to an Afghan Soldier. Partnership is the last thing on the mind of a young eighteen-year-old infantryman. He joined the Army to do a lot of things: to be a killer, to fight the Taliban, to get money for school, to get a job. But training the Afghan military is not one of them. The typical American Soldier did not understand that the Afghan standing next to him knew more about hardship, death, conflict, family, and religion than he did. The Afghan Soldier tended to see a skinny boy in a ragged uniform who did not know how to handle his weapon. But the reality is that the Afghan Army was our partner and that ragged Afghan Soldier was our best hope for never coming back.

The Afghan Soldier and the American Soldier were partners against the Taliban, and we were expected to stand shoulder to shoulder together, *Shonna Ba Shonna*. Alas, Afghanistan is not the United States, and our methods and fighting techniques only go so far. Afghanistan was the Afghan Soldiers' home, and despite what we said otherwise, they had a vested interest in their country's future. But their vested interest and our interest were not necessarily the same. Subsequently, expectations had to be managed. As Americans we could only do so much in the time we are given.

Being deployed consists of long days that bleed into late nights. There just are never enough hours in the day. There is always one more thing to do. During a deployment you have a finite amount of time to make a difference. There is only so much time to accomplish the mission, which can range from destroying the enemy of the United States to helping a fledgling government. The goal is not to go out and win medals and be some sort of hero but to prevent yourself from having to come back again.

In Afghanistan, we had less than one year to accomplish a lot: separate the Taliban from the local population, build infrastructure, partner with our Afghan Army partners to build their capabilities so that they could sustain the fight in our absence, and set conditions for our replacements. These tasks are not easy and require a team effort. No single person can do it all. The STRIKE Brigade transformed its organic task organization of two infantry battalions, a reconnaissance squadron, one field artillery battalion, and two support battalions, all together totaling nearly 3,500 Soldiers, into Combined Task Force (CTF-STRIKE) consisting of 8 U.S. Army Battalions and 8 Afghan Army Battalions, which all totaled nearly 10,000 Soldiers. Our combined task force in early July was larger than some divisions, and we were still growing.

The Brigade constantly pushed Soldiers out from KAF and into the districts of Arghandab, Zharay, and Maiwand so that the STRIKE Brigade had Soldiers out living among the local population and fighting the Taliban. In the Arghandab we had two battalions splitting the district into two battle spaces with the 1st Battalion, 320th Field Artillery, who was functioning as infantry, in the north and 2nd Battalion, 508th Infantry Regiment, 82nd Airborne in the south based out of the district center. In eastern Zharay we had 1st Battalion, 502nd Infantry Regiment while 2nd Battalion, 502nd Infantry Regiment was in western Zharay.

In Maiwand we had the 3rd Squadron, 2nd Cavalry (Stryker) Regiment from Vilseck, Germany, and were concentrated out of FOB Ramrod. At FOB Wilson in central Zharay we had our Special Troops Battalion and Support Battalion while 1st Squadron, 75th Cavalry was feverishly working on pushing our newly formed Afghan Army partners out of the relative luxury of Camp Hero near KAF and into

Zharay and Maiwand where our Soldiers were fighting and functioning unilaterally.

No form of technology in terms of robots, computers, imagery, and biometric sensors can replace local knowledge. Not just the knowledge of who lives where but the cultural understanding of how the people live and how the people and villages interact. Despite our exceptional skills as Soldiers, we lacked knowledge of the people, local customs, and tribal and sub-tribal relation. We needed all of our Afghan partners. Our battalions in the Arghandab and in Eastern Zharay had Afghan Army partners from 1st Brigade, 205th Corps, however the rest of the Brigade remained unpartnered at the time because the 3rd Brigade, 205th Corps refused to leave Camp Hero.

As we surged into Afghanistan there was a simultaneous internal surge to rapidly build its Army's capabilities. This surge led to the formation of the 3rd Brigade, 205th Corps. Most of the Soldiers in the newly formed Afghan Army Brigade had just completed their basic training and skill training, comparable to the military occupational specialty training in the U.S. military that differentiates the jobs of each Soldier from clerics to infantry to engineers and so forth, near Kabul and were newly assigned to Kandahar. For many of these young Afghan Soldiers, it was the farthest and the longest they had ever been from home. Talking to the Afghan Soldiers, many of whom were farmers and young men, there was sense of wanting to do more. The Afghans had signed up not for educational or health benefits. There was no Montgomery G.I Bill or Tricare health plan for these Soldiers. These Soldiers had signed up to help end a destructive era they had grown to loathe. These Soldiers wanted to fight. Meanwhile their Brigade Commander did not.

Colonel Abdul Fatah Azizi, the first Commander of 3-205 ANA, was a large, unfit man. I suspect his waistline matched his height, which was over six feet. He had a thick dark black mustache that he dyed with shoe polish. He reminded me of a Central American revolutionary from the 1980s. Despite his physical presence, he was a weak, tepid man that refused to leave the sanctuary of Camp Hero where the streets and sidewalks were paved, where eucalyptus trees lined the roads providing shade and a sweet perfume that hid the stench of sewage. Here at Camp Hero, Colonel Azizi could live like a king, eating gluttonously amounts of rice, lamb, and sweets while watching satellite television in his air-conditioned office and quarters.

Colonel Kandarian had Colonel Azizi flown out to FOB Wilson to inspect the shared operating base and tour the Afghan Army living quarters. Colonel Kandarian personally escorted Colonel Azizi on a foot tour of FOB Wilson. Colonel Azizi constantly complained it was too hot, too dusty, and that the living quarters were not satisfactory for his men.

The reality, however, was the American taxpayers had paid millions of dollar to set up tents; install shower trailers and latrines; build dining facilities, and provide a containerized housing units for each of his Officers yet he scoffed at the efforts. While Colonel Azizi was upset about his quarters, American Soldiers were sleeping on the ground, rarely had water to shower let alone hot water, and dealt with constant power outages. Despite the hardships the American Soldiers were enduring it was only Colonel Azizi was the one complaining. Our living areas were intermixed so that partner battalions lived and worked next to each other to foster trust and a constant learning environment. I frequently heard young American Soldiers complain to each other about why they are sleeping in old over-crowded tents when the Afghans had brand new tents that sat empty.

We spent millions of dollars more to get more gravel down on the dusty roads while American Soldiers were dying on unpartnered patrols. On July 2, 2010, the Taliban attacked a small outpost on the eastern edge of Zharay detonating a vehicle-borne improvised explosive device that decimated the tiny structure that held a platoon from 2-508 Infantry. This bombing wounded six and forced the STRIKE staff to scramble for contingency forces. Ultimately, the Brigade air assaulted a platoon from Charlie Company, 1-75 CAV out of Kandahar Airfield to secure the site and recover all U.S. military gear. The Taliban were on the offensive. The summer was the Taliban's fighting season, and until the STRIKE Brigade could convince its Afghan Army partners to get into the fight with us, American Soldiers were going to be forced to continue to operate, and potentially die, alone.

Only after days of relentless pressure through RC-South and by the 205th Corps Commander did Colonel Azizi capitulate. He finally ordered his troops to begin moving to FOB Wilson and the outlying outposts. The presence of the Afghan Soldiers was a critical start to our partnership and to the people of Zharay. The local population needed to see fellow Afghans out working for them and not foreign troops that reminded them of the Russians of yester year.

I struggled to work with Colonel Azizi and dreaded having to talk to him. He literally refused to leave his office. He literally did everything there. He choose to sleep there along with his three young clerks/body guards/servants. In those first few days I would go to talk with him in an effort to build trust while Colonel Kandarian would try and discuss future operations, yet all he did was complain. For Colonel Azizi, leaving the office was a significant activity. He sat in his air-conditioned office while his partner, Colonel Kandarian, went daily to see both American and Afghan troops at FOB Howz-e-Madad and all of the other outposts throughout the large battle space. Colonel Azizi commanded through his cell phone and listened to updates from his kandak/battalion commanders.

Instead of worrying about his Soldiers and their needs, Colonel Azizi worried about his personal financial health. He frequently asked about ISAF contracts such as lucrative construction and logistics agreements. His lack of leadership and unwillingness to do the right thing was disheartening.

I, and others, suspected his corruption and refused to award any contracts to his "preferred vendors," let alone listen to him talk about how he could help "manage" the contracts. Unlike the American military where promotions and commands are based on merit, the Afghan system is based on politics, which is to be expected in a developing nation but was a pressing issue, which the STRIKE needed to contend. Our Army for decades was based on a similar system but over time our evaluation system evolved, and promotions and positions became less about who you knew and more on merit and experience. Even in the most horribly corrupt system, there is still a means to remove ineffective and corrupt commanders, but it is a difficult and tedious one.

On July 19, 2010, STRIKE held an uncasing of the colors ceremony with Colonel Azizi and all of his kandak commanders as well as the district leadership. We wanted to announce officially our presence in the district, our partnership with the Afghans, and our mission to help the people of Zharay. Colonel Azizi struggled through the short ceremony. His struggle has nothing to do with his speech, rather he struggled to remain upright like a Soldier. It was a warm morning and Colonel Azizi was not accustomed to be being out of the air conditioning. He was sweating profusely and wobbly the entire ceremony. Meanwhile, following the ceremony, Colonel Kandarian held a Banam Shura or "together council" with the leaders of the district to hear their views and dreams for the district. Notably, Colonel Azizi was absent.

While Colonel Kandarian and I openly struggled with Colonel Azizi and his actions, we also fought a smart, subversive political fight against him. Prior to STRIKE's arrival in Afghanistan, the U.S. Marine Corps offensive in Helmand had been the main effort of ISAF. Kandahar, however, was of greater strategic significance and ISAF leadership was intent on seeing action. The new ISAF Commander, General David Petraeus, having taken over for General Stanley McChrystal about the time I flew into Afghanistan, was paying close attention to Kandahar and STRIKE's presence, particularly because of our daily fights with the Taliban and our struggles with Colonel Azizi. General Petraeus was reading our daily situational reports that were sent to Regional Command - South and the initial Commander's Update Assessment Tool (CUAT) on our ANA partners.

The CUAT was far from glowing, and it was extremely harsh on Colonel Azizi. Colonel Kandarian even let him read what had been written about him. It was an honest and straightforward assessment of Colonel Azizi that left him flabbergasted. His face turned bright red with anger as he read the translated version. Colonel Kandarian pulled no punches. Political and military decisions in Kabul were being made because the offensive in Kandahar needed to begin and Colonel Azizi was impeding the mission. Had the same words written in the CUAT about Colonel Azizi been written in an American Officer's evaluation report that Officer would easily have been kicked out of the military. It was that devastating. The Afghan system is vastly different. Colonel Azizi, instead of being removed from power, was promoted to luxurious job in Kabul so that he could save face.

Just in time to see Colonel Azizi leave 3-205 ANA, the ANA Brigade's executive Officer arrived from Helmand where he had been fighting with the Marines against the Taliban in Marja. Colonel Quandahari was the leader the Brigade needed. He was from the

Arghandab and had fought against the Russians there in the 1980s, having laid ambushes along Highway One using the grape walls and beautiful green vegetation for cover. Colonel Quandahari would regale me with stories of sheltering in underground bunkers for days as Soviet artillery shells rained down on the Mujahideen positions southwest of Nalgham. Being a local, Colonel Quandahari aptly understood the significance of the fight in Arghandab and Zharay. Symbols and gestures are important in Afghan culture, and there was no greater symbol that fighting the Taliban in its birthplace.

Through Colonel Quandahari, I came to fully understand and appreciate the concept of local Taliban and foreign Taliban. The local Taliban are those who pick up arms and fight because they have no other choice. Sometimes, local Taliban fighters are forced to fight when a foreign fighter threatens him or his family. Sometimes, local Taliban must fight to seek revenge against NATO under their code of honor, Pashtunwali. The foreign Taliban, in simplistic terms, is not a local; some come from other parts of Afghanistan, some form other countries such as Pakistan, Yemen, Saudi Arabia and others in the name of jihad. The foreign Taliban are believers and seek nothing more than to kill infidels.

The learning curve with Colonel Quandahari was steep but relatively easy. From my perspective, Colonel Quandahari was disgusted with Colonel Azizi. He viewed Azizi as a thief and had no shortage of harsh words to describe his former commander. As Colonel Azizi left FOB Wilson, he attempted to convince his subordinate commanders and Officers that his removal was Colonel Kandarian's fault and that the STRIKE Brigade was holding the ANA back and preventing them from doing their job in the district. His words could not have been further from the truth. Colonel Quandahari recognized Azizi's corruption and immediately held a meeting with the ANA brigade staff and kandak commanders. For the first time our partnered ANA brigade had a leader. Colonel Quandahari pushed his staff to work with the STRIKE staff and for his kandak commanders to do the same with their partners.

Colonel Quandahari was a charismatic leader whose decisions were based on common sense, a rarity in Afghanistan. He stressed to his subordinate ANA leaders that we (the Americans) would not be there forever and that unless they wanted to keep fighting here in Kandahar and away from their families, then they needed to defeat the Taliban. Colonel Quandahari understood the assets the STRIKE Brigade could bring to the fight. During his Mujahideen days he had wished for a greater commitment from the U.S. Now against the Taliban he was getting that commitment and in a position to make a difference.

Seeing Colonel Quandahari in action, Colonel Kandarian petitioned 205th Corps through RC-South to keep Colonel Quandahari as the Brigade Commander. The STRIKE Brigade had won the fight for Colonel Azizi's removal but would not win this fight. Despite the many nepotistic aspects of the Afghan military and government, there is a degree of order. Rank means everything, and Colonel Quandahari was a junior Colonel in the system.

Colonel Quandahari was a natural leader and a fighter for decades having been a Mujahideen. He lacked, however, the formal training to rise through the ranks. The new Brigade Commander had already been selected and was on his way to Kandahar having recently completed the Afghan equivalent of the U.S. Army's War College in Kabul.

Colonel Murtaza was a short, fit man who looked like a Soldier and who, like most Afghan men his age, hid his graying hair with dye. Warriors do not have gray hair. Colonel Murtaza arrived a couple weeks after Colonel Azizi's departure and came ready to work.

Unlike Colonel Quandahari, Colonel Murtaza had formal military training, having been conscripted into the Afghan Army under the Soviets. Colonel Murtaza was from the northern province of Panjshir. After the Soviet withdrawal, he had fought under Ahmad Shah Massoud in the Northern Alliance against the Taliban. Despite their divided pasts under the Soviets and ethnic differences, Colonels Murtaza and Quandahari shared an extreme hatred for the Taliban.

Colonel Murtaza did not hesitate to follow the old adage of "when in charge, be in charge." Colonel Murtaza was small in stature but large in action, proving to the STRIKE Brigade that there are many capable leaders in the Afghan Army. He immediately took over and began going on battlefield circulations with Colonel Kandarian. He understood the necessity to see his Soldiers, something Colonel Azizi had refused to do. Instantly the kandak commanders were held accountable, and he worked to get his rogue and corrupt 6th Kandak Commander under control.

Despite being assigned to fill out the 3rd Brigades task organization, still the 6th Kandak Commander refused to work for Colonel Murtaza. The 6th Kandak had originally been part of 1st Brigade, 205th Corps and was referred to as the "Highway Kandak" due to their mission. They refused to recognize the new task organization. The 6th Kandak was spread out along Highway One from the northwest edge of Kandahar City through Zharay and Maiwand to the Helmand border. There, the kandak commander controlled commerce along Highway One. He was essentially tariffing people who wanted to pass. He was no better than the warlords that the Taliban had risen up against. He was also suspected of stealing fuel from our depots and selling it on the black market. As Americans, our suspicions and disgust at the corruption meant nothing to the Afghans. For many it was a part of doing business, as long as it was not overburdening. But we kept a constant presence around the 6th Kandak checkpoints in an effort to stem the blatant corruption, and we sent the issue up the chain of command.

As the days and weeks progressed the 6th Kandak Commander continued to refuse to even acknowledge Colonel Murtaza as his commander. He would often go complain to the 1st Brigade Commander and the 205th Corps Commander about his treatment. In a sense the 6th Kandak Commander had been correct. He had been given a verbal order from General Hamid the 205th Corps Commander, and since he did not have an official order from the Ministry of Defense (MOD) he choose to ignore his division commander. The Afghan concept of following a superior Officer's orders is very different than ours.

In building trust and partnership Colonel Murtaza asked Colonel Kandarian and me to help. Colonel Murtaza needed the order from MoD to rein in the 6th Kandak and officially reflag the 6-1-205 Kandak to 6-3-205, under Colonel Murtaza's complete control. The process took several weeks but upon receipt of the order Colonel Murtaza immediately consolidated the 6th kandak in Maiwand and off Highway One, which drastically hurt the kandak commander's profit margin. Highway One, once the kandak commander's financial thoroughfare, was now off limits. He could no longer justify any presence along the highway.

Colonel Murtaza was not afraid to take risks. He pushed his Soldiers to conduct combined patrols with the STRIKE Brigade and encouraged his Soldiers to take pride in their efforts. I often listened to him talk to his Soldiers at the distant outposts and frequently heard him tell his Soldiers that, "It is easy for the Americans to do the work, but it is *our* country and the Taliban are cowards who *destroy* our country."

Colonel Murtaza was also very intuitive and learned a great deal from Colonel Kandarian. The daily interaction between the two leaders caused many of the American leader's traits to be instilled into Colonel Murtaza, especially in leading by example and implementing discipline. Colonel Kandarian had a brilliant habit of picking up any errant trash he discovered around the FOB and criticizing those nearby saying that the trash was a sign of poor discipline. He would often make a show of picking up the trash, remarking, "Don't worry. This is Colonel trash, I'll get it."

Colonel Kandarian's actions embarrassed the Soldiers who are nearby and motivated them to do the right thing. Colonel Kandarian would do this not only on FOB Wilson but also on the tiny patrol bases and outposts letting the Soldiers there know that standards are the same for everyone no matter where they lived. After a few months, I would see Colonel Murtaza inspecting the ANA living areas and admonishing his Soldiers for their trash and filth just as Colonel Kandarian did. Colonel Murtaza would tell the Soldiers that "the Qur'an does not tell them to live this way so why were they?"

Colonel Murtaza was not perfect, but he truly cared about his Soldiers. He would often ask me for things not to improve his quality of life but to improve that of his Soldiers. Still, as Americans, we had restrictions on what and how we could give to the ANA. Personally, I was not going to bend the rules to make a friend. Bending the rules for the sake of convenience was not going to make the ANA better Soldiers and would only likely end up with me in trouble.

If the Afghans wanted something, I wanted something in return. My favorite quid pro quo request back to the ANA was for a camel. The interpreter did not initially understand my comments but finally caught on that I was asking for something ridiculous of the ANA just as I perceived their requests to me.

I knew that for the ANA it was easier to ask the Americans instead of going through their own channels. I had also learned there was a warehouse full of supplies at Camp Hero if the ANA would simply request the goods. So before I would even entertain them asking me for something, I wanted a copy of their denied request form from the 205th Corps headquarters. This not only dropped the number of requests, but when in hand, the denied request gave me something to send to the ANA mentors at RC-S to fix on their end.

I spent many days and nights reading through Afghan training manuals that had been translated to English, which for the most part resembled the American system. I sent notes out daily to subordinate commanders on how the Afghan systems worked and on ways to get the ANA to use their internal systems. As a Brigade, we learned the ANA systems for maintenance and supplies because the ANA did not know it themselves. For example, the ANA did not like taking vehicles out on patrols because if a vehicle broke down or was damaged they couldn't fixed it. The ANA did not know how to request a replacement part. Consequently the ANA hid damaged vehicles on the FOB in a state of disrepair and would report all vehicles operational.

At times I would walk around to the back corners of FOB Wilson and find dozens of Afghan Army Ford Rangers and armored vehicles wasting away. It took us teaching them how to order parts and to fix the vehicles through their own contracting system before the number of broken vehicles began to diminish. The Afghans have their own systems that worked if you forced them to use it. So we taught the ANA about their own supply system.

As the 3rd Brigade Soldiers began patrolling and sharing the hardships of the daily patrols with their STRIKE partners, as a staff, STRIKE started to look at the ANA Brigade staff. We did not have mentor teams for our Afghan Army counterparts so it was up to us to teach them as we went, aka on-the-job training.

A major problem we had to endure was ourselves. The STRIKE staff was full of sections and individuals who would drag their feet and avoid their counterparts because they didn't want to work with them. My fellow Americans Soldiers would complain that the Afghans smelled or were lazy ergo they did not need to work with them.

From the Afghans, I would hear that their counterparts talk down to them. I was stuck in the middle. I became the conduit of complaints as each side would come to me for mediation as if I could mend their relationship by making an Afghan bathe more or stopping someone who out ranked me from being a bigot. I am never one for sensitivity and when Colonel Kandarian would ask about certain sections or tasks, I would be honest and say that Major so-and-so refused to work with his partners and to do his job. An infuriated Colonel Kandarian would generally fix the situation with a few choice words, which at the very least would facilitate a minimal effort of certain STRIKE staff sections.

A few Officers, however, understood how to work with the Afghans and had tremendous success. LTC Stader and Major Cox worked extremely well with their counterparts, held combined Afghan and American meetings that led to the production of combined plans and combined operations.

The Afghans, involved in the process, actually cared about the outcome. They had a vested interest and did not feel like our puppets. The Afghans understood more than they let on and were capable of accomplishing anything when they needed to but why should they if the Americans provide everything for them. Throughout their training and prior experiences with American and NATO mentor teams the Afghans were not given the opportunity. Americans are impatient and want instant results and would often prefer to throw money at a problem or do it themselves; this instant solution rarely allowed the Afghans to succeed. As a Brigade we had to balance finely the needs of the mission with our patience.

We knew we were part of the surge. Our presence represented the most contact the people of Arghandab, Zharay, and Maiwand had ever had with Americans and coalition forces which would immediately diminish with our replacement unit, 3rd Brigade, 10th Mountain. We were taking a lesson from David Kilcullen's *28 Articles* and already preparing our handover. Frequently, I heard Colonel Kandarian ask others, and me "if I (we) wanted to keep coming back to Afghanistan?" and the honest answer was an emphatic NO!

As each day ground on, the more I missed home just as every other Soldier in the Brigade missed home. The long-term exit strategy is the presence of an Afghan Army. An Army that does not only exist on paper but is also capable of protecting the people and the Brigade worked persistently with our ANA partners. We sought to build their combat skills, their ability to plan and execute missions, and their ability to support themselves through their own logistics channels; the Taliban however had a vote in our success.

The Taliban was born in Zharay and has used Maiwand, Zharay, and Arghandab to influence Kandahar City and Afghanistan as a whole since the Taliban's inception. When STRIKE arrived the Taliban effectively controlled Highway One and used the thick hedge row-like vegetation to keep ISAF forces at bay and away from the population. The Taliban had the freedom of maneuver; controlling the local population through fear and intimidation. So while we allocated resources and efforts to build our Afghan partners in the 3rd Brigade, 205th Corps, we simultaneously, with our fledgling ANA partners, also set out to strip the Taliban of their birthplace.

Chapter 8
Operation Unify Arghandab

In the early morning hours of July 30, 2010, the Soldiers of 1st Battalion, 320th Field Artillery Battalion "Top Guns, began their movement to secure the intersection Route Mariners and Highlife, which connected COPs Nolen, Tynes, Terra Nova, and Jelawar. This intersection was critical to freedom of maneuver for both the Taliban and our forces. If the operation were successful, our presence would separate sufficiently the local population from the Taliban so that the people could have the opportunity to access their fields and harvest their grapes and pomegranates. The physical intersection was named Objective Bakersfield and for five straight days, Top Gun Soldiers and their Afghan Army partners endured indirect fire, small arms fire, and sniper attacks. Gaining and holding Bakersfield would be costly.

On the first day, Sergeant Kyle Stout, Specialist Michael Stansbery, and Master Sergeant (Retired) Robert Pittman of the Asymmetric Warfare Group were killed by IEDs and small arms fire. The close fighting last nearly five days, leading to the destruction over 25 IEDs around the area and the establishment of COP Stout, in honor of the fallen Top Guns Soldier.

It was nearly two weeks after the heavy fighting that I went to COP Stout with the acting Brigade Command Sergeant Major John White. Within minutes of dismounting our armored trucks, explosions concussed around us. We were in the open as the Taliban began firing 30mm high explosive rounds at the outpost. We quickly moved to cover and ended up in a small fighting position near a tree along the canal on the southern edge of the COP. On the other side of the canal lay an open farm field nearly a hundred meters in length with a small compound and heavy vegetation on the other side. The field was no man's land as the Taliban had emplaced dozens of IEDs.

Unbeknownst to us in the foxhole, close air support had been called. Suddenly the tremendous ripping sound of fifty caliber machine guns tore through the chaos as two OH-58D Kiowa helicopters made strafing runs at the suspected Taliban firing positions. The pilots flew at top speed just above the treetops, giving me the eerie sense that I could reach up and touch the helicopter's skids. After the first pass the helicopters circled around for another run, this time firing high explosive rockets.

The helicopters invigorated the partnered ANA platoons from 1-205 ANA. The ANA sat up from their adjacent foxhole and fired 40mm rounds from their attached M203 grenade launcher back at the Taliban. It had little damaging effect on the Taliban but was equally as harassing as the fire we were receiving. The ANA fired so many rounds so rapidly that two of the launchers jammed from their own heat.

Suddenly a massive explosion cut the vigor of the ANA and American Soldiers at COP Stout. The explosion came from a couple hundred meters away near COP Nolan. Everyone knew it was an IED but wondered if it was deliberately detonated or if someone stepped on it. This was life and death in the Arghandab.

The Arghandab District lies directly north of Kandahar City and is roughly separated from the city by the Arghandab River as well as a large steep hill. On the south side of the hill I could look out and see the low-lying mud houses and buildings of Kandahar City that spread out like a dust-encrusted spider web. Immediately at the base of the hill on the south side is the former home of Mullah Omar when he was the leader of the Taliban during the 1990s. On the north side and, barely visible through the thick, vegetation are pockets of houses and villages, however most residents in the district live at the base of the hill along the Arghandab River.

The first time I saw the Arghandab was from high above as I rode in a Blackhawk helicopter with Colonel Arthur Kandarian, Major Clint Cox, and Major Bo Mixon (the Brigade Intelligence Officer) to the district center, which sits about two-thirds of the way up that steep hill and overlooks the district to the north.

Since the STRIKE Brigade arrived in Afghanistan and into the districts of Arghandab, Zharay, and Maiwand, the Regional Commander, Major General Vance of the Canadian Army, had wanted action. He wanted a combined operation against the Taliban in the Arghandab. The district provided the Taliban close proximity to Kandahar City. The Taliban were detrimentally affecting local governance, development, and general security in the city, which is one of the largest cities in Afghanistan.

The dense pomegranate orchards and high grape walls provide the Taliban ideal cover and concealment from coalition forces. Walking through this area was akin to walking through a jungle as a predator lays in wait for its prey to pass. Despite modern tactics and military capabilities, STRIKE Soldiers were still the prey. The Taliban, at home in the green zone, had the advantage. The Taliban encircle their camps and buildings with defensive belts of improvised explosive devices so that when coalition troops attempted to approach, many Soldiers would be either maimed or killed. There were very few fields large enough to land a helicopter and those that did exist were similarly booby-trapped. The Taliban had observed NATO troops for long enough to know how our Soldiers moved and acted around the battlefield.

In early July, as elements of 1st Battalion, 320th Field Artillery (Top Guns) settled into combat outposts in the Arghandab, they began to understand the needs of the local population and the difficulty of the terrain. The locals complained about not being able to harvest their grapes and pomegranates, which left unattended would rot as the summer heat persisted. The Taliban used the farmers' fields and orchards for cover. The less the green zone was harvested, the more cover the Taliban could maintain.

Under the cover of darkness on July 10th, Alpha Battery moved 1,200 meters south of COP Nolen and established a new patrol base in the dense pomegranate orchards near the village of Noor Mohammad Khan Kalache. The next morning Bravo Battery conducted a similar operation and established a patrol base in a compound northwest of Khosrow Sofla, which is just south of intersection of Route Highlife and the 2nd Canal crossing point along Route Mariners. Despite their names as routes, which would seem to imply large roads, both Route Highlife and Mariners were little more than trails but were still heavily used by the Taliban and the locals alike.

Heat and the exertion of climbing over eight-foot walls and through grape orchards that trapped the humidity and moisture close to the ground, all while wearing body armor and other combat gear during a combined counter-reconnaissance patrol on the afternoon of the 11th, led to several heat casualties. As the platoons called in a medevac helicopter to remove the heat-stricken Soldiers from the battlefield, the insurgents began driving off the helicopters with intense machine gun fired from the trees that lined the nearby canals.

Only after suppressive fire from nearby attack helicopters were the medevac helicopters able to land and evacuate the heat casualties. Soldiers constantly train to complete their mission in a wide-range of scenarios and difficult situations, yet despite all the training available some Soldiers fold under the stress. The heat, terrain, and fatigue led to distrust between the Soldiers and the Officers in the battery, and it was only through the presence and leadership of Lieutenant Colonel Flynn, the Battalion Commander, that order could be reestablished. With a small security detail, LTC Flynn moved from his headquarters to the tiny patrol base in the searing heat. Once onsite, LTC Flynn assessed the situation, and in the best interest of the unit and its morale, he relieved the young platoon leaders who had lost the trust of the men they were charged to lead.

A few days later, a unit from the 75th Ranger Regiment was attempting to kill or capture a high value target in the Arghandab. As the Rangers began their insertion during a night operation, the rotator wash from their Chinook helicopter detonated a series of improvised explosive devices and wounded several men who were standing on the rear ramp in preparation for a rapid exit. These booby traps damaged the helicopter and forced the Rangers to abandon their mission and limp back to Kandahar Airfield.

As a consequence of the failed mission and the realization of the amount of IEDs around the field, Colonel Kandarian with approval from ISAF command sent dozens of GPS-guided artillery rounds into the field in order to destroy any other possible IEDs awaiting future operations. This was not so much an act of revenge as of necessity. With a limited number of possible landing zones in the area large enough to support helicopter landings, open fields such as this one was necessary for use as a potential medevac site. Clearing an IED from a field while a medevac helicopter circles overhead wastes precious time that could mean the difference between life and death for those on the ground and in the air.

In Zharay and Maiwand the majority of the STRIKE Brigade was focused on building the capabilities of our 3-205 ANA partners, while the STRIKE Battalions in Arghandab were partnered with two Afghan infantry battalions from 1-205 ANA.

The 1st Brigade, 205th Corps had been established of a few years prior to our arrival, so each of these ANA battalions had its own embedded mentor team from the Canadian Army, which for years had been in charge of Kandahar. With the help of the Canadian mentors, the 1-205 ANA leadership took the lead in coming up with the plan for clearing the Arghandab. Colonel Kandarian, Majors Cox and Mixon as well as myself sat with them several times to offer recommendations such as how to coordinate fires and when operations should begin. We also discussed areas were our assets such as artillery and attack aviation air support could be a factor and ensured we would have the necessary support from RC-South.

The idea for the operation was fairly simple. The 2nd Battalion, 508 Infantry Regiment, also known as "2Fury," and their 3-1-205 ANA partners would conduct a small clearing operation from the southwest toward the northeast and push the Taliban away from Kandahar City and Highway One. Then 2Fury and its ANA partners would establish what would amount to a blocking position, denying the Taliban direct access to the city and Highway One. The concept of a blocking position is similar to that of a construction crew closing down a series of roads or routes into a city. A detour is established, but in this case, it would take time for the Taliban to reach it and would force them into a specific direction.

Following the establishment of the blocking position, the Top Guns Battalion with their 1-1-205 ANA partners conducted a clearing operation back the northeast to take away the Taliban's main support network in the villages of Jelawar and its surrounding area. Based on the initial planning, success of the 2Fury operation, and knowledge of the area, the STRIKE staff assessed that the operation would take no longer than a week or two and the Taliban would be gone.

The Taliban and the environment proved us wrong.

On July 21, 2010, 2Fury began its part of the operation and cleared the area around the village of Kakaran and began the construction of combat outpost (COP) Ashoque to deny permanently the Taliban access to Highway One and to Kandahar City. This phase of Operation Unify Arghandab took approximately four days. While the Brigade was patting itself on the back, however, the Taliban were preparing. The Taliban were planning to use the same tactics the Mujahideen had used in the Arghandab against the Soviet Union.

On May 22, 1987, the Soviet Union with Government of Afghanistan troops launched an offensive operation against the

Mujahideen residing and operating in the Arghandab district. Their offensive operation consisted of over 6,000 men and began with intense artillery barrages and aviation strikes. It is believed through later reporting that the Mujahideen used stinger missiles to shoot down several aircraft forcing the Soviet and Afghan ground forces to continue clearing the district without air support against an entrenched enemy that was dug into camouflaged bunkers.

By the end of June the Soviet offensive had stalled and defections by the Afghan government troops left the remaining Soviet forces decimated as they attempted to take Charqobla Olya. It is estimated that nearly 1,200 Soviet Soldiers defected and another 500 were killed, not to mention the number of Soldiers that were wounded during the operation.[29] Nearly one-third of the initial clearing force was off the battlefield.

Thirteen years later, it was the Top Guns Soldiers clearing the Arghandab. Despite the initial losses of the Soldiers at Objective Bakersfield, the Soldiers captured the objective and denied the Taliban access.

Many Soldiers from Top Guns distinguished themselves throughout the fight, together earning multiple Silver Stars, Bronze Stars with Valor, and Army Commendation Medals with Valor. One such Soldier was Sergeant First Class Kyle Lyon, who led his platoon through the fight at Objective Bakersfield and was first to establish positions on the north and south side of the objective. His platoon, composed of Soldiers from the Battalion's Headquarters Company, began taking sustained fire from the Taliban from the south and southwest. Realizing that the accuracy and volume of enemy fire would decimate his men, SFC Lyon moved from a covered and concealed position through enemy fire to reposition a grenadier and mark targets for attack aviation. Throughout the first day, SFC Lyon directed his men and their lethal fires to repel repeated attacks by the enemy.

On the next day SFC Lyon's platoon began receiving indirect fire from Taliban 30mm grenades, which wounded four Soldiers almost immediately. With complete disregard for his own safety, SFC Lyon ran to the point of impact and conducted an impact crater analysis to

---

[29] Urban, M. (1990). *War in Afghanistan*. Palgrave MacMillan Press.

determine the enemy's position so that he could redirect fires onto the Taliban. On August 1st as SFC Lyon and his platoon moved from Objective Bakersfield with a squad of Sapper engineers to reduce nearby structures that the Taliban were using for cover, the unit again began receiving heavy and sustained small arms fire from within 50 meters of their position. SFC Lyon charged forward without hesitation through the heavy fire and engaged the enemy position with his M4 rifle. Together with his Soldiers, he immediately established a defensive perimeter around the structures, enabling the Sappers to complete their mission. SFC Lyon and his men continued to repel multiple Taliban counterattacks.

And again on August 2nd, SFC Lyon and his platoon were receiving heavy, sustained small arms fire from structures to the southwest of the objective and with coordinated efforts of the attached Joint Tactical Air Controllers from the Air Force were able to direct the fires of Air Force A-10s onto the Taliban, destroying their positions. SFC Lyon's performance during Operation Unify Arghandab was nothing short of heroic as he demonstrated great leadership, poise, conviction, and courage under constant enemy fire. What is truly unique about SFC Lyon is that he was not even trained as an infantryman. SFC Lyon's primary military training was in field artillery meteorology. In other words, his job was to determine the effects of weather on the flight of artillery rounds. For his heroic actions throughout the Battle for Objective Bakersfield, SFC Lyon was awarded the Silver Star.

As Lieutenant Colonel David Flynn, the Top Guns Battalion Commander, summarized about the significance the objective, "It falls on the road that leads to our COPs and it was one of their strongholds, but we fought through attacks, IEDs, and everything the Taliban had in the Arghandab River Valley. The Taliban no longer had control over the area."[30] LTC Flynn would also be awarded the Silver Star for his actions and leadership under fire in the Arghandab.

The fight, however, did not end in the Arghandab with the establishment of COP Stout at Objective Bakersfield. The fight would rage for another month as the Soldiers of Tops Guns Battalion and its

---

[30] LTC David Flynn. (2011). In *Book of Valor Combined Task Force STRIKE Operation Enduring Freedom 10-11*. Page 69.

ANA partners continued to push and expand its presence westerly into villages like Charqobla Olya and Babur. The Taliban had suffered heavy losses during the establishment of COP Stout. As the Top Guns began its continued push into the Arghandab the Taliban's resistance in terms of small arms and indirect fire began to tapper off. The threat of IEDs, however, remained high.

On August 13th, I went to the Arghandab with the acting Brigade Command Sergeant Major John White who had been filling the role since mid-June when CSM Smith was wounded. SGM White needed to assess the morale of the men and to determine what additional assets the Brigade could provide and brought me along to take note and help facilitate re-directing assets upon our return.

We arrived at COP Nolen as a patrol was pushing south from the COP into the thick pomegranate fields to create a lane into Charqolba Olya, some 300 meters away. Looking south from a machine gun position on the roof, I could see nothing but green, leafy treetops. It was as if the ground had been lifted to the tops of the trees. There were no breaks in the dense foliage.

I knew there was a patrol out there yet the Soldiers remained invisible. The vegetation was so thick that the Taliban could have been standing below me and I would have had no idea. The Soldiers had been using chainsaws, axes, and even detonation cord to clear the trees back and prevent the constant attacks, but it wasn't enough.

I sat there in COP Nolen talking to a young Soldier who had arrived at COP Nolen less than twenty-four hours prior and like all young Soldiers, was ecstatic to be down range. The young Soldier told me he had been with that Top Guns Battery for over a year but his first child had been due right when the Brigade was to begin deploying. So in order for him to be with his wife for the birth he had been left behind at Fort Campbell for a couple months and had finally caught up with his unit.

After a couple hours, SGM White and I moved on to COP Stout. Nearly twenty minutes after arriving and after the Kiowas had completed their strafing runs a loud explosion erupted in the distance near COP Nolen. Minutes later my fears were confirmed that someone had stepped on an IED.

Over the radio while simultaneously watching the medevac helicopter land below the distant tree line, we learned the name of the victim. The young man I had just been talking to, Specialist Luis Lugo, had stepped on the IED. The explosion amputated one of SPC Lugo's legs and shrapnel peppered the face of the Battery's First Sergeant Nathan Bryant who was nearby to Lugo in the patrol.

The small building where SPC Lugo stepped on the IED would be turned into a patrol base bearing his name. The battle for Charqolba Olya would ultimately cost one American his life and wounds to 11 others. Operations to secure the village of Babur would lead to the death of two other American Soldiers.

The indirect fire from the Taliban was not extremely accurate, but it was persistent, keeping the Soldiers at COP Stout on edge. At the time COP Stout was little more than a dust bowl surrounded by HESCOs, which Soldiers worked around the clock to fill. The indirect fire destroyed tents and other equipment that the Soldiers needed to protect themselves from the sun, heat, mosquitos, and the Taliban. As SGM White and I sat there in our foxholes and later a small concrete bunker with the Soldiers from Top Guns as the indirect fire continued, Kiowa helicopters raced just above the treetops firing rockets and machine guns at the suspected enemy positions.

Looking around I could see the controlled chaos of continued combat. Sitting around and constantly being attacked can be numbing. Soldiers had priorities of work that kept them constantly busy and ready for the next encounter with the Taliban. Soldiers are constantly improving their defensive positions, preparing for the next patrol, and pulling security. Rest and relaxation, however, are also necessary to prevent fatigue. Leaders have the difficult job of maintaining that balance and assigning tasks evenly.

Soldiers with too much time are susceptible to minds that wander to thoughts of home, of spouses, of bills and the combined stress of combat, and the more amazing thoughts of home can easily break a Soldier's spirit and will to fight. Soldiers took turns constructing tents, filling force protection barriers, digging fighting positions, cleaning their weapons, pulling security, and sleeping. You could see those who had been asleep when the barrage of indirect fire began. They now stood in bunkers with their body armor and helmets barely on over their Army-issued physical training shorts and shirts. Some were waiting for a lull to go back to their tents and others gave up and choose to sleep in the shade of the concrete bunkers. As the barrages subsided, Soldiers would return to their assigned duties only to race back to cover with each new round of attacks.

I was impressed with the resiliency of the Soldiers. The Soldiers at COP Stout had been in a constant fight for the last two weeks and yet they remained cool and collected. Back at FOB Wilson, I had managed to secure a cot in an overcrowded tent for sleeping, which was far more than these Soldiers had. I could occasionally catch a cold shower very late at night; they did not even have that small luxury to look forward to. If I waited in a long line, I could eat hot food in the dining facility tent where these Soldiers sat in the dirt eating a meal ready-to-eat that had likely been prepared and packaged years prior. I empathized with their conditions and realized despite my hardships there is always someone who has it worse, and SGM White and I took note of their conditions and would help where we could.

While I observed the actions and the morale of the Soldiers SGM White quizzed the Battery First Sergeant about his Soldiers, asking if as First Sergeant certain things such as more force protection, more generators, and more water for the Soldiers had been requested as well as things to just make their lives better in general. SGM White wanted to make sure the First Sergeants throughout the Brigade were doing everything possible to protect their Soldiers and to help them survive and if not then he would direct them on what they should be doing. Several First Sergeants failed to live up to the standards and expectations of SGM White, and while I am not sure of the exact number, I had heard a total of six First Sergeants were fired and replaced in the first couple months of the deployment.

Watching the ANA fire their 40mm grenade rounds, I often wondered what they were seeing to shoot at but am not sure it mattered. The ANA and American Soldiers at COP Stout were suffering equally. Through the unforgiving heat, the humidity, and through the constant Taliban attacks the Afghan Soldiers of the 1st Brigade, 205th Corps demonstrated a resilience and willingness to fight that was light years beyond our 3-205th ANA partners. I wondered how the Soldiers of 3-205th Corps would hold up in similar conditions when clearing operations began in Zharay.

The Soldiers of Top Guns and the ANA refused to allow themselves to be drawn out and chase the enemy into their terrain. They instead used combined arms and coordinated assets to attack the Taliban on their terms, not the enemy's. The hard and painful lessons that the Top Guns Battalion learned in the Arghandab would be incorporated into the future plans of the STRIKE Brigade and how future units that follow STRIKE will operate along the green zone.

While the Taliban and Top Guns were engaged along the north side of the Arghandab, 2Fury was beginning its trip home to be replaced by the 1st Battalion, 66th Armor Regiment. It would be from this unit on August 30th that the first Chaplain since Vietnam, Captain Dale Goetz, would be killed when a vehicle he was traveling in to see Soldiers at an outpost in the Arghandab struck and detonated an IED. This IED was so large and powerful that it destroyed the entire vehicle, leaving only the engine block burning on the ground. All five occupants in the armored mine resistant vehicle were killed instantly.

Toward the end of August 2010 the operational tempo in the Arghandab was dying down, and the relief in place between 2Fury and 1-66 Armor was almost complete when I flew to the Arghandab District Center again. Colonel Kandarian and Major Cox were to meet with the Arghandab District Governor and later with the 1-66 Armor Battalion Commander to ensure the transition between his unit and 2Fury had no enduring issues to be resolved. The meetings did not prove to be of any significance, however, the Taliban reminded us that they were still there.

As I walked from the combined ANA-ISAF operations center behind the district center to the 1-66 Battalion TOC, I happened to be looking down into the river valley when I saw the smoke of a rocket as it streaked up toward the district center. I remember watching in awe, paralyzed as if life were suddenly in slow motion. The white smoke of the rocket contrasted beautifully against the dark green foliage of the valley below. There was nothing I could do in that instant. I was caught in the open. I hoped the rocket would miss and luckily the rocket exploded with a thunderous concussion nearly 75 meters ahead of me, close to the tiny path that leads to the HLZ. No one was hurt in that attack, which is lucky considering that when a relief in place, the population of any given FOB or COP is nearly doubled.

Progress was measured in the meters and yards that were gained in the Arghandab through the use of combined arms to overwhelm the enemy. Combined arms is generally considered the use of infantry, artillery, and aviation support in concert with each other. However it is the intangibles, like the leadership of men such as SFC Lyons and LTC Flynn, that make these effective. Leaders know how to use the right force at the right time to achieve the mission.

On August 31st, elements from Delta Company, 1-66 Armor came under intense enemy fire while patrolling near the Afghan National Police (ANP) checkpoint in the town of Haji Towr Kalacheh. The American unit was pinned down at the checkpoint due to the heavy enemy fire and unable to maneuver on and destroy the enemy; support for the patrol fortunately came in the form of combined arms as two OH-58D Kiowa helicopters raced to help the troops in contact.

Unable to easily distinguish between friendly and enemy positions in the thick vegetation, the Kiowa pilots repeatedly flew extremely low just over the treetops exposing themselves to heavy automatic fire from the Taliban. The Kiowas made multiple strafing runs across the enemy positions, suppressing the enemy long enough for the Delta Company elements on the ground to maneuver away from the checkpoint. When out of ammunition, the Kiowas flew to FOB Jelawar and quickly re-armed to provide further support for the Delta Company element that was still engaged as the patrol attempted to break contact. The continued and near constant runs by the Kiowa pilots inflicted multiple enemy casualties and forced the Taliban to withdrawn into the dense orchards. These Kiowa pilots would all be awarded the Army Commendation Medal with V-device for Valor for their low flying and constant actions.

Further north in the Arghandab, while conducting a disruption operation to stem the Taliban's movement in near the village of Noor Muhammad Khan Kalacheh, the Alpha Battery, 1-320th patrol base came under sustain enemy small arms, mortar and rifle launched grenade attack. The Company Commander, Captain James Thomasson, who was out with one of the patrols quickly identified the fortified position near the village that Taliban was using to attack the patrol base, CPT Thomasson reacted immediately, exposing himself repeatedly to heavy enemy fire to direct volumes of accurate suppressive fire from his Soldiers on to the Taliban positions. His actions motivated his Soldiers as they moved as a team to close with and destroyed the Taliban positions.

After securing cover, the Taliban launched an immediate counterattack, massing its assets on CPT Thomasson's exposed position with indirect fire, rocket-propelled grenades, and small arms fire. Once again CPT Thomasson further exposed himself to enemy fire and directed one of his Afghan Army partners to fire two RPGs at the enemy positions, killing two Taliban fighters.

The initial attacked on the patrol base had seriously wounded Sergeant First Class Allen Manley who required immediate medevac. Moving back to the patrol base, CPT Thomasson received a report of four personnel moving to once again attack the patrol base so he led his men to interdict the Taliban personnel who could potentially destroy the medevac helicopter as it attempted to land for SFC Manley.

With close combat aviation assets now in support of the troops in contact, CPT Thomasson was able to direct two Kiowas on the Taliban positions providing suppressive fire while his Soldiers maneuvered secure the landing zone for the medevac. CPT Thomasson also directed a Hellfire missile strike on the compound the Taliban was using. SFC Manley was medevaced and during the fighting four Taliban were killed while another two were captured. For their actions, CPT Thomasson along with five others members of Alpha Battery were awarded a Bronze Star with V-device for Valor and three others were awarded the Army Commendation Medal with V-device for Valor.

As August rolled into September, a sense of relief began to emerge in the Arghandab. Not that the fight was over but that somehow the Soldiers of Combined Task Force STRIKE and of the Top Guns Battalion in particular had managed to break the enemy's will. The Soldiers of Top Guns, 2Fury, and then 1-66 Armor with their ANA partners had pushed the enemy back. The combined task forces demonstrated an innate tenacity to destroy the enemy using a multitude of means to, which the Taliban was unable to respond. Patrols were still going out daily but contact with the enemy became less and less, allowing the Soldiers and their ANA partners to interact more and more with the local population. Intelligence reports speculated that many of the Taliban had withdrawn from the area by either blending back into the local population or moving into other sanctuaries like Zharay. The Taliban that did stay were far fewer in number and choose not to engage the Soldiers of STRIKE directly, instead choosing to use indirect fire and IEDs to disrupt our deterrent operations.

The constant threat and action also fostered a unique bond between the Afghan and American Soldiers as both sides demonstrated a willingness to risk their own lives for one another. On September 30th, a patrol from the headquarters battery of 1-320th was conducting an area reconnaissance west of COP Stout. The Taliban had placed an unknown number of pressure-plate improvised explosive devices throughout the grape furrows and pomegranate orchards. Because of the IED threat an attached squad of Sappers were used to breach a route through the vegetation so that the ANA and American Soldiers could move unimpeded.

The cleared route was marked with bright orange and fluorescent pink VS-17 panels and the platoon moved onward. Specialist David Bixler was the last man in the patrol to cross through the breach and he carefully picked up the panels, which marked the cleared path to prevent the Taliban from using the same trail or booby-trapping it behind the patrol. Still as the patrol moved onward, more IEDs were found. As the patrol moved around IEDs, it was ambushed by the Taliban from two separate locations with sustained fire from PKM machine guns. Unable to maneuver through the IED-laden field, the platoon attempted to break contact with the enemy so that it could use another field to maneuver and flank the entrenched enemy positions.

Heading in reverse, SPC Bixler now found himself leading the platoon back through the breach point and path, which he had marked with the VS-17 panels. As the platoon approached Route Mariners, SPC Bixler noticed an Afghan Army Soldier had strayed of the cleared path and into an uncleared area. With complete disregard for his own safety, SPC Bixler quickly ran through the field to the ANA Soldier and threw him back onto the cleared path. In the process of saving the ANA Soldier from imminent harm, SPC Bixler detonated a pressure plate IED. The blast instantly took both of his legs above the knee. The ANA Soldier that SPC Bixler gallantly saved suffered only minor injuries, and for his actions to save a fellow comrade in arms SPC David Bixler was awarded the Silver Star and Purple Heart.

In a sense STRIKE had cleared the Arghandab of the Taliban, something the Soviets had failed to do in the 1980s against the Mujahideen. But clearing, while dangerous, is relatively straightforward compared to building governance, developing economic growth, and preventing the Taliban from returning. Despite the lower levels of direct contact by September, STRIKE Soldiers were still being wounded and killed but our resolve remained steadfast. While the kinetic focus had been on the Arghandab in the first few months of the deployment, STRIKE was also looking to Zharay and Maiwand. While not the Brigade's main effort in August, the districts were proving to be extremely dangerous and deadly nevertheless.

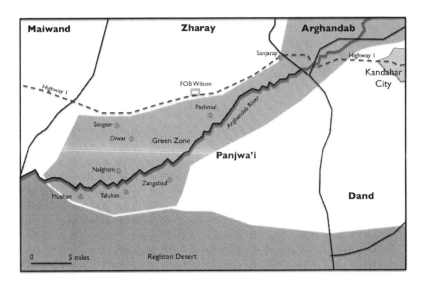

A typical sketch of the area of operations (AO) used to discuss operations with the ANA and ANP

A member of the ANP with his RPG standing guard at a checkpoint just south of Highway 1.

Examples of typical vehicles used by the locals, as seen on Highway One.

A local Afghan and his children walk to a *shura* at FOB Howz-e-Madad.

The author with COL Murtaza and some of his Soldiers at a small compound in Zharay during Operation Dragon STRIKE.

District Chief of Police Bismullah Jan discusses the role of checkpoints with a STRIKE Soldier.

COL Murtaza relaxes in the office of one of his Battalion Commanders.

STRIKE Soldiers adjust field artillery in support of troops in contact.

The blast of a MICLIC and IEDs detonates in Zharay. STRIKE used dozens of MICLICs to clear roads and paths in order to access Taliban controlled areas.

The remnants of a combat outpost destroyed by a vehicle-borne improvised explosive device that killed several STRIKE Soldiers

COL Murtaza maneuvers through a thick pomegranate grove, discussing an operation with his subordinates.

Colonels Kandarian and Murtaza with the leadership of Zharay to include the district governor, the chief of police and the NDS chief.

STRIKE Soldiers run along Highway One in order to seek cover during a clearing operation.

STRIKE Soldiers build COP Nalgham during Operation Dragon STRIKE.

An Afghan-built bridge across a canal just north of the Arghandab River that separates Zahray and Panjwa'i

A portable bridge used by STRIKE to cross the canal just north of the Arghandab River. This bridge was approximately 100 meters from the Afghan version shown above.

Chapter 9
A New Plan

You know how Mullah Omar came to power? He
controlled Highway One!

Karim Jan
Zharay's District Governor

The Battle for Objective Bakersfield and the fight in the Arghandab taught Combined Task Force STRIKE a great deal about our enemy and how they fight. It showed Soldiers how the Taliban used the thick vegetation for cover and taught them how, through the use of combined arms, to best deny the Taliban their intrinsic advantage.

We also came to recognize just how little we controlled in Zharay. It was like the Wild West where anything goes. Our outposts were being attacked constantly. Private security companies hired to protect civilian convoys moving along Highway One were constantly shooting at anything they deemed a threat to include both civilians and sometimes military units on the ground. STRIKE was on its heels in Zharay and struggling to gain the initiative, which the Brigade was not going to achieve through daily patrols. STRIKE needed to change its thought process about how it operated in Zharay. In the Arghandab, the people had come forward to ask for help in order to get to and harvest their crops. In Zharay, however, the Taliban dominated the landscape and the people were scared of both the Taliban and ISAF.

The majority of the tactical infrastructure that the Brigade occupied in Zharay laid within a few hundred meters of Highway One, yet these did little to deter attacks along the highway. In fact, their proximity to the highway almost encouraged attacks. The outposts were too far apart to be mutually supportive, and the enemy was not only able to attack them at will but bypass them to reach Highway One. It was a near daily occurrence that outposts such as FOB Howz-e-Madad, Asoque and Spin Pir received small arms and RPG fire while FOB Wilson sitting on the north side of Highway One also received constant indirect fire.

Only a few outposts such as COP Gundy Ghar and Lakhokel were away from Highway One in July and August. The combat outposts were arrayed to protect the population and Highway One, and insurgent attacks were terrain-dependent. We could protect ourselves by building our outposts in the middle of the desert so that the Taliban could not reach us, however the people were the mission and they did not live in the desert.

Ghundy Ghar, due to its elevation, was more immune to daily attacks, although the road running to and from the hill where the outpost stood was laden with IEDs. As soon as route clearance cleared the route, the Taliban were back to reseed it with new IEDs. On the other hand, Spin Pir, slightly southeast of FOB Howz-e-Madad, was battered constantly by Taliban attacks in their effort to force STRIKE Soldiers to withdraw from the outpost. If STRIKE gave up Spin Pir, the Taliban would have direct access to the population around Howz-e-Madad.

On August 20th, an element from the 2nd Battalion, 502nd Infantry Regiment, 2-502 Infantry "STRIKE Force," Headquarters was at the Spin Pir strong point assessing the outpost to plan for improvements when the outpost came under attack. Heavy small arms fire and rocket-propelled grenades battered the HESCO-enclosed outpost. The Taliban had used nearby ditches, bunkers, and grape huts that the previous unit had failed to destroy and were firing from within 150 meters of the outpost. The fierce fight raged for hours and one of the clear heroes of the day was Command Sergeant Major Troy Henderson, the Battalion's Command Sergeant Major, who was leading the assessment team to the outpost when the fighting broke out.

During the fire fight CSM Henderson commanded the defense of Spin Pir enabling Captain Timothy Price to lead a second ground element. CPT Price was able to maneuver on and destroy the nearby enemy positions. CSM Henderson repeatedly exposed himself moving from guard tower to guard tower to direct suppressive fires. He also redistributed ammunition and marked target locations for close combat air support and vehicle-mounted gunners. The actions of CSM Henderson enabled CPT Price to not only maneuver his combined U.S./Afghan Army patrol to a better vantage point over the enemy, but once there and while drawing enemy fire CPT Price coordinated multiple guided bomb units (GBU) and 30mm gunfire from aircraft onto the Taliban positions.

The next day a patrol from Delta Company, 2-502 Infantry moved to conduct a battle damage assessment of the GBU strikes. As the patrol moved 800 meters through thick vegetation in the scorching Afghan sun, five Soldiers became heat casualties. Moving under the weight of their equipment and body armor beneath the relentless sun and humidity of the lush green zone drained the Soldiers of water and energy. The heat also damaged two mine detectors, rendering them ineffective. First Sergeant Eric Allen from the patrol led a small four-man security element through 600 meters of uncleared terrain to reach a unit sent from Howz-e-Madad to evacuate the heat casualties. During the movement 1SG Allen's small security element was engaged by Taliban small arms fire. First Sergeant Allen coordinated and directed rotary wing assets to destroy the enemy positions enabling his four Soldier element to link up with the ground casualty evacuation element where 1SG Allen then led the entire element back to the five heat casualties. The moving element once again was engaged by effective small arms fire as 1SG Allen worked to evacuate his Soldiers. For his leadership, heroism under enemy fire, and willingness to lead through dangerous conditions, 1SG Allen would be awarded the Bronze Star Medal with V-device for Valor.

In an effort to take the initiative away from the Taliban in Zharay Combined Task Force STRIKE began assessing our understanding of COIN operations and how best to secure the population of Zharay.

Life in Zharay is centered along Highway One. Farmers sell their goods in the stalls of the small bazaars that line it and the majority of the locals live near it. Highway One slices through contrasting areas. In the west, the road is surrounded by arid, dusty fields; in the east, it cuts starkly against the thick vegetation. Highway One in central Zharay highlights the rapid transitions between life and desert.

As the assistant Brigade planner I was charged with developing a concept of the operation for Operation Economic Corridors. In July and early August, that concept was little more than a name on a PowerPoint slide meant to be presented to Colonel Kandarian. It was an attempt to delude Colonel Kandarian into thinking the plans section was thinking ahead but little if anything had gone into actually developing the plan. I only found out I was in charge of the named operation minutes before the presentation.

So following the meeting I set to work on what the operation should accomplish. The operation needed an end-state. The operation was to focus on improving development and local governance along Highway One. I had no special skills or experience in planning these types of development operations, and other people in the plans shop saw it as busy work. They wanted to be planning the large-scale kinetic operations because for lack of a better explanation high kinetic operations have greater visibility.

I quickly realized that there would be no means to improve the economic condition for the locals or ensure deliverance of local government such as education to them without improved security along Highway One. So through STRIKE's intelligence section a historical template was generated highlighting all of the IEDs and small arms fire engagements along Highway One in the past year. Using this I pinpointed about fifteen locations south of Highway One where the Brigade could install watchtowers to provide oversight along Highway One and to improve security instantly so that the real thrust of Operation Economic Corridors could commence. The concept was for the watchtowers to be run by the local Afghan Police as sub-stations to the district police station, which would be further supported by the Afghan National Army garrisoned throughout the district at the local combat outposts.

Critical to this plan's success was the watchtowers' location: they had to exist at the historical engagement sites. Moreover, support for the towers had to be feasible. As such, the watchtowers needed to be able to withstand Taliban attacks and be supportive of each other so that if one tower was engaged by the Taliban, then another could support it by either rapidly sending troops or through interlocking machine gun fire. The sum of these watchtowers created an engagement zone that was important south of Highway One. The zone would protect the local population and lead to economic development that was centered along the highway.

With the concept in hand, the Brigade Engineers Major Kevin Moyer and Captain Colby Krug came up with three potential watchtower designs composed of HESCOs, containers, and sand bags that could support a small detachment of police. Using the estimated height of the watchtowers, the intelligence section was able to refine their locations based on the terrain and to maximize the field of view and ultimately fields of fire. The simplicity of the watchtower also enabled the Brigade to contract out their construction to a local Afghan company so that we would simultaneously provide a boost to the local economy while improving security.

With a refined concept of the operation, I presented the plan to Major Cox, and after some further refinements, the operational concept was presented to Colonel Kandarian. As the operation was being discussed and dissected for its merits and potential drawbacks it became clear that this operation could provide STRIKE with the long-term initiative necessary to affect serious change and stability to Zharay. With the emplacement of watchtowers Combined Task Force STRIKE would also launch a large-scale clearing operation to knock the Taliban on its heels so that if/when they recovered their access to Highway One and the people, the Taliban would ultimately be denied.

On September 1st, Operation Economic Corridors, or as the Afghans called it "*Amaliat Dalize Aqtesad*," began with several benign programs. Combined Task Force STRIKE began cleaning up Highway One by hauling away destroyed vehicles and the rubble of collapsed buildings along the highway. This first phase was necessary to create standoff between the Taliban and the population by removing the cover and concealment in the historic engagement zones used by the insurgents. Local contractors largely completed this phase. Additionally STRIKE prepared to build the watchtowers by ensuring all necessary supplies were on hand at FOB Wilson and that the local Afghan Police were prepared to guard the towers as soon as they were established. As a Brigade we did not want to limit ourselves by building a bunch of watchtowers and then suddenly being forced to guard them ourselves because the police were not prepared for the task. Colonel Kandarian and I further coached the Afghan Army into developing a better relationship with the district police because after the United States departed Afghanistan all that would be left would be the Afghan Army and Police.

More importantly, however, STRIKE and its partners prepared for the upcoming clearance operation known as "Operation Dragon STRIKE" that would begin in the middle of September. Soldiers continued to conduct daily patrols, presenting a familiar face to the Taliban every day, while also establishing patterns of "business as usual."

Immediately south of FOB Wilson on September 5th, elements of Charlie Company, 1st Squadron, 75th Cavalry Regiment "Widow Makers" conducted a small clearance operation in the village of Tiranan to disrupt Taliban influence and IED construction in the area. The small battalion-led operation would not only disrupt the Taliban's activities prior to the upcoming operation but also presented the facade that no large-scale operation was pending. As the platoon arrived at a suspected Taliban cache site, the patrol received small arms and machine gun fire from enemy positions that were across an open field. Intelligence previously suspected approximately 20 fighters were operating in and around Tiranan.

To maneuver and engage the Taliban, SPC Cody Chandler led his four-man team approximately 200 meters through a wadi north of the insurgents' position. An hour into the fight, as he was moving through exposed terrain to direct the fires his Soldiers, SPC Chandler was shot in the abdomen. Remaining calm he assisted in his own medical care so that his Soldiers could continue to hold the Taliban at bay and SPC Chandler managed to do so until he was evacuated.

As the battle continued, Sergeant Zachary Fraker identified 10 Taliban fighters moving to reinforce the fighters who were already engaging his platoon, and he quickly reorientated his team's fire and suppressed the reinforcements with his 40mm grenade launcher. His actions prevented the additional Taliban forces from getting into the fight. Ultimately through the combined use of rotary wing assets and indirect fires, the 1-75 CAV platoon was able to route the enemy. The platoon estimated it killed approximately 15 Taliban fighters. The gun battle last nearly three hours and many Soldiers, both American and Afghan alike, distinguished themselves.

Patrols continued to face Taliban fighters in green zone south of Highway One, and while patrols went out daily, there were behind-the-scenes coordination occurring at all levels in the Brigade. Both American and Afghan Soldiers were shifting around the battlefield into different task organizations as well as learning new equipment. STRIKE was preparing to conduct a combined Brigade-size air assault with both American and Afghan Soldiers but first we needed to teach our Afghan Army partners how to get on and off the helicopters without getting hurt. STRIKE had also learned valuable lessons in the Arghandab. Our Brigade engineers while searching the Army's inventory found just the tools required to defeat the defensive IED-laden fields the Taliban had constructed to the south to protect their bases of operation.

STRIKE's engineer company learned how to utilize the M58 Mine Clearing Line Charge, which is commonly referred to as a MICLIC. This device consists of a rocket fired from a trailer that pulls along what appears to be a long string. The string, however, is an explosive line charge that upon detonation clears a 100-meter-long and 8-meter-wide path. The engineers also found the APOB system, which is a smaller version of the MICLIC and clears 45-meter-long and 1-meter-wide path. The APOB is portable and can be carried in a backpack by a Soldier on a dismounted patrol. The MICLIC comparatively requires a trailer for transportation and employment.

Economic Corridors had simple origins. As a plan it was to provide a minimal amount of security to the people of Zharay traveling along Highway One and for the greater long-term development of commerce and government outreach. The simple origins grew and evolved, however, and Operation Economic Corridors became STRIKE's campaign plan for the deployment. Under the Economic Corridors construct all subsequent operations such as Operation Dragon STRIKE were designed. Economic Corridors and the long-term hope that it promised was, in a sense, the Brigade's exit strategy.

Chapter 10
Unsustainable Success

Many have walked where we walked. Alexander the Great, the British military, the Soviets, and the Canadians had all attempted to do what we sought to do. We were fighting in a different era, but the insurgency and the fight in southern Afghanistan remained timeless.

When STRIKE Soldiers on patrol asked locals about "which district they lived in?" in an effort to determine how the locals perceived their local government, the common response the Soldiers were likely to hear was "Panjwa'i." Up until the end of 2006, the district of Zharay did not exist; it was carved out of Panjwa'i by the government in Kabul to separate and appease Pashtun sub-tribes within Kandahar Provence. The Arghandab River, cutting west of Kandahar City, ran through the middle of what was then Pankwa'i. Like many rivers it made a natural border to separate a new district, Zharay, from what was left of Panjwa'i to the South.

Prior to the establishment of the new Zharay and Panjwa'i district borders, the old district of Panjwa'i was controlled by the 1st Battalion of the Royal Canadian Regiment, led by Lieutenant Colonel Omer Lavoie who assumed control in early August 2006. In the weeks and months prior to the Canadians' arrival in Panjwa'i, a tremendous shift across Afghanistan had occurred as the North Atlantic Treaty Organization (NATO) expanded its command and control.

The NATO mission transformed from a mostly unilateral U.S. military-led coalition to a NATO-centric operation with the Canadian military granted command of the Regional Command-South. Canadian Brigadier General David Fraser led the NATO coalition from Kandahar Airfield in RC-South, and the Taliban watched the shifting of troops play out around Afghanistan and in Kandahar particularly.

Intelligence reports at the time rumored that more than a thousand Taliban fighters were moving into Panjwa'i district, specifically around the village of Pashmul. The district borders in 2006 covered from the southwestern edge to the northwest edge of Kandahar City. The thick vegetation we now fought in provided the Taliban with direct routes to infiltrate the city. Just as my unit was pushed to act in 2010 against the Taliban in the Arghandab, the Canadians had also been forced to mobilize against the Taliban in 2006. The direct encroachment into Kandahar City and associated threat was too great to be ignored. The Canadians' clearing effort was called Operation Medusa.

Operation Medusa was, at the time, the largest operation in Afghanistan since Operation Anaconda in 2002. It was the first-ever ground combat operation under NATO's operational command and control as well as the largest operation Canadian forces had conducted since the Korean War. The goal of Operation Medusa was to disperse or destroy the hundreds, if not thousands, of Taliban fighters who had gathered in Panjwa'i. In total, LTC Lavoie would command nearly 1,400 hundreds Soldiers to set up two critical blocking positions. One position was along the high ground of Masum Ghar and Mar Ghar, which are steep, high hills west of Kandahar City that border the edge of Panjwa'i. And the other key position was further north along Highway One, orientated south into the green zone.

The two positions together formed a counterclockwise V-facing formation in which a main fighting element from the Canadian Battle Group's Charles Company would assault from the south toward the east into the blocking positions to destroy the enemy. The movement of Charles Company would resemble a hammer against the blocking position's anvil with the Taliban caught in the middle. The main objective, named Objective Rugby, was centered around the village of Pashmul where intelligence indicated the largest mass of Taliban fighters was located.

The operation began on September 2, 2006, at six in the morning, and the forces emplacing the blocking positions met little to no resistance from the Taliban. The positions were set within fifteen minutes. The Canadian Army forces had been littering Panjwa'i with fliers and radio messages for days about the impending operation so that the local villagers not associated with the Taliban would hopefully leave before the fighting began. The downside to the Canadians' public service campaign, of course, was that the Taliban knew about the impeding operation. The rationale behind their messaging was to reduce civilian casualties since the plans for Operation Medusa called for a series of airstrikes to destroy 10-20 known insurgent nodes. The airstrikes were slated to commence immediately once the blocking positions were set, leaving the Taliban confined to the small area of the green zone south of Highway One and north of the Arghandab River.

This area was considered a "free fire zone," permitting Soldiers and aircraft in the area to shoot freely at any suspected Taliban target when the opportunity arose.

As the blocking positions sat and waited for the main ground assault that was scheduled to begin nearly 96 hours later, the Canadian Soldiers witnessed a horrific sight. A British Nimrod MR2 spy plane caught fire mid-flight and crashed into Panjwa'i. The Soldiers from their positions watched the fireball streaked down like a meteor and exploded on impact against the unforgiving land. The Soldiers in the blocking position at Masum Ghar raced to search for survivors and secure the crash site. Fourteen British Soldiers had been onboard the surveillance aircraft, tragically, all were killed as a result of what was later determined to be an electrical fire on the aircraft.

To make matters worse the brigade leadership, for unknown reasons, changed its plan to wait for the planned bombardment of the area. The main clearing operation would instead begin immediately.

The next morning, September 3rd, at first light, the main thrust of Operation Medusa shifted from the south and across the Arghandab River towards Objective Rugby. The decision to change the plan would prove disastrous to the Canadian Army.

Brigadier General Fraser later gave an interview to Adam Day of *Legion Magazine* about the decision to change the plan and his order for the assault to commence in advance of the predetermined timetable. "You fight the enemy guided by a plan," General Fraser tried to explain. "You don't fight a plan. If you fight a plan and ignore the enemy, you will fail. You will incur lots of casualties and you will fail. A plan only gets you thinking and gets you to the enemy. And the enemy has a vote. So, on September 1 or 2, I had decided the situation was changing so that we could attack. I gave the orders on the 2nd to attack. It was in advance of what the plan said. Well, I don't care about the plan."[31] Now without a new plan, the Canadians rushed across the Arghandab River where the enemy did vote.

On the morning of September 3rd as Charles Company crossed the Arghandab River from the south and as the lead elements entered

---

[31] Day, A., (2007, September 7). *Operation Medusa: The Battle for Panjwai.* Legion Magazine. Page 7.

Objective Rugby, no Taliban fighters were in sight. Initial elation was that of easy success. As the lead vehicle neared the white school, which was located at the center of Objective Rugby on the edge of Pashmul and believed to be the headquarters of the Taliban in Afghanistan, an insurgent suddenly shot up a signal flare. The plan suddenly collapsed along with any hope of ease.

Seconds later a rocket-propelled grenade crashed through the lead vehicle's windshield, instantly killing Rick Nolan, a platoon warrant Officer, who was sitting in the front passenger seat. Badly wounded in the vehicle were the platoon's medic and a local national interpreter who both had been sitting in the back.

Another vehicle in the lead assault element was struck with an 82mm recoilless rifle round, instantly killing Sergeant Shane Stachnik, an engineer assigned to the platoon. Inside the vehicle, all of the other Soldiers were wounded, some lying unconscious.

The main effort of Operation Medusa had maneuvered directly into the enemy's kill zone. The Canadians were easy prey in the Taliban's ambush. The Taliban fought, like the Mujahideen had fought against the Soviet Union, lying in wait for their prey to come into preset ambush sites. The insurgents were hidden in trenches and fortified buildings, firing onto Charles Company from three sides. Adding to the Taliban's tactical advantage was the thick marijuana and hashish fields that provided a convenient array of intersecting canals used by the local farmers to water their cash crops. Using these canals, the Taliban easily maneuvered undetected around the Canadian forces.

The Canadians quickly regrouped and moved forward to collect their wounded and prepare the casualties for evacuation. A Canadian armored vehicle full of dead and wounded Soldiers reversed at high speeds out of the kill zone only to crash backward into a ditch. Mistakes on the ground compounded the mistakes made echelons above the Soldiers in the fight. The Canadian armored vehicle continued to be assaulted, hit multiple times by rocket-propelled grenades. The well-laid plan that began with the establishment of the blocking positions was rushed to a hasty assault and further collapsed into chaos as Soldiers fought to stay alive and to help their wounded comrades. Private William Cushley and Frank Mellish, a warrant Officer for 8th platoon, would be killed rushing forward to help their friend Rick Nolan.

Major Mathew Sprague, the Charles Company Commander, struggled to control his men and direct their fire over the radio as he himself was under constant fire. The Canadian force was encapsulated by unrelenting enemy fire as the Soldiers struggled to coordinate air support that seemed to have little effect on the entrenched enemy. To further add to the chaos, a 1,000-pound bomb dropped by a coalition aircraft missed its intended target and came crashing through the Canadian lines. With four Soldiers already dead and 10 wounded of the 50 that entered Object Rugby, there was little that could be done except withdraw from the objective. Of the Soldiers who fought at Objective Rugby that day, five would receive the Medal of Military Valor, Canada's equivalent to the Silver Star and one, Corporal Sean Teal, would receive the Star of Military Valor, the equivalent to America's Distinguished Service Cross, the second highest award for valor.

As the Canadian forces withdrew from the objective, others prepared for another assault. Things continued to grow worse for Charles Company, which still sought to complete the mission. The next morning in the predawn light, an American A-10, used for close air support, made a catastrophic mistake. The pilot mistook the rising smoke from burning trash at the Canadians' assembly area for a Taliban location. The pilot fired his 30mm chain gun strafing the Canadian position, instantly killing Private Mark Graham, a former Olympic sprinter and wounding more that 30 others. Between the losses the previous day at Objective Rugby and the erroneous strafing run, Charles Company was now combat ineffective. The Canadians Battle Group lost the force designated as their main effort. The hastily launched assault and misguided efforts of the American A-10 pilot cost the Canadians their initiative in Operation Medusa.

LTC Lavoie and his staff were forced to redesign quickly the operation. The operation had stirred a hornet's nest and the Canadians needed resolution, not only for their fallen comrades but also for stability in the district. Operation Medusa was no longer the quick operation it was expected to be. The Canadians had hoped to rapidly close on and destroy the enemy rather enter into a drawn out, phased attack. The new Medusa began by bolstering the Canadian forces on the ground with additional troops with elements from Alpha Company, 2nd Battalion, Princess Patricia's Canadian Light Infantry, a company of American Soldiers from the U.S. 10th Mountain Division, elements of U.S. Special Forces, and the consolidation of the remaining elements of Charles Company with a Canadian Intelligence and Surveillance squadron into what became known as "Task Force Grizzly," which was led by Colonel Steve Williams of the U.S. Army.

Under the new plan, the Canadians would still conduct the brunt of the phased clearing operation, however, the addition of American troops and consolidation of others elements into Task Force Grizzly freed up a larger force of Canadian for the assault back into Objective Rugby. Also after the heavy losses on September 3rd, the Canadian plans incorporated better air support to cover the advancing troops and destroy the Taliban in advance of their Soldiers.

Operations are a fine balance between intelligence and movement of forces. Too little intelligence and the operations are seen as reckless or too aggressive, but if you wait too long for precise intelligence, then you risk overcautiousness and can provide the enemy a better opportunity to establish a defense. The movement of Charles Company could be seen as reckless due to the lack of intelligence and certainly because of the lack of air support. The later refined phases of Operation Medusa would create tension between Colonel Williams, who worked to advance Task Force Grizzly against the Taliban in southern Panjwa'i, and LTC Lavoie, who despite being outranked by the American Colonel still commanded the operation and did not wish to have another catastrophic engagement with the Taliban.

In adding to his discussion of why he pushed the ground assault earlier then scheduled, Brigadier General Fraser said, "The intelligence I was receiving, and also the information I was receiving from my other task force commanders that were part of this battle, not just Omer Lavoie, and talking to Afghans: We were ready. We were at the point where we could press this thing home. Yeah, we could have stuck to the plan, but again, you start to ignore the enemy, what he's doing, what intelligence is on the ground."[32] In hindsight, Brigadier General Fraser's initial assessment of the situation fails to appropriately address the Taliban's disposition and despite initial failings, the revised plan could be judged a success.

---

[32] *Ibid.*

Ultimately the new plan was a balance between intelligence and force commitment and other available resources. Through tactical patience, the Canadians were able to clear Panjwa'i, and in the basic sense of their mission the Canadians accomplished the objectives of Operation Medusa, hence it was a tactical success. The operation, however, did not destroy the Taliban and their resurgence was inevitable. The combat operation phase of Medusa ended on September 14th while the construction of routes and outpost for a sustained presence in the district continued until October 14th, which roughly corresponds to the end of the fighting season.

The Taliban are dependent on the thick vegetation for their cover and concealment, not only to attack ISAF but also to hide their base of operations from ISAF reconnaissance. As winter sets in and as the full, thick leafs on the trees begin to thin so does the Taliban's advantage. The Taliban have understood how to use the terrain to their advantage since the Mujahideen were fighting the Soviets throughout the 1980s. The fighting in Panjwa'i likely died out not because the Canadians decimated the Taliban rather because the season changed. The Taliban, when done fighting, hide their weapons and slip back into their villages either in Afghanistan or across the border in Pakistan where the fighters live with their families, claim glory for fighting the infidels in Afghanistan, and prepare for the next fighting season.

Throughout the brutal 16 weeks of Operation Medusa, the Canadians lost 19 Soldiers. To put this loss in perspective, during previous years of combat operations in Afghanistan, the Canadians lost only two Soldiers due to direct enemy fire; the loss of life during Operation Medusa was nearly a 10-fold increase in 5% of the time. Counting the British Soldiers that were killed in the Nimrod surveillance aircraft supporting Operation Medusa, a total of 33 NATO Soldiers were killed.

Sitting on FOB Wilson, four years later in the heart of Zharay just a few kilometers from the village of Pashmul and on the verge of Operation Dragon STRIKE, I took stock of the Canadian losses. Their efforts and sacrifices would be lessons applied to the upcoming operation.

As a staff, we wondered if we had planned enough and coordinated enough so that STRIKE did not repeat the same mistakes as the Canadians. As a Brigade, our mentality was that we did not want to be fighting the same fight for years to come over the same strips of land. Success, we knew, would come at price but we did not want any loss to be in vain. STRIKE needed a decisive victory so that the Taliban would be broken and that units to follow us in the years to come would not be sitting in the same seats and planning similar operations and trying to learn from previous mistakes. The victory STRIKE sought needed to be sustainable.

Chapter 11
Sand Tables, Briefings, and Tim Hortons

Synchronizing efforts among a small group of people can be difficult. It is a process to ensure that everyone knows their job and when to do their job. Typical missions at the platoon level, such as patrolling through the streets of Baghdad or the mountains of eastern Afghanistan, have thirty to forty personnel, and synchronization requires deliberate effort and rehearsals. A platoon is four levels down from a Brigade, and the level of complexity is not necessarily linear to the size of the unit rather the number of units, the number of enablers, and the number of headquarters required for its execution.

Operation Dragon STRIKE was, on paper, a brigade-level operation, and with additional assets our organic unit swelled from about 3,500 to over 8,000 Soldiers directly involved in its execution. The operation would be the largest combined operation in Afghanistan, over four times the size of Operation Medusa in 2006, which had roughly 1,700 Soldiers, and nearly three times larger than Operation Anaconda in 2002, which had almost 2,700 personnel attempting to trap Osama bin Laden in the mountains of Tora Bora. Success of Operation Dragon STRIKE would depend on our ability to ensure all units and assets were in the right place at the right time. We could not afford to repeat the mistakes of Operation Medusa.

The words resonant in my head like it was yesterday: "Go build a sand table." The order came from Major Cox, the Brigade's Operations Officer. Of course, I knew what it was but had never built one before. I stared at him dumbfounded for a second hoping it was a mistake, hoping that he was talking to someone else. Then I stared silently at him hoping for further guidance and got "make it as big as you can, set it up for Dragon STRIKE, and go see the Sergeant Major for a detail when you need it."

I remember thinking to myself, "I must have really screwed something up to be relegated to this task." I felt like it was beneath me. All Officers and senior non-commissioned Officers are familiar with sand tables: they are a tool to provide visualization of the operation or mission at hand. Maps are good places to start with briefs but do not provide a spatial perspective of the terrain. Maps are not three-dimensional. Sand tables are a means to rehearse an impending operation without actually walking the terrain.

Officers early in their careers are taught what sand tables are and how to brief operations orders from them almost immediately. I remember doing so during the first few weeks of Officer Candidate School at Fort Benning, Georgia, and then later at the Officer Basic Course well before ever getting to my first unit in Germany. The ability to brief an operation order is critical to being an Officer and must be done right. Briefing a mission from a sand table is advantageous over maps because other subordinate elements and adjacent units can see where and how they fit together in the large scheme of maneuver. It also provides a perspective of how failures affect other elements and the overall success of the mission.

I spent about an hour wandering around the outside of the Brigade operations center and the surrounding buildings, vehicles, and containers looking for a spot. I felt dejected having been assigned the sand table task but told myself that at the very least, I would do it right. I would demonstrate to Major Cox that I was worthy of more than just menial tasks.

I ultimately settled on a patch of dirt on the southeast side of the TOC along the 18-foot HESCO outer wall that paralleled Highway One and the adjacent wall that separated the Afghan National Police and district center compound. I marked the area off using white engineer tape so that no one would come park a vehicle or drop a container there while I coordinated with the Sergeant Major for a detail of Soldiers to help with the construction. The area was roughly a square, each 50-foot side making the whole sand table 2,500 square feet.

I then showed Major Cox the selected area and he said that it would work, before adding, "Oh, by the way, it's for the combined arms rehearsal next week, and the CG (Commanding General) will be there so make it look good. Also all our Afghan partners will be there so you will need to ensure that all labels are in Dari as well." I asked Major Cox why I was the one stuck building the sand table and was told that it was because unlike others in the TOC I knew the terrain. Unlike the Soldiers manning the radios and coordinating assets, I routinely went on patrols.

In a combined arms rehearsal, broadly described, subordinate units synchronize their plans and the higher headquarters conducts a review to ensure that the Commander's intent has been achieved. At the company level, it is generally a small group of a few platoon leaders and platoon sergeants, the fire support Officer, and the Company Commander and First Sergeant, some nine people. Operation Dragon STRIKE was far from a company-level operation. In terms of combat power we had five U.S. Army Infantry Battalions (1st and 2nd Battalions, 502nd Infantry Regiment, 1st Squadron, 75th Cavalry, 3rd Squadron, 2nd Stryker Cavalry Regiment, and 1st Battalion, 187th Infantry Regiment) as well as seven Afghan National Army Battalions. In addition to our two internal support Battalions and the Afghan support battalion, STRIKE, for further support of the operation, received an engineer company from the U.S. Marines Corps out of Helmand Province and a National Guard route clearance company, and served as the priority for all lift and attack aviation assets available from Regional Command-South out of Kandahar Airfield. Much to the chagrin of other Brigade Commanders in RC-S, STRIKE got all the assets we were requesting, even at the expense of other units.

I sat that night at my desk in the plans cell and tried to picture the terrain, the units, the objectives, phase lines, and phases of the operation in my head. I printed off the concept of the operation and had the intelligence section print a map for me. I had to put Dragon STRIKE into context in my head and then build it on the ground. Major Travares worked on writing the script with Major Cox while they further coordinated with all of the units that were themselves requesting more information and assets.

The next morning the detail was on hand and ready to build, and I attempted to explain what we had to do. It's tough to tell a Soldier who has spent the past couple of months in the Brigade TOC that he needs to build a giant sand table that mimics what is on the other side of the wall and lay out an operation when he has not seen the plans, let alone even heard the name of the operation.

So we started simple, spending the next couple of hours smoothing out the ground and acquiring (Army slang for stealing) additional supplies. I provided the Soldiers with a basic list of what we needed and knew better than to ask questions when material appeared. We got camouflage nets, two-by-fours, string, yarn, cones, paint, empty ammo boxes and just about anything else we thought would be useful.

Over the next couple of days we built the sand table. The camouflage nets were strung up along the HESCOs and the adjacent buildings, and the two-by-fours were nailed together to create a giant pole, making the whole thing look like a circus tent. Hills such as Masum Ghar and Ghundy Ghar were formed from the fill from the miniaturized Arghandab River that we had dug up. Highway One and the FOBs and COPs were in place as well as all of the major routes and objects. We critiqued and refined as much as possible. We ensured the curve of the roads and the river on the model matched the real things. We situated villages and houses in their correct locations and as much to scale as possible. We made unit symbols down to the company level for both U.S. and Afghan forces and had everything translated to Dari. We were also able to get a hold of headsets that the Afghans could wear to hear the translation and ask questions in real time. When the sand table was finished it reminded me of the large tables in the movie the "Longest Day" used to brief the paratroops on their objectives before Operation Overlord during World War II.

Operation Dragon STRIKE was to begin during the pre-dawn hours of September 13, 2010, and the combined arms rehearsal took place nearly 48 hours prior so that if there were any major concerns or issues identified, then enough time remained to address and fix them.

Everyone had a part in the rehearsal. Major Cox led the rehearsal and controlled the script. The intelligence section of the Brigade updated the suspected enemy course of action while other sections such as fire and aviation stated what assists would be available. As Major Cox led the Brigade through the operation sequentially the Battalion and Company commanders played their role. They described their actions, task, and purpose every step of the way from the initial air assault to the seizing of an objective to the follow-on logistics. The scripted sequence enabled Colonel Kandarian and the other leaders to de-conflict priorities of effort and fires to prevent the operation from collapsing.

Timing of phases was refined and all leaders could see the entire scope of the battle as the Brigade's intelligence section played the Taliban. The rehearsal lasted nearly four hours stretching into the night. Portable lights had been set up just for such a contingency. Colonels Murtaza and Kandarian ended the meeting with closing remarks about the significance of the impending operation on the future security in Zharay and how success will only be achieved through partnership.

The crowd of company commanders, battalion commanders, first sergeants, sergeants major slowly dispersed, then the intelligence and operations Officers. A few hung back. I watched a group of company commanders work out timing details and another group tried to get the latest intelligence updates for their area. STRIKE was spread out over multiple districts and at a variety of combat outposts. It was rare to have all the leaders in the Brigade together; so they took advantage of the occasion. I observed a feeling of anticipation. Many knew this would be a large operation, and despite all the intelligence on hand, the Commanders would only really know the truth about what the Taliban had in store for them after the operation commenced.

It would be a learning experience for U.S. Soldiers and Afghans alike. Combined arms rehearsals are a part of military doctrine and widely taught at the basic and career courses, but few Soldiers ever actually do one. In many ways the success of Operation Dragon STRIKE hinged on the final coordination and deconfliction of efforts that occurred on the sand table built by a group of young privates who had no idea what a sand table was a week prior let alone what Operation Dragon STRIKE would be. Soon the brigade would launch the largest combined operation of the war, where American and Afghan Army partners would conduct air assaults over the Taliban's defense and into their strongholds. Soldiers would be surrounded by the Taliban as they cleared objectives and waited for ground assault forces to push through the Taliban's defensive belts littered with IEDs. The brigade would carve out new roads and build new outposts to deny a Taliban resurgence.

I was focused on answering additional questions when I was called over by Colonel Kandarian who had just seen off the RC-S Commander, Major General Carter. "Stephen, you need to pack a bag. You are going to KAF to liaise with the Canadians," Colonel Kandarian said, walking away before I could comprehend fully what the order entailed or get more information.

I found Captain Meyers, who ran the aviation cell, and explained my new task to him and asked him to get me a flight to KAF. He managed to secure a flight the next day at around noon, so I went back to my office feeling even more dejected. Not only had I been relegated to building a sand table but now I was being sent to KAF to liaise with the Canadians when we had a liaison from the Canadian Army in our tactical operations center. It seemed redundant to me. I wanted to be in Zharay where the fighting was, not on KAF. A few couple hours later, while talking to Major Cox, I came to understand the reason I was heading to the super FOB and what my job would entail.

Through our conversation I learned that the Canadians were not happy about Operation Dragon STRIKE. Brigadier General Milner, the Canadian Battle Group Commander, had requested that Major General Carter send a liaison to brief him and his staff on the our plan. In hindsight, I suspect the Canadians were worried about our plan given their past experiences in Panjwa'i and Zharay and were concerned they would be forced to respond to our troops in contact.

Thankfully, I also learned that this would not be a permanent job for me. One of the Company Commanders for the Top Guns Battalion was coming out of command in the next 24 hours and would take over once he got to KAF, which would be in nearly 72 hours. Major Cox told me that I had done a good job and now I could go brief the Canadians and relax for a couple days before getting back into it. I appreciated the sentiment but KAF was still the last place in the world I wanted to be. It was a paradise of a target for indirect fire, known as a place for lazy Soldiers to conveniently disappear, smelled horribly, and was overcrowded. Before I even left FOB Wilson, I couldn't wait to be back.

The bonus side of liaising with the Canadians was that they were going to let me stay in their compound. So instead of my current tent with spotty air conditioning and occasional showers, I would be put up in a containerized housing unit with consistent air conditioning and running water. It would be nice to take a shower on a regular basis, if only for a few days.

The next morning I caught a flight on a Blackhawk to KAF and began my short liaison stint. Working with the Canadians was unlike anything I had ever done previously. Having spent time on the United States Army Europe Staff I had worked with military leaders from many former Soviet states, and their mentality was generally very formal whereas the Canadians, likely due to the small size of their military, was much akin to a tight knit family. So walking into their command and control area was surreal, compared to my dusty existence on FOB Wilson and our open work environment.

In the heart of KAF adjacent to the RC-S Headquarters was the Canadian Army Brigade's Headquarters, which was a separate walled off compound. The Canadian TOC was an exclusive compound in an already exclusive fortress. There was gravel to keep the dust down, paved sidewalks, and trees, and everyone was extremely polite and surprisingly informal. In fact, most of Afghanistan was a "no salute zone." FOB Wilson was one of the few exceptions since we wanted our Afghan Army partners to mimic our good order and discipline.

The Canadian area consisted of close to a dozen small buildings, a mix of concrete and stone structures whereas STRIKE could boast only three, hastily built structures made of plywood and tin roofs.

The purpose of a tactical operations center is to track everything going on within the unit's area of operation, and as technology has evolved, so have TOCs. In World War II, Officers tacked maps on a board with pins denoting troop locations. Now with electronics and GPS, the internet and televisions and projectors have replaced static maps. Exact troop locations and actions are updated instantly. Gone are the days of radio updates and moving pins on a static map. Radios are still used for coordination but use is limited since GPS signals are automatic and continuous. The Canadian tactical operations center was also like walking onto the bridge of the Starship Enterprise.

The Canadian TOC, dimly lit and relatively small, was arrayed in a U-shape, with one wall supporting several large flat screen TVs that illustrated troop movements and UAV feeds. In the middle of the horseshoe was a giant map of their area of operations. Around the U-shape were a variety of stations for their intelligence sections, fires, medical, and so forth, but the biggest difference between ours and theirs was the utter dearth of Afghan involvement. To STRIKE, the ANA were our partners, and we considered any exclusion of them a missed training opportunity. The Canadian's ANA partners lived south of KAF on Camp Hero. Additionally, despite our best technology, the ANA had better human intelligence than we did. The Canadians' presence on KAF and the lack of contact with their ANA partners, in my opinion, left the Canadians extremely isolated. These Canadian Soldiers and Officers who were supposed to be supporting Soldiers in the field were completely disconnected from the reality beyond the wire.

I'm sure I came off more cowboy than a Soldier to them. My uniform was covered in dust and sweat, and my hair was long and matted down. I was unkempt for a Soldier, not exactly a model for the U.S. Army. The last haircut I had had was in June right before I left Fort Campbell but at least I had been able to shave. My boots also had holes from constant wear and tear and sported more than a few dark spots of dried blood. Yes, I was hardly a picture of spit and shine at that moment, but frankly, I did not care.

My daily priorities at FOB Wilson were to stay alive and do everything in my power to come up with better plans and assist the ANA. These Soldiers appeared to be working in eight-hour shifts. There was a sense of relaxation as if the Soldiers were working a nine-to-five job. I was introduced to both the Battle Captain and Battle Major, and the Battle Captain gave me a cold stare like I did not belong there. I surmised that she probably had not been off KAF since landing in Afghanistan. The Battle Major was very welcoming and seemed to understand what life was like off of KAF.

I gave them a quick brief on Operation Dragon STRIKE and would, in a couple hours, give a more detailed brief to Brigadier General Milner when he returned from the Panjwa'i district center.

While I waited for General Milner, I prepped some notes in my green notebook since I did not have a PowerPoint slide to highlight the overall operation. Due to differences in networks, I had been unable to plug my U.S. government laptop on to the network at KAF. It was not an auspicious start for my task of assuaging doubts and concerns about Operation Dragon STRIKE. But, I figured, at least maps and pointers never fail, and I could make due with whatever I had.

A few hours later, General Milner arrived in his TOC and received an update from the Battle Captain about their units in the field and the latest intelligence about Taliban movement. He quickly noticed me standing nearby as my gray digital Army Combat Uniform was quite distinguishable from the Canadians' tan uniforms. Neither uniform is ideal for blending into the lush green zone. The troops often joked that the only thing the ACU blended into was gravel. The Battle Major introduced me to General Milner, and I quickly jumped at the opportunity to brief him on the plan. I walked him through the phases of the operation, which included 3-2 SCR with 6th Battalion, 3-205 ANA moving out to establish an observation post and sniper positions to the southwest along the rim of the Registan Desert that shoots up nearly a couple hundred feet above the Arghandab River as well as their movements to seal off the western edge from Highway One to the Arghandab River.

Moving further east, 2-502 Infantry with 1st Battalion, 3-205 ANA would air assault into two main objectives taking Nalgham and Sangsar, which is the home of Mullah Omar and the white mosque where the Taliban was founded. In central Zharay, 1-75 CAV with 2nd Battalion, 3-205 would air assault in to Siah Choy and Pashmul, which was the Canadians Objective Rugby during Operation Medusa. Sealing off the east would be 1-502 Infantry with 3rd Battalion, 3-205 ANA, which together would move through the thick pomegranate fields south of Sanjarey, Asoque, and Kandalay and across the Arghandab River. I also explained that all air assault forces would be supported by ground forces that would cut roads through fields to reach the objectives. We had named all of our objectives after towns in Tennessee, in accordance with the STRIKE Brigade's standard operating procedures, which further added to the confusion. The only names the Canadians recognized were Nashville and Lynchburg. I also informed General Milner about STRIKE's intent to establish combat outposts to control these areas and keep the insurgents away from Highway One.

As I briefed Brigadier General Milner and his staff, I could sense an uneasiness developing about the plan and was asked how we planned on cutting through all of the suspect IEDs in the fields. In my rush to brief, I had assumed they had followed our actions in the Arghandab and the use of MICLICs and APOBs. To the best of my ability, I explained that both MICLICs and APOBs were rockets with a string of trailing explosives that were launched into high-IED zones and then detonated, initiating all potential IEDs in the blast area and creating a clear path. I could tell they remained skeptical. I suspected the Canadians presumed STRIKE was overreaching and under-assessing the enemy's capabilities but they were satisfied nevertheless with the brief. It was a lot of information to digest, but the Canadians, in fact, had no say in the operation. My presence was a mere courtesy.

The next morning, I arrived at the Canadian TOC at close to 0700 and was quickly met by the battle captain who seemed frantic. Their outpost on Masum Ghar was reporting loud explosions for the past couple hours from just north in Zharay. The battle captain thought we were engaged in some horrific close combat and demanded that I immediately call our TOC to see if we needed assistance. I assured her that it was a MICLC being detonated but called anyway just to confirm. I briefly talked to my battle captain about the explosions and learned that they were indeed the MICLICs and that we were moving forward according to the timetable. Initial contact had been light due to darkness. The Taliban did not have the night vision capabilities we did and would rather hide until daylight and then attack.

As I talked to my battle captain back on FOB Wilson, I could see the impatient look on the Canadians' faces wanting an answer so I took my time. I finally got off the phone and told the Canadian battle captain that those explosions that Masum Ghar was reporting were indeed MICLICs and that the operation was moving along. I was deliberately vague since her impatience annoyed me.

I understood that the Canadians wanted situational awareness of the operation, however there were four U.S. Infantry Battalions with ANA partners conducting missions all at the same time. I ultimately apologized that I was not able to provide the visibility they desired because everything in combat is fluid and ongoing. Having been a battle captain before, I knew the last thing my Brigade had time to do was to call me prior to every MICLIC explosion or some other controlled detonation of an IED. If the Canadians wanted real-time information they could simply monitor the feed at RC-S headquarters since we were required to notify our higher headquarters at every instance that we cleared our air space to initiate a detonation.

Over the next couple of days, I tried to spend as little time in the Canadian TOC as possible. There was nothing for me to really do. I could call and get information, but I did not have a computer on their network so I ended up drinking a fair amount of Tim Hortons coffee and managed to acquire nearly ten pounds of the coffee grounds to take back to FOB Wilson with me. My replacement would be arriving on the night of the 15th and I would meet him on the morning of the 16th and fly back later that day. I was also pretty sure the Canadian Battle Captain would be happy to see me leave and perhaps have a better working relationship with someone potentially who wanted to be there instead of with the Soldiers. Being at KAF made me feel isolated. The reality visible on screens and monitors and through reports is not the same reality in the field. In spite of the comforts of a real bed and consistent showers at KAF, I wanted to be back at FOB Wilson. I missed being able to go out on patrols and working for the Soldiers who were out constantly in harm's way.

While I was at KAF, I was missing the fight. I was missing the evolution of the plan as the Taliban fought back. As General Fraser had said about Operation Medusa, "The enemy has a vote," and I wanted to get back to hear and see its opinion. Upon returning to FOB Wilson another area would come into STRIKE's sights following the Taliban's initial vote or counter-action to Dragon STRIKE.

Just south of western and central Zharay is a swath of land that is formed by the Arghandab River to the north and the Registan Desert to the south. The flow of the river and desert wind create a shape that resembles a rhinoceros' horn. Technically this area is part of Panjwa'i district but the Canadians had left the area alone for such a long time that the Taliban freely controlled the villages of Mushan, Talokan, and Zangabad. The air assault into the Horn of Panjwa'i was not part of the original concept of the operation. The idea was that the displaced Taliban lacking a support in the area would move into the Registan Desert and toward Pakistan were armed drones and attack aviation could easily engage the Taliban away from civilian populations. As Operation Dragon STRIKE commenced we realized that we would ultimately need to go into the Horn of Panjwa'i to clear the Taliban out from the three villages to prevent them from resettling back into Zharay. The Brigade, however, at the time lacked the organic combat power to clear further, and we requested more troops through RC-S and ISAF Headquarters.

Operation Dragon STRIKE was already the largest operation in post-September 11th Afghanistan so our request was quickly granted. Within a couple weeks we were welcoming the 1st Battalion, 187 Infantry Regiment from 3rd Brigade, 101st Airborne that had rapidly displaced from eastern Afghanistan and three additional Afghan Army Battalions, which came from all over Afghanistan. The Soldiers of 3rd Brigade are known as the "Rakasans," which comes from the Japanese word for umbrella. During World War II, the Rakasans jumped into Japan as part of the occupation force, and the locals were heard yelling "rakasans" as the Soldiers glided to the ground from the falling umbrellas that their parachutes resembled. Subsequently, while attached to us, the 1-187 Soldiers would be known as "Strike-asans."

To commence the Strike-asans air assault into the Horn of Panjwa'i, two conditions had to be met. One, 2-502 Infantry and their ANA partners needed to be set in Nalgham where they were rapidly establishing an outpost, and two, STRIKE needed a bridge. Running parallel to the Arghandab River was a deep canal just on the north side of the river that was nearly twenty feet deep and twenty feet wide. Simply air assaulting 1-187 Infantry and their partners into Zangabad, Talukan, and Mushan would leave them to the mercy of aerial resupply and reinforcements, and if the Taliban massed enough forces against the isolated units, then the Strike-asans would surely endure heavy casualties before coalition forces could arrive. STRIKE examined two options to support the operation: one was to cut a road through the fields directly south of what would be COP Nalgham and use a tethered balloon with a camera to watch the road constantly. The other option was to cut a road from Masum Ghar west along the northern edge of the horn. Colonel Kandarian argued against this option due to our inability to guard or keep eyes on the road at all times to prevent IEDs. The latter was also the simpler option and one the Taliban would expect. We had learned almost immediately in Afghanistan to take the harder route because it invariably would save lives. The terrain favors certain actions, and the Taliban understood this so they emplaced IEDs and mines and established ambush sites along those common routes. Cutting a road from COP Nalgham to the Horn of Panjwa'i would be possible with the use of MICLICs and would rewrite the Taliban's narrative that NATO forces are constrained by the terrain.

Operation Dragon STRIKE would be a pivotal and defining moment for the STRIKE Brigade and ultimately for the success of Kandahar. For the first time in four years, coalition forces were making a concerted effort to clear the Taliban not only from their current strongholds but from their historical birthplace. The success of the operation would be measured and viewed in many different lights ranging from the heroism of the Soldiers, the effects on the Taliban, and the effects on the local population.

Chapter 12
Dragon STRIKE: Heroes Among Us

It behooves every man to remember that the work of the critic is of altogether secondary importance, and that, in the end, progress is accomplished by the man who does things.

Theodore Roosevelt

Exhausted, hungry, and ready to relax, a small squad-size patrol from a 1st Battalion, 502nd Infantry on November 1, 2010, was nearly within sight of its patrol base in eastern Zharay when a motorcycle parked nearby exploded. Shrapnel tore through the air in a wave of heat and pressure. The shrapnel pierced men, body armor, buildings, and trees alike. Specialist Jonathan Curtis and Private First Class Andrew Meari were killed instantly and six other Soldiers, including Specialist Felipe Pereira, were wounded. The explosion was just the beginning of the attack.

Private First Class Philip Wysocki immediately moved to help the wounded. He applied tourniquets to both legs of Sergeant Ryan Louviere. PFC Wysocki needed to control the bleeding to save his team leader and friend.

As he worked, the squad came under intense enemy small arms fire from seven different positions. With complete disregard for his own safety, PFC Wysocki pulled SGT Louviere to a safe position behind cover before returning through enemy fire to recover the remains of SPC Curtis. PFC Wysocki then exposed himself again to the enemy a third time to recover his fallen comrade's equipment and to prevent it from falling into the hands of the enemy.

For the next 35 minutes, the squad remained pinned down under heavy Taliban fire. In the absence of team leaders, PFC Wysocki took charge. He directed sectors of fire to his fellow Soldiers and controlled their rates of fire while pointing out Taliban fighters as they presented themselves. The patrol fought under PFC Wysocki's control and leadership until re-enforcements arrived at which point he provided a detailed assessment of the situation including status of both enemy and friendly elements. His actions are a testament to his character and his skills as a Soldier. His actions undoubtedly saved the lives of his fellow Soldiers. For these actions, PFC Wysocki was awarded the Silver Star, the nation's third highest award for valor.

"Anyone who says that the U.S. Soldier cannot fight anymore has not seen what is going on ... There is extremely close fighting going on," commented ISAF Commander General David Petraeus about Operation Dragon STRIKE during a visit to FOB Wilson. Operation Dragon STRIKE lasted 84 days as the over 8,000 U.S. Soldiers and Afghan National Army partners of Combined Task Force - STRIKE conducted over 800 combined patrols, dropped 86 tons of high explosive ordnance, distributed nearly 9 million dollars for improved local infrastructure, and killed over 130 Taliban fighters.

Patrolling in the green zone was far from easy. The lush green vegetation, high grape walls, intersecting canals, and over-planted fields hid everything. Movement was slow but meticulous. Roads south of Highway One were virtually nonexistent. The tiny trails cannot support the weight of the large up armored vehicles that protect Soldiers, so to reach the tiny villages, Soldiers walked. The Taliban hid IEDs along the trails and set up ambushes along points where the green zone canalized movement so Soldiers avoided these points and took the path of greatest resistance.

Under the weight of body armor, helmets, weapons, ammunition, water food, grenades, flares, smoke, radios, night vision goggles, and batteries, the Soldiers moved methodically through the vegetation that trapped humidity close to the ground. Avoiding trails and paths, Soldiers walked through canals and used ladders to climb over grape walls. Movement was slow and deliberate as the path ahead was cleared with metal detectors and bomb-sniffing dogs. Patrols regularly began under the cover of darkness and proceeded through the morning and into the heat of the day.

On September 16th, a patrol of Soldiers from 3rd platoon, Alpha Company, 2-502 Infantry was sent out to conduct a battle damage assessment of Taliban casualty following an attack on their newly established outpost near Nalgham. Their initial movement forced them to cross an open area. As the platoon bounded forward under heavy gear in small teams, the insurgents attacked the platoon from multiple directions with small arms and machine guns. The platoon established a base of fire and Sergeant Aaron Kramer moved his squad across the field to link up with the lead elements and maneuver on the enemy. During this movement, SGT Kramer was shot in the upper right arm and fell to the ground. Seeing SGT Kramer fall, Private First Class Thomas Pedigo, Specialist Kevin Clafton, and Specialist Adam Lipski raced forward to aid their leader.

PFC Pedigo and SPC Clafton immediately provided suppressive and continuous fire on the enemy forces as rounds impacted nearby, which enabled SPC Lipski, the platoon's medic, to evaluate and treat SGT Kramer under direct enemy fire and with no cover in the open field. It was after several minutes of stabilizing SGT Kramer that SPC Lipski was able to move him 25 meters to a covered position and ultimately to evacuate him from the battlefield.

For their effective suppressive fire, which enabled SPC Lipski to treat SGT Kramer, SPC Clafton and PFC Pedigo were awarded the Army Commendation medal with Valor. For his efforts to save SGT Kramer under direct enemy fire, SPC Lipski was awarded the Bronze Star Medal with Valor. Sadly, SGT Aaron Kramer died of the wounds he sustained from the Taliban's small arms fire.

Further west on September 16th, elements from Charlie Company, 2-502 Infantry were patrolling in support of engineers who were building blocking positions to prevent Taliban movement near the "Super Wadi." The Super Wadi is an open streambed that runs between western Zharay and Maiwand and had not been patrolled by ISAF for several years. As the platoon moved south across the Super Wadi, ahead of the engineers, the platoon was engaged by small arms from the south and southwest.

As the platoon struggled to find cover in the open area, Specialist Matthew Zaragoza raced forward 75 meters to a short wall and began to engage the enemy with his M240B Machine Gun. Despite being grazed by a bullet on the inside of his leg, SPC Zaragoza aggressively and accurately engaged the enemy so that the remainder of his unit could move to a covered and concealed positions. Once it had an established base of fire at SPC Zaragoz's position, the platoon was able to maneuver and destroy the enemy positions. The platoon's effort and clearance ahead of the engineers enabled the construction of the blocking positions.

Soldiers are taught to place the mission first, and Specialist Zaragoza, in the character of every Soldier, continued the mission that day. He carried his load of more than 60 pounds for the balance of the patrol, another six-and-a-half hours. His actions under fire enabled the patrol to destroy the Taliban forces that would have attacked the engineer unit establishing the blocking obstacles. Their ability to complete the mission stemmed the insurgent flow of men, weapons, and other equipment in and out of the Brigade's area of operation. Specialist Matthew Zaragoza was awarded a Purple Heart and a Bronze Star with Valor.

Unlike Operation Medusa in 2006, Dragon STRIKE was not meant to be a quick clearance operation but rather a phased attack to illustrate to the Taliban our resolve and capabilities to reach the people. Despite the phased, methodical nature of the operation, there was still an inherent risk and necessity to take risks. STRIKE Soldiers were willing to expose themselves and put themselves at risk to complete the mission. The following day, September 17th, Second Lieutenant Taylor Murphy was leading a 30-man platoon on a movement to contact mission in an area where recoilless rifle and small arms fire had been rampant.

While just north of Makuan village, his platoon came under heavy fire including machine gun, small arms and recoilless rifle from multiple locations nearly 150 meters south of their location. Due to the thick vegetation, his platoon was unable to identify the exact location of the incoming fire, and so to assess the situation 2LT Murphy selflessly exposed himself to enemy fire and within seconds was engaged with an accurate burst of machine gun fire. A round struck him in his right wrist and lodged in the chest plate of his interceptor body armor.

With complete disregard for his wounds, 2LT Murphy continued to lead his platoon and coordinate air strikes on the enemy positions gaining fire superiority and destroying the enemy's will to fight. Only after the arrival of his Company Commander did 2LT Murphy remove himself from the front line for treatment. Less than twenty-four hours later, 2LT Murphy was again leading his platoon to secure a site where a double IED strike had resulted in a mass casualty situation. As his platoon moved to the site, they detonated an IED, which resulted in the death of Staff Sergeant Jamie Newman, the platoon's platoon sergeant and the wounding of 11 others including 2LT Murphy.

Despite his additional wounds, 2LT Murphy continued to fight and lead his Soldiers. He quickly established security around the wounded against a potential Taliban small arms attack to protect the wounded while they were hastily treated. He then assisted in carrying his fallen platoon sergeant over 800 meters back to the strong point so that all of the wounded could be evacuated. As stated in the citation for his Army Commendation Medal with Valor and Purple Heart, "2LT Murphy's courage and leadership under fire and dedication to duty are unquestionable. He consistently continued to lead, maneuver and coordinate close air support, close combat air, and indirect fires expertly and with complete disregard for his personal safety and wounds, thus driving off and securing the enemies' fighting locations."[33]

Including Staff Sergeant Jamie Newman, the STRIKE Brigade would lose two other Soldiers that day. First Lieutenant Eric Yates would die of wounds sustained by an improvised explosive device and Corporal Deangelo Snow would die of wounds sustained when his vehicle was attacked with a rocket-propelled grenade.

Critical to Operation Dragon STRIKE, and to counterinsurgency doctrine more broadly, was the necessity to gain the support of the local population. Implicit within the commander's intent was the necessity of conducting key leader engagements, commonly known as KLEs, with the leaders of the villages to both draw them closer to the Government of Afghanistan and away from the Taliban. The Taliban, however, were not going to allow this to be easy. The local population was also just as necessary for the Taliban's own survival.

On September 19th, LTC Thomas McFadyen and his ANA partner battalion commander conducted an engagement with the leaders of Zendanon, just north of Pasmul. As the personal security details for the battalion commanders were leaving the town, their dismounted patrol was engaged in what can only be described as a complex attack with coordinated IEDs and small arms fire. The attack was initiated by an IED that instantly wounded several Soldiers. Captain Matthew Crawford, the squadron's intelligence Officer, and Sergeant Zane Cordingly were both within the initial blast radius but quickly regrouped.

---

[33] 2LT Taylor Murphy Citation. (2011). In *Book of Valor Combined Task Force STRIKE Operation Enduring Freedom 10-11*. Page 139.

Captain Crawford immediately moved forward through an uncleared IED-laden area and found SGT Cordingly providing life-saving first aid to Private First Class Robert Trujillo who had extensive lacerations and trauma to both legs from the blast. Together and while still under small arms fire, they worked as a team and stabilized PFC Trujillo and carried him to a waiting medevac helicopter. Their combined action saved PFC Trujillo's life, and both were subsequently awarded the Army Commendation Medal with Valor. Sergeant Cordingly also received the Purple Heart for his wounds.

The ability to mass firepower quickly and accurately, using both rotary and fixed wing aircraft, indirect fire, and infantry, made Dragon STRIKE extremely lethal to the Taliban. Critical to this capacity was the role of the embedded Air Force personnel that function as a "Joint Terminal Attack Controller." On September 26, the scout platoon from 2-502 Infantry conducted a partnered air assault into an unsecured helicopter landing zone and moved 900 meters through overgrown grape fields and dense woods to establish observation post, Dusty. At dawn the newly established OP came under heavy fire from rocket-propelled grenades, PKM machine guns and small arms from Taliban positions to the southeast and the east. The Taliban had created a lethal crossfire.

Without hesitation and under intense enemy fire, Senior Airman (SrA) Nathan Archmbault, who was assigned to the scout platoon for the mission, positioned himself outside of the compound so that he could communicate with rearward elements and requested immediate close air support. He quickly and efficiently informed the aircrews of the dire ground situation and the close proximity of the enemy. Senior Airman Achambault controlled 10 strafing passes from supporting aircraft, five of which were danger close and within 50 meters of his platoon's position, and yet despite the strafing passes, the enemy continued to maneuver aggressively on the observation post in an effort to overrun the position.

With complete disregard for his own personal safety, SrA Archambault climbed on top of the compound roof at the OP and low-crawled to get a better vantage point of the enemy movements. Under heavy machine gun fire and sporadic RPG fire impacting within 50 meters, he was able to control eight precision guided munition strikes on several enemy fighting positions and with weapons impacting within as close as 170 meters of his own location; a danger close situation again. Over the next 48 hours, he continued to repel 20 separate enemy assaults by controlling additional strafing runs, including four that were within 100 meters of his position.

The combination of precision-guided munitions and multiple strafing runs ended all enemy fire and prevented the observation post from being overrun. After-action estimates put the enemy killed at 13 with an additional 30 Taliban wounded. As his Army Commendation Medal with Valor citation states, "without SrA Archambault's bravery and leadership while controlling close air support, it is highly probable the 27 coalition and Afghan soldiers would have died during the multi-day battle."[34]

The complexity of attacks and determination of the Taliban did not diminish as Operation Dragon STRIKE moved into October. Following a meeting near Pashmul in central Zharay between battalion leaders for 1-75 CAV and its ANA partners with their partnered subordinate companies, an ANA HMMWV struck a pressure plate initiated IED as it was being repositioned for their exfil. The IED was immediately followed by enemy small arms fire from a tree line nearly 150 meters away. Staff Sergeant Christopher James was approximately 20 feet from the IED blast and caught in the open as he had been moving to his vehicle when the fight commenced.

Regaining his bearings, he kneeled and began providing suppressing fire on the enemy positions while the ANA Soldiers began exiting the destroyed vehicle. One of the severely injured ANA Soldiers was unable to crawl so SSG James, further exposing himself to enemy small arms fire, ran through the engagement zone and pulled the ANA Soldier by his body armor over 20 feet to cover. His actions during the complex attack were critical in saving the ANA Soldier's life, and for his complete disregard for his own safety he was awarded the Bronze Star with Valor and the Purple Heart for the injuries he sustained in the initial blast.

The Taliban attacks, however, did not deter the Soldiers from continuing on with their daily missions. On October 8th, elements of

---

[34] SrA Nathan Archambault Citation. (2011). In *Book of Valor Combined Task Force STRIKE Operation Enduring Freedom 10-11*. Pages 161 – 162.

Charlie Company, 1-75 CAV were conducting a partnered, intelligence-driven clearance of a two compounds near Pashmul when the platoon began receiving effective small arms fire from locations to the south, east, and north of their positions. With most of the platoon pinned down in a wadi under sustained enemy fire, Sergeant Jesse Hattesohl led his fire team to maneuver on the enemy and gain a more advantageous position. Once in a dominant position, SGT Hattesohl directed his team's small arms and machine guns to suppress the enemy to the south. This, however, did not alleviate the heavy fire from the east and north, and so under intense fire, he left his covered position and maneuvered further to the north side of the wadi and began suppressing the enemy there.

With rounds impacting nearby, SGT Hattesohl continued to give fire commands to his machine gunner, direct fires, and direct high explosive grenades on the enemy's position so that the remainder of the platoon could concentrate their fire on the enemy's main element to the east. Throughout this engagement, SGT Hattesohl was exposed to enemy fire on two sides. And once close air support was available, he marked the enemy positions with smoke grenades and moved back and forth between his two elements controlling their fires until the enemy was suppressed. The actions of SGT Hattesohl were unparalleled in the fight and necessary for the defeat of the enemy ambush, leading to no friendly losses. Additionally, Kaka Abdul Hadi, a Taliban leader in Zharay and a high value target, was killed in the ambush. For his leadership and bravery under intense enemy fire, SGT Hattesohl was awarded the Bronze Star with Valor.

While some Soldiers demonstrate heroism, leadership, and bravery under direct enemy fire, others do so in the face of the unknown. Soldiers are trained to react to dangerous situations and what motivates many Soldiers in the face of unknown danger is the fear of letting their fellow Soldier down. Further west the next morning, elements of Alpha Company, 2-502 Infantry were clearing an objective near a vital route intersection when a platoon struck a house-borne IED. Two IEDs were initiated in the house in a five-minute span in an attempt by the Taliban to wound as many Soldiers as possible who were rescuing those wounded in the first explosion. The combined results of these two blasts were 12 wounded Soldiers.

Despite being within three meters of the second IED blast, Sergeant Dustin Hennigar quickly regained his situational awareness and sprinted to the aid of PFC Comer who was within a meter of the blast. Ignoring the possibility of any further IED threat, he rushed through the smoke and the crumbled remnants of the compound to save his fellow Soldier. SGT Hennigar threw PFC Comer over his shoulder and carried him out of the immediate threat area to the casualty collection point where he began assessing and treating his wounds. Similar actions were carried out by Specialist William Blair, who like SGT Hennigar, received the Bronze Star with Valor and Lieutenant Colonel David Easty, the battalion surgeon was also on the clearance operation to assist the Soldiers and who received the Army Commendation Medal with Valor.

By the middle of October, 1st Battalion, 187th Infantry and their three ANA partner battalions were ready for their push into the Horn of Panjwa'i. This task force was called "Gad Zawak," which is Dari for "Great Force." As Command Sergeant Major Eric Crabtree, the 1-187 BN CSM, said, "the horn of Panjwa'i is the last bastion of hope for the Taliban right now and they thought they were untouchable in there and we have touched them in every corner of that horn. The best news of all is the people there are hungry and ready to see us out there and more importantly, they're ready to see the Afghan National Army."[35]

Gad Zawak was organized into four forces with each infantry company partnering with an ANA battalion in a true 1 to 3 (U.S.:ANA) ratio and the Headquarter and Headquarters Company. Alpha Company and its partners would air assault and operate along the western part of the horn in Mushan, Bravo Company and its partners in the east at Zangabad, Dog Company and its partners in the central area of Talukan and the Headquarters would establish observation and firing positions along the southern edge in the Registan Desert to eliminate the Taliban option of retreat. With the continued push towards the south in Zharay and the Strike-asans in the horn of Panjwa'i, the Taliban were cut off and surrounded. As LTC Robert Harman, the Strike-asan Battalion Commander, said, "How we came in

---

[35] 18 October 2010. (2011). In *Book of Valor Combined Task Force STRIKE Operation Enduring Freedom 10-11*. Pages 188 – 189.

here [was], we surprised the enemy. The several things leading up to the conditions we see right now and the method on how we came in here, on their terrain, has put the Taliban off."[36]

Despite being caught off guard, the Taliban were not destroyed and were demonstrating a capability to fight. As clearing operations continued in all directions, elements of 3rd Squadron, 2nd Stryker Cavalry Regiment were clearing compounds near the village of Shalghamay to enable Marine engineer assets to breach and establish a new route south. During the early hours of the operation, a platoon halted next to a compound while the route clearance conducted a controlled detonation of an IED. One of the dismounts triggered an anti-personnel mine along the wall of the compound. The blast wounded three, and Specialist Steven Dupont ultimately died of the wounds he sustained in the blast. Sergeants Curtis Crew and Brennan Lagemann raced to the roof of the compound to help the wounded Soldiers and to assess the situation.

Both Soldiers began treating the wounded when they recognized their dire situation. They were surrounded by multiple anti-personnel mines. Despite the great risk to themselves they feverishly continued to recover the remains and equipment of their fallen comrades. An EOD team later confirmed the compound was designed to be a house-borne IED and the casualties would have been much greater had the unit actually entered the compound instead of just setting up an overwatch position on the roof. For their dedication to their fallen comrades, Sergeants Crew and Lagemann would each earn the Bronze Star with Valor for their actions.

For the month of October, the STRIKE Brigade would lose 10 Soldiers killed in action and 60 Soldiers would receive Purple Hearts as a result of action with the Taliban. The weather in southern Afghanistan was starting to turn cooler, and the Taliban would end its fighting season, according to history. It was a technique learned from the Mujahideen to survive and to fight another day. This year, however, the Taliban would not be allowed simply to walk away. Coalition forces were now living and patrolling with relative ease in the historical birthplace of the Taliban movement. The Taliban leadership could not

---

[36] *Ibid.*

ignore STRIKE's presence. Their actions grew increasing desperate, devolving from complex engagements to IEDs and suicide attacks in desperation. Still, we hoped that the Taliban's withdrawal would enable us to solidify our gains in Zharay and Panjwa'i.

Patrols and fighting continued daily by every element in the STRIKE Brigade as we fought to find caches of weapons and ammunition and to further clear the Taliban out of Zharay and the Horn of Panjwa'i. On November 11th, another suicide bomber would strike again in eastern Zharay. As a combined patrol was returning to COP Senjaray, a motorcyclist approached with other traffic along Highway One. The patrol saw the motorcycle, and the cyclist abided the requests for him to halt. As the patrol maneuvered around him in order to enter the outpost's gate, the bomber detonated. The blast instantly killed two Soldiers and wounded four others, including the squad leader and the other team leader. The blast was then immediately followed by small arms fire and RPG fire from multiple positions.

Despite shrapnel wounds to his spleen, liver, and left lung sustained in the blast, Specialist Felipe Pereira raced into the outpost and commandeered an all-terrain vehicle and moved back into heavy enemy fire to provide an evacuation platform for his wounded comrades. Several Soldiers were pinned down under heavy enemy fire 20 meters away and using the vehicle he positioned himself so as to provide effective suppressive fire on the enemy and allow his fellow Soldiers to move two casualties to the vehicle. His actions also permitted the Soldiers to egress to the relative safety of the COP's entrance. Medics were then able to treat the wounded. Specialist Pereira is credited with saving the lives of two of his fellow Soldiers while risking his own life on multiple occasions. His commitment to others, selfless service, and bravery under fire defines heroism, and for his actions, SPC Felipe Pereira would be awarded the Distinguished Service Cross, a valorous medal second only to the Medal of Honor.

Less than 48 hours later, another suicide bomber would attack the STRIKE Brigade this time in western Zharay. On November 13th, 1st platoon, Bravo Company, 2-502 Infantry began a clearing operation of 20 buildings near the village of Maligan. During the operation, the platoon received sporadic small arms fire until they completed their mission and were heading back to their outpost. During a short rest halt so that other elements of the patrol could catch up, the platoon established a security perimeter when a suspicious individual began approaching the patrol from the hashish fields to the north and worked his way south toward the platoon.

Closely observing the man's action as he came out of the field, Staff Sergeant Juan Rivadeneira grew gravely skeptical. His instincts proved correct: the man was a Taliban fighter dressed as a local farmer and even carried a bundle of poppy stalks to further accentuate his disguise. The man approached, passed two ANA Soldiers who attempted unsuccessfully to speak with him, and continued across a ditch towards the U.S. positions. SSG Rivadeneira moved to intercept the individual, placed himself between the suspicious man and his Soldiers, and raised his weapon at the disguised fighter. Realizing that he could not advance any further, the fighter raised his head and shouted "Allahu Akbar" as SSG Rivadeneira fired two rounds from his M4 rifle into the suicide bomber's chest. The bomber fell back away from the Soldiers as he detonated. The explosion, however, killed SSG Rivadeneira, SPC Jacob Carver, PFC Jacob Carroll, and two other ANA Soldiers.

Staff Sergeant Rivadeneira's actions were above and beyond the call of duty. His situational awareness, leadership, and bravery saved countless lives in his squad. For his actions, SSG Rivadeneira was awarded the Silver Star. Others within the platoon seemingly emulated his leadership and reacted quickly to treat the scores of others wounded in the attack.

The month of November would close with 8 Soldiers killed in action and another 33 Soldiers receiving Purple Hearts for wounds sustained in combat. Operation Dragon STRIKE transitioned to Operation Dragon Wrath on December 7, 2010, as the winter set in and our resources from RC-S were being reallocated. The fighting was still far from over.

STRIKE measured a sharp decrease in significant attacks along Highway One since Operation Economic Corridors and Dragon STRIKE had begun nearly three months prior. STRIKE attributed this decrease to the success of Operation Dragon STRIKE while a Taliban would likely argue, "It was the end of the fighting season so we returned to Pakistan." Regardless of the reason, we needed to maintain the pressure and prevent the Taliban from reoccupying the villages and compounds that many Soldiers had died to secure.

As the quote from Theodore Roosevelt goes, "Progress is accomplished by the man who does things." And nearly a decade after the first Americans went into Afghanistan the STRIKE Brigade was making progress in southern Afghanistan and in the home of the Taliban. For the last decade, Soldiers were fighting and destroying Taliban fighters in hordes yet the Taliban's will was not broken. So STRIKE did the unprecedented. Operation Dragon STRIKE removed the Taliban from their birthplace through a combination of lethal force, skill, and persistence. Many STRIKE Soldiers paid the ultimate price while striving to finish America's work. The fight was not over, however.

The Taliban would be back. The Soldiers of the STRIKE Brigade were still in the Taliban's home and their attacks in December alone would be just as deadly as the height of Operation Dragon STRIKE. During that month, 10 Soldiers were killed in action and another 39 Soldiers would receive the Purple Heart. Of the Soldiers killed, two were by a suicide bomber on December 8th and another 6 Soldiers on December 12th when a newly established outpost near the village of Diwar just east of Mullah Omar's village Sangsar was attacked. The attack at Diwar was executed with a vehicle-borne IED, eliciting a blast so powerful that it shook every building at FOB Wilson, where I had been sitting at that very moment with Colonel Murtaza and his staff during their morning Afghan National Army meetings. The blast created a crater nearly five feet deep and the shock wave collapsed the roof and walls of the outpost, crushing the Soldiers.

The Taliban had a vote.

Chapter 13
Dragon STRIKE: The Taliban Vote

The air assault put the Soldiers of Combined Task Force STRIKE behind the Taliban's support zones and defensive belts of IEDs, allowing ground units to subsequently punch through using MICLICs. STRIKE converged on the trapped Taliban fighters from multiple directions while air support in the form of drones and attack helicopters provided both visual cover and armed support.

The Taliban's ability to reach Highway One was now limited at best.

Both Operation Medusa four years prior and Dragon STRIKE saw the clearance of the green zone south of Highway One, but unlike our Canadian counterparts, we also established new infrastructure including outposts and roads by which we could regularly patrol to the small villages deep in the green zone that had been and still were pro-Taliban. Operation Dragon STRIKE left the Taliban in Zharay with two choices: fight or flight.

The Taliban that stayed to fight were desperate and dwindling in numbers as we continued to push both with military might and with humanitarian aid for the people of Zharay. The insurgents were now on the defense and trying to maintain their base of support. The villagers, in this area, had rarely, if ever, seen coalition and other Afghan forces. Seemingly overnight our platoon leaders and company commanders were holding Shuras with them and finding out what the locals needed in terms of medical care, security, government assistance, and access to their own fields. Due to the depth of our bases in the green zone and our ability to maneuver through the defensive belts of IEDs using MICLICs and APOBs, STRIKE was able to visit these villages constantly. The people quickly realized that we were not going to simply disappear into the night after a few days.

Our persistent presence in the green zone empowered the people and began stripping away the Taliban's control and power. The village of Sangsar in the heart of central Zharay is the birthplace of the Taliban and should have been the one place in the world where the Taliban's control was absolute and unquestioned but it wasn't.

The Taliban, which comes from the Pashtu word *talib* meaning "student," rose to power through the chaos of the Afghan civil war. The withdrawal of the Soviet Union from Afghanistan in the spring of 1989 had led to a power vacuum. The puppet government of Mohammad Najibullah in Kabul collapsed shortly after the Soviet withdrawal, and leading Afghans and former Mujahideen leaders soon became warlords fighting each other. Unlike the American Civil War, the Afghan civil war was without any easy delineation between geographic locations. The war was warlord versus warlord for power and control, not for an overarching cause or belief.

The Taliban emerged in the Afghan civil war as an antithesis to the warlords. Lawrence Wright highlights in his book *The Looming Tower* that the Taliban, in the context of being students of Islam, have existed for decades. It was first seen within the religious schools, *madrassas*, in Pakistan during the Soviet-Afghan war, not as a political movement but rather a term to describe a group of young men who immerse themselves in the Qu'ran. These same students picked up the fight against the Soviets and continued to refer to themselves as Taliban.[37]

The present day Taliban's rise in Afghanistan began with a group of farmers who in September 1994 came to Mullah Mohammed Omar's mosque in Sansgar in the heart of the then Panjwa'i District. The men reported that their children had been beaten and raped at a checkpoint on Highway One by men loyal to a local warlord. As the story goes, Mullah Omar led about 30 men with barely half that number of rifles to the checkpoint, confronting the armed bandits. It is unknown how the events actually occurred, but the legend holds that Mullah Omar had the local commander hung from the barrel of one of the many burnt-out Soviet tanks rusting away along Highway One west of Kandahar City. By such an obvious show of aggression, Mullah Omar clearly wanted the other warlords to fear the Taliban, to see that there was a new sheriff in town.

With this single act of righteousness and revenge against thieves and rapists, the modern Taliban movement was born. Regardless of which events are real and which are legend, the results were the same. Mullah Omar became a figure around whom the people of Kandahar could rally. A religious leader, Omar promised to rule the people by

---

[37] Wright, L., (2007). *The Looming Tower: Al-Qaeda and the Road to 9/11*. Vintage.

sharia or Islamic law. In the face of lawlessness and banditry under the feuding warlords, his movement gained the support of the people as word of his deeds spread from village to village. Soon Mullah Omar controlled all of Kandahar province, and with each subsequent victory, the movement harnessed more and more military power through personnel, weaponry, and financial pledges from business and religious leaders around the country. The Taliban campaign to rid Afghanistan of its warlords and institute Sharia across the country then moved west into Herat and eventually north. Over the course of the first few months of its movement, the Taliban gained control of 12 of Afghanistan's 34 provinces. Within two years, the Taliban controlled Kabul.

During the distant fighting, Mullah Omar appointed himself "Head of the Supreme Council of Afghanistan" and relocated the movement to Kandahar City.

The physical origin of the Taliban movement held a powerful place in the Taliban's psyche. The Taliban's sense of righteousness was tied closely to its humble beginnings. The Taliban viewed themselves as men upholding religious beliefs. They were David to the Goliath that was the warlords and corruption of Afghanistan. The post-9/11 Taliban may have altered their tactics to fight their new enemy, but Sansgar and Kandahar province remained the spiritual home. It is the center of the Pashtun tribe and a pivotal node from which their power is derived.

The tactics employed by the Taliban against ISAF and the STRIKE Brigade, however, are most comparable to those of the Mujahideen against the Soviets and not the tactics of the open conflict of Taliban versus warlords. The ambush on June 13, 2010, that wounded Command Sergeant Major Smith mimics those conducted by the Mujahideen.

In the book *The Other Side of the Mountain: Mujahideen Tactics in the Soviet-Afghan War*, Commander Mullah Malang, a former Mujahideen Commander in Kandahar, describes in Vignette 11 the effectiveness and routine of these ambushes:

> "Hardly a day would pass without a Mujahideen attack on the enemy columns along the main highway connecting the city with Ghazni in the northeast and the Girishk in the west. The enemy columns were most

vulnerable on a stretch of the road between the western suburbs of the city and Howz-e-Madad, located about 40 kilometers west of Kandahar. In this area, the Mujahideen were able to hide in the orchards and villages to ambush enemy columns. As the road leaves Sanjaray on the Arghandab River, the green zone runs parallel to the highway in the south and an arid plain, that gradually rises toward the mountains, flanks the road to the north."[38]

During one such attack on a Soviet column in September 1984, approximately 250 Mujahideen were split into "several groups" with RPG grenade launchers and 82mm recoilless rifles. The fight lasted about 30 minutes, and Mullah Malang claims that 50 Soviet vehicles were damaged including several gasoline trucks that caught fire. The Mujahideen were able to blend back into the lush green zone before the Soviets could scramble aircraft pursuit. The Soviets were under constant attack along this stretch of road until their withdrawal in 1989 as the Mujahideen would "set up road blocks, conduct ambushes, mine long stretches of the road and demolish bridges, underpasses, and viaducts using unexploded aerial bombs."[39]

For the most part, the post-9/11 Taliban used the same techniques along the same stretch of Highway One because the Mujahideen had shown them to be highly effective. The success of such attacks also bred a Taliban overconfidence that NATO would be unable to reach them deep in the green zone. Operation Medusa laid bare the folly of that overconfidence. The Canadians struck the Taliban but were unable to sustain the fight. As Antonio Giustozzi illustrates in *Koran, Kalashnikov, and Laptop: The Neo-Taliban Insurgency in Afghanistan*:

> "Based on the experience of anti-Soviet jihadis and on their own interpretations of the strategy and tactics of the Soviet army, the leaders of the Taliban seem to

---

[38] Jalali, A. A., & Grau, L. (1995). *The Other Side of the Mountain: Mujahideen Tactics in the Soviet-Afghan War*. Military Bookshop. Page 43.
[39] *Ibid.*

have identified the solution to their dilemmas in the vineyards of the area of Pashmul, between the districts of Panjwa'i and Zhare, a mere 20 kilometers from Kandahar City. The local mujahideen were convinced that the Soviet army could never take Panjwa'i because its grapevines, drainage ditches, high walled compounds and 'scores of escape tunnels and trenches' built during the 1980s offered good protection from air bombardment as well as shelter from air reconnaissance. Why would the ruse not work against the U.S. Air Force? Moreover, the deployment of Taliban among the villagers of Panjwa'i and Zharay was probably seen as a deterrent against large-scale air bombardment. During March-July Pashmul had been the staging area of most attacks against Canadian troops, but in August the Taliban tried to make their presence as obvious and as provocative as possible, turning up in large numbers in full daylight, establishing training centers and giving out every signal that they intended to turn the area into a stronghold that could be used to scale up activities in central Kandahar province, including Kandahar City itself."[40]

The Taliban's gamble against the Canadian and NATO troops ever entering Pashmul failed. In the end, NATO estimated that nearly 1,500 Taliban fighters were killed during Operation Medusa. It is likely that the Taliban overestimated the defensibility of Pashmul since the Soviet army in the 1980s chose not to launch an operation into the village.

The Taliban suffered heavy losses during Operation Medusa. It was the result of these losses that the Taliban was unable to launch any major operations until the spring and summer of 2007. The Taliban's disastrous experience against a numerically superior force in the green zone forced them to revert back to the old Mujahideen tactics: small

---

[40] Giustozzi, A. (2008). *Koran, Kalashnikov, and Laptops: The Neo-Taliban Insurgency in Afghanistan.* Columbia University Press. Page 124.

ambushes followed by immediate retreat back into the protective green zone. As we launched Operation Dragon STRIKE we saw a change in the tone of the Taliban's attacks and operations in Zharay. No longer were their IED belts and ambushes effective. They had to resort to suicide bombers, a sign of their desperation.

As with all insurgencies, the base of support for the Taliban was the people. Following the U.S.-led invasion of Afghanistan in October 2001, the Taliban leadership fled to Pakistan where the sovereign border not only provided them with protection but access to the large Pashtun population along it, made up of refugees of the Soviet invasion decades earlier.

The Taliban leadership was initially dispersed in late 2001 and early 2002 along the Afghan-Pakistani border, having scattered in all directions. The leadership ultimately reconnected near the village of Quetta. The Taliban began its resurgence in 2003 by sending emissaries back into Paktika and Zabul provinces to scout out villages and towns supportive of the Taliban. Following the emissaries back into Afghanistan from Pakistan were more Taliban who left written intimidation messages under doors late at night in what were referred to as "Night Letters." The Taliban's support was ultimately re-established not only through fear but also anti-government sentiment. "Even where the Taliban had little direct support, the unpopularity of the government and what was perceived as the 'disrespectful' behavior of foreign troops, fueled by lack of understanding for the local culture, had the effect of dividing and demoralizing the opposition to the insurgents and creating some nostalgia for the time when the Taliban were in power."[41]

My personal perception of the local population was that most did not care who was in power as long as they were able to live their lives peacefully. Naturally, foreign troops driving in large, noisy vehicles and the unintentional killing of civilians was a major disruption in the lives of the local farmers in Zharay. Concurrently, many also saw the Taliban and their use of intimidation, roadside bombs, and strict interpretation of Sharia as a significant disruption in their lives.

---

[41] Giustozzi, A. (2008). *Koran, Kalashnikov, and Laptops: The Neo-Taliban Insurgency in Afghanistan*. Columbia University Press. Page 70.

Most locals were, understandably, disgusted with the two groups vying for their allegiance. Still, with both entities brandishing guns as they competed for their loyalty, the locals had little choice but to make a decision about whom they supported. This is why, particularly during the Shuras conducted as part of Operation Dragon STRIKE, we sought to underscore the ideological differences between the Taliban and the government of Afghanistan. During these Shuras we always tried to downplay ISAF's presence and highlight the role of the Afghan National Army and the local government leaders.

In a typical Shura, the local Afghans sat under the shade of a tent on large plush rugs and faced the local Afghan Army and government officials. Through the local leaders, we, as a brigade, imparted our message to the people. We stressed that despite the Taliban movement's origin in Zharay, the Taliban fighters who were destroying their homes and villages were really not locals but outsiders from Pakistan and other regions that supported al-Qaeda. It was, we added, Mullah Omar who offered protection to Osama bin Laden, making him complicit in the attacks of September 11th in our country.

We additionally underscored the hypocrisy of Mullah Omar. While Mullah Omar forbade their sons and daughters from going to school, his own daughters were at that very moment going to school in Quetta. "How is that fair?" we asked. We even had fliers featuring the picture of a little girl carrying a book to school and the question, "How come the Taliban won't let your kids go to school?"

The Shura, most importantly, was an opportunity for the Afghans to solve and discuss Afghan problems. The local leaders talked about the role of government and the opportunity to live peacefully, for their children to go to school, to get their crops to market, and receive compensation for damages caused in clearing the Taliban out. The Shuras lasted hours, and the refreshments were often served by Afghan Army soldiers wandering around the tent, their M-16s slung across their backs and trays of Cokes and orange soda and rice and lamb they made in hand.

The Shuras were open to all and provided us with an understanding of the local village leaders and their culture while also allowing the district leadership to connect with the village elders. The Shuras were deliberately not held at the district center but rather in the remote outposts to show the people that governance was reaching out to them.

165

Operation Dragon STRIKE was extremely effective in clearing the Taliban from Zharay but it was also causing a great deal of physical damage. One of the biggest mistakes would have been to ignore that damage. The use of MICLICs, while highly effective in destroying IEDs and mines, also tore up large swaths of fertile farmland. Many houses and grape huts were destroyed with bombs, artillery, and shoulder-fired rockets during combat because they were rigged with Taliban IEDs. STRIKE could have explained that the damage was the Taliban's fault because they were hiding in them or placing IEDs near their houses and in their fields, but what sense would such logic have made to the farmer without land for his crops or a home for his family?

The families living in the small villages were large: parents, children, other relatives. Every time we destroyed something, whatever the reason, whether right or wrong, we were affecting their livelihoods, their ability to provide. That's what mattered to them. So we paid for the damage we inflicted. Rough estimates put the total at nearly $100 million. Families would come to the district center adjacent to FOB Wilson and file their claim with the district leadership under the watchful eye of an Army civil affairs team that would process the claim. The money was then given to the district governor, who would promptly deliver the compensation to the family and give them blankets and food. We monitored the district leaders for corruption and pushed the leaders to be out front, putting forward an Afghan as the solution to the local villagers problems.

The only alternative for the locals would have likely been to pledge support to the Taliban, who would pay them a small amount of money to plant IEDs or conduct other attacks against us and our Afghan partners rather than reimburse actual damage caused by the fighting. STRIKE had to make the contrast between working with us and working with the Taliban as stark as possible.

Between our kinetic clearing operations and our engagements with the local population, the Taliban's influence in Zharay was shrinking at a critical time. Winter was approaching. There is a typical fighting season in Afghanistan between April and October or November, depending on how early winter arrives. The fighting corresponds with the foliage on the trees, which provides the Taliban with their advantage of maneuver. When the thick green leaves begin to fall off the trees and vines, the Taliban withdrawal to Pakistan or their stronghold villages elsewhere in Afghanistan.

Despite tacit support from the locals, the Taliban were not capable of sustaining themselves through a winter that would expose them to extreme weather. The Taliban that arrive from Pakistan come with what they can carry and demand support at the end of a weapon. The Taliban did not have shelter or food supplies capable of sustaining them through the winter. So historically the Taliban hides their weapons and ammunition in small caches to retreat for the winter, returning to Zharay and other districts in the spring to dig up their caches and fight. The Taliban against the Canadians in Operation Medusa attempted a feat unusual for their character: to surge against a conventional force. They lost heavily.

Against us in Operation Dragon STRIKE the Taliban chose to follow their traditional fighting methods. But with our Soldiers living in their home and gaining support among the people, the Taliban could not afford to walk away and wait for the spring, per their usual fighting schedule. The locals were sensing the Taliban's defeat, and the Taliban needed to alter that perception.

Desperation increasingly became the tone of the Taliban's tactics. It is likely that the Taliban sat huddled around at night without a fire for fear of alerting our surveillance drones and balloons while we ate warm food and slept in warm tents just a few kilometers away. The Taliban lashed out. In December 2010, we saw this desperation in a series of suicide bombers against our forces across the district with two suicide bombers around Sanjaray, two in the Sangsar and Diwar area, and one in western Zharay.

Despite the Qu'ran's prohibition against suicide, as dictated in Sura 4 "And do not kill yourselves, surely God is most Merciful to you," the Taliban defied their beliefs in wretched fashion. It was not the first time suicide bombers made an appearance in Afghanistan but their sudden existence in Zharay toward the end of Operation Dragon STRIKE demonstrated the Taliban's need for dramatic statements to alter the growing perception of their demise.

The bombings killed a total of 13 U.S. Soldiers but not our resolve. In fact, they only solidified our relation to the people of Zharay. The local population, who are Muslim like the Taliban, believed the use of suicide bombers was sinful and came to see the hypocrisy of the

Taliban for themselves, independent of the ISAF messaging. These acts also further underscored what their future would be like under the Taliban.

The most obvious gains from Dragon STRIKE can be readily catalogued: terrain under coalition control, the prevention of Taliban attacks along Highway One. But perhaps the most substantial gain was with the local population. The Taliban's access to the people was now limited, and the public's perception was changed forever. We could never change Zharay's status as the birthplace of the Taliban, but after Dragon STRIKE, the people there no longer saw the Taliban as a legitimate answer to banditry and lawlessness. Diminishing power was only accentuated by the Taliban's willingness to defy their beliefs and employ suicide bombers. The Taliban's losses and STRIKE's gains would be solidified in the winter.

Chapter 14
Dragon STRIKE: The People

Faces linger in my mind, the faces of those who I spent time with, talked to, and saw on a daily basis. The faces of some people with whom I had little interaction are imprinted forever on my mind.

I remember the face of Specialist Luis Lugo with his closely trimmed hair, dirt on his face, and a radiant smile of excitement for being in combat with his friends and fellow Soldiers. Sitting up against the wall of the small compound that was COP Nolan, he puffed on his cigarette as the smoke lingered in the humid, sweaty air while he talked about being there. Moments later he put his body armor back on and returned to work. In that moment I remember innocence. Neither of us knew it would be his final mission. One of the few missions SPC Lugo would ever embarked on. Minutes later he was being medevac'd out of the Arghandab to a hospital on Kandahar Airfield after an IED blast ripped his leg off.

It is the face of Sergeant Michael Beckerman who I saw virtually every morning on FOB Wilson. Whenever I traveled with Colonel Kandarian and Colonel Murtaza to conduct partnered battlefield circulation, there he was: serious and determined. Sergeant Beckerman was not part of the Colonel's personal security detail but worked for the Brigade Support Battalion and would assist in ensuring the road was cleared as we traversed FOB Wilson to begin our daily battlefield circulations. Sergeant Beckerman died of wounds he sustained when an IED was exploded near him. On the day he died, I did not know it was him. Sadly I had not even known his name when he was alive. I just knew his face, which was all I ever saw of him through the tiny window of ballistic glass on my vehicle. It was only weeks later when I was talking to one of the drivers and asked "where the serious guy was" that I ashamedly learned of Sergeant Beckerman's death.

The faces that will also never pass from my mind are those of the local Afghans. Faces of all types and expressions. Faces of joy, pain, excitement, pure hatred, and despair.

I have seen delight on the face of a small Afghan child as we handed out backpacks with coloring books. I recall the stony faces of old Afghan men that bore the struggles of years of war, poverty, and hardship as they worked their fields, a generation of Afghan men who for their entire lifetimes have known nothing but war: with the Soviets, with themselves, with NATO and the Taliban and al-Qaeda in their villages, fields, and homes. Despite our best intentions over the past decade, the local populations have been ridiculed by night raids and searches, had their fields destroyed by vehicles and bomb. They have lost loved ones, killed by both the Taliban and NATO.

Late in the deployment I remember riding in our up-armored vehicle, heading east on Highway One towards FOB Wilson as we returned from Maiwand. Off to the left I saw a man walking, carrying a burlap sack. His face was deeply tanned from working in the fields for years, and his beard, like his hair, was grey and scraggly. His dark eyes were filled with despair and fatigue. As we roared by in our several-ton vehicle with air conditioning and pointed weapons, our own eyes scanning for threats, I was able, just barely, to make out what was in the sack. It was the body of a young child, a small leg extending from the folds of the cloth. It might have been his son. It might have been his grandson. His eyes expressed the weight of his heart.

In that passing instant, I was vulnerable. I thought of my son who was only four. The man's heartbreak was unimaginable for me. For a moment, I imagined what it was like to be that broken man, like so many other devastated people in Zharay, in Afghanistan as a whole, who had lost a loved one. It was wrenching.

The faces in Afghanistan all in some way resemble the different invasions and hardships. The Hazaras look Mongol, while further north and west you see a Persian influence especially in those with red hair, the same color as Alexander the Great.

The faces of the people of Zharay depict a very different life from those of Americans. The people of Zharay do not spend their days playing video games and complaining that there is nothing on T.V. or that the internet is too slow. They do not go to McDonald's or eat fast food at all. Their days are spent focusing on survival. Not only do they need to tend to their fields to grow grapes, pomegranates, and wheat to eat but they also need to produce enough to sell to have money for their families. There are no retirement plans. You simply work hard and take care of your responsibilities until you no longer can.

Each and every day, Afghans go to work in their fields wondering if it would be their last. Death lurks constantly. As an Afghan, will you step on an old Soviet land mine or a Taliban IED? Will you be caught in the crossfire between ISAF and the Taliban? Will the Taliban come harass you and demand your support? Will the Americans raid your home in the middle of the night because you are suspected of supporting the Taliban? Will a missile fall from the sky because someone miles away sees your picture on a screen and thinks you are planting an IED when, in reality, you are just plowing your field?

The hardships that the people of Zharay endure on a daily basis would make the typical American wither. We are not used to that kind of daily struggle for our very existence. Afghans of all ages have fought for basic necessities and have only wanted a better life amid the incessant conflict. After years of conflict and strife many are willing simply to choose any side so long as stability and peace are the end result.

The blatant indifference we often saw from the people of Zharay was rooted in the fact that both the Taliban and NATO forces disrupted their lives. The Taliban, prior to September 11th, kept the people under tight control, forcing them to live according to Sharia and shun the outside world. When its influence waned, the Taliban regained support through intimidation and murder. The presence of NATO to prevent the return of the Taliban further disrupted the locals, even their ability to survive.

Clearing the Taliban from Zharay meant more than physically forcing them out; it had to entail breaking the prevailing mindset that the local population only had one choice. The Taliban, despite the atrocities they committed, remained an entrenched element in the culture of Zharay. The Taliban are Pashtun in origin and from the villages of Zharay.

Pashtun-wali, which literally means "the way of the Pasthuns," is perhaps the most dynamic aspect of the local culture. It is a code of 10 unwritten principles. These principles reveal the Pashtuns' beliefs about hospitality, asylum, justice, bravery, loyalty, righteousness, trust in God, courage, protection of women, and honor. The unspoken principles of Pashtun-wali make winning the support of the locals extremely difficult for outsiders who do not understand the customs and culture. It was under the principle *Nanawatai* (asylum) that Mullah Omar pledged his word to Osama bin Laden to protect him against his enemies.

Under the principle of *Tureh* (bravery) a Pashtun is expected to defend his land, property, family, and women. A Pashtun is expected to seek justice (*Badal*) or revenge, no matter how long it takes, against any wrongdoing. The intersection of these two concepts alone can lead to eternal blood feuds. From a military perspective, Pashtun-wali makes operations difficult. If you kill a Taliban who is the family member of a local or if you damage the local's property, then under Badal that local is expected to seek justice.

Under *Sabat* (loyalty), there is a hierarchy of allegiance to family, friends, and tribe, and to be disloyal to this hierarchy would bring shame to a person's family. Afghans from different parts of the country are also considered outsiders since they most likely are not Pashtun, let alone part of the sub-tribe. This reality severely limited the Afghan Army's ability to gain the support of the people. Trust, we learned, could only be built over time, and we needed to fulfill our promises to the people so that they recognized our determination and support for them.

Counterinsurgencies and insurgencies, in general terms, are about the people and their will. No entity can survive without the support of the people. The Taliban movement formed from the will of the people. The locals wanted stability and protection from robbing and raping warlords whose agenda was profit and power. The Taliban, however, did not prove to be the solution or to provide the stability the people had craved. Mullah Omar's harsh enforcement of Sharia led to a degradation of Afghan society. Nothing could challenge the Taliban's way of thinking. Schools were closed. Contact with the modern outside world was limited. Moreover, the people did not understand that by supporting the Taliban they were in fact supporting al-Qaeda, which would not be permitted by a post-September 11 world.

The kinetic aspects of Dragon STRIKE allowed us to separate the Taliban physically from the local population, which, though expensive in terms of lives, military assets, and collateral damage to houses and such, was relatively easy compared to driving an ideological wedge between the Taliban and the local population. With every step of the operation we sought opportunities to harness our momentum from the clearing assaults and to capitalize on Taliban missteps to win over the local population. We paid for damage caused, held Shuras, and were visible to the people.

Within our operational design we sought to reduce the number of civilian casualties. Our rules of engagement required positive identification of a Taliban fighter, in other words the guy who is actively fighting us or showing intent to fight us such as burying an IED next to a trail or road. Despite reducing the number of civilian casualties, STRIKE inflicted a large amount of property damage throughout Zharay. Homes, grape huts, fields, and livelihoods were destroyed to such a large degree that President Karzai sent a delegation to Zharay to view the damage amid concerns that the local population's claims of damage were not being paid properly. The cynics among us, to include me, concluded that Karzai and his cronies in Kabul were upset that they were not getting their share of the millions of dollars. But the money was for the people of Zharay, not for the government in Kabul.

Under the 1982 Foreign Claims Act, the locals were able to seek justice and submit claims for the damage we inflicted. We had an obligation and legal standing to pay for the damage we inflicted. The claims process was fairly quick and could provide immediate justice for property loss. It did not, however, alleviate the immediate needs for shelter for those whose homes had been destroyed. We simply gave the locals money for their loss, and it was up them to rebuild a house that had taken in most cases generations to build.

STRIKE hosted Shuras in Nalgham, Howz-e-Madad, and Sangsar so that the local population could meet their government officials and that the district leaders could hear their concerns directly. The locals needed Afghan leadership more than they needed American military leadership. For the first time, the people of Zharay were seeing American forces in the far corners of the Taliban's homeland and suddenly given a choice to either continue their support of the Taliban or to support the government of Afghanistan. The people saw our operation as different from previous ones because we were building roads and outposts for a permanent security presence. These outposts would ultimately be for the Afghan Army and police to live in, to work like police sub-stations system in a major city.

Previous operations by previous units had been short-lived and ultimately counterproductive. NATO forces and the Afghan Army defined a target or objective to clear and would, upon completion, claim success and retreat back to Kandahar Airfield or some other distant operating base before the Taliban could launch a counter-attack. The Taliban simply walked in behind the withdrawing victors and returned to their bases, bunkers, and compounds they had abandoned prior to the operation. Safe and relatively sound, the Taliban would seek out the locals again and gain more support, citing damage the NATO forces had left in its wake of the operation as a reason to join their cause.

Through Colonel Quandahari, the executive Officer of the 3-205 ANA, STRIKE as a team was in many ways, able to overcome the local loyalty, *Sabat*. Since he was from the Arghandab District, he was more local than any other member of our partnered Afghan National Army Brigade. As a young man, Colonel Quandahari had fought in the ambushes along Highway One and in Nalgham. During his Mujahideen days, he sat with the future would-be leaders of the Taliban as the Soviets laid siege to Nalgham with large clearing operations and days of shelling.

During one of our many conversations, Colonel Quandahari told me how the Mujahideen had sat underground for days in large bunkers that they had dug out, topped by a steel reinforced roof created with stolen Soviet material used in construction of their buildings and bases. It was in these bunkers that the Mujahideen planned their missions and where they returned for medical treatment after battle. Throughout his time as a partner with STRIKE, Haji Commander, as Colonel Quandahari was known, attended the Shuras and talked to the people, and through his personality and reputation, he was able to drive a wedge between the Taliban and the people. The respect that the people had for him could supersede the Pashtun-wali loyalty to family and tribe.

Colonel Quandahari would also meet with the village elders on his own and slowly won them over to support the local government. I once asked him why he didn't just target the Taliban, just "go and take them out?" He smiled at me, recognizing my lack of understanding of the Pashtun culture, and in a calm, thoughtful manner explained why he couldn't, that in doing so he would violate the trust of their families. He was from the area and knew who supported the Taliban, but he also knew that they supported the Taliban not necessarily out of ideological blindness but for lack of options. Assassinating the local Taliban would turn a relative or a family against us. He needed to present a better solution. When he left to go talk to the villagers of Pashmul and Siah Choy, he simply got in his car and drove out the gate to go talk to them in their homes. Colonel Quandahari did not fear for his life. He had been invited to talk with the elder, and so his protection was guaranteed, lest the Taliban wanted to further lose the support of the local population. Though he went there under the elder's promise of protection, I know Colonel Quandahari was not reckless and never went anywhere unarmed.

Colonel Quandahari was not STRIKE's only face of reason when talking and listening to the locals but likely our most significant. Leaders at all levels within the STRIKE Brigade and our Afghan Army partners constantly engaged the people from the individual farmer to a group of children to a meeting full of elders because everything and everyone was an opportunity to garner support. Some local elders were more influential than others, but we had no prior information to enlighten us about who the true leaders were, so we treated all the villagers equally with respect. The platoon leaders, company commanders, and battalion commanders drank more chia than they probably ever thought they would, yet with each cup of tea and hour of conversation, they learned more and more about the locals and how to exploit the failures of the Taliban. STRIKE leaders also learned of the previously failed promises by and problems from other units that had been in the area. The 5th Stryker Brigade, 2nd Infantry Division, for example, had been stretched over too large an area with too few forces and therefore rarely made it to all of the villages in a consistent manner, let alone fulfill all the promises it made.

Distinct from 5/2 Infantry Division, STRIKE was fully partnered at all levels, so each conversation done was with our Afghan Army partners. Those villages that had seen Canadian and U.S. forces previously were now seeing U.S. forces with Afghan forces.

The faces of many individuals and locals may reside in my mind, but I am sure that from a local's perspective, Soldiers' faces are all the same. Each year units rotate in and out of an area, and so the faces change but what's important is that the message does not. Americans have a tendency to over-promise and under-deliver. Those that actually do deliver to the locals are remembered and praised. Trust is a difficult thing to earn, and we are not helped by the constant merry-go-round of faces that our deployment cycle produces. I remember being at my first unit, 1st Squadron, 1st U.S. Cavalry, in Germany and seeing the 13 campaign streamers from Vietnam on the squadron colors and thinking about the number of deployments the squadron must have gone through to receive that many streams.

I later learned the squadron was in Vietnam continuously from 1967 to 1972. Being there continuously for five years, conducting of counterinsurgency operations, is in many ways ideal. Rotating units through means a constant rotation of forces. Just as trust is being built between the unit and the people, the unit disappears to return home. By rotating Soldiers from the same unit through, there is always continuity and a core that permits trust to develop between the locals and the unit.

There is more than one way to conduct counterinsurgency operations, but security of the local population is the most important element since it is their will that will decide the fate of COIN's success. By seeing the locals on a daily basis and being there, the counterinsurgent can see the anguish, trust, fear, and hatred on the locals' faces. Ultimately the counterinsurgent can see how their actions affect the lives of the local population for better or for worse. The counterinsurgent is invested in the lives and the success of the locals because that ultimately means success for the counterinsurgent and the opportunity to go home.

Despite the massive destruction of property we caused during Operation Dragon STRIKE, by being present and being proactive as much as possible STRIKE was able to assuage their anger and attempt to rectify any injustice. Our means and capabilities surpassed those of the Taliban, but notwithstanding our tactical success, we would still have lost and it would have all been for nothing if we had not been present day in and day out, face to face with the people.

Chapter 15
Dragon Wrath

The best way to attain peace is to combine force with politics. We must remember that destruction must be used as a last recourse, and even then only in order to something better in the end ... Each time an officer is required to act against a village in a war, he needs to remember that his first duty, after securing submission of the local population, is to rebuild the village, reorganize the local market and establish a school.

General Joseph Gallieni
Fundamental Instructions, 1898

The use of "Dragon" in an operation name seemed like a horrible idea to me. I was never fully sold on the dragon moniker for Operation Dragon STRIKE. Major Travares derived the term from the dragon-shaped area we controlled around Highway One. Continuing the "Dragon" theme for naming operations seemed childish, but my rank precluded me from any opinion. In hindsight I suspect Major Travares wishes there was a better name but great ones like Operation Overlord, the invasion into France during World War II, and Operation Desert Storm, Gulf War 1991, were already taken, so we strove to be original at least and avoid the snake themes of Operation Anaconda, the 2002 operation for Osama bin Laden in Tora Bora, and Operation Medusa.

Continuing under the Brigade's campaign plan, Economic Corridors, Operation Dragon Wrath, which began on December 7, 2010, was the non-kinetic, counterinsurgency continuation of Dragon STRIKE. The operation was meant to be both the "hold and build" of Zharay. "Clear, hold, and build" is the military mantra for conducting counterinsurgency operations.

The problem with many clearing operations is that once completed, there is no plan to prevent the insurgents, in this case the Taliban, from returning to those areas. The final phase, "build," refers to developing the governance and economic aspects of a community. The "build" phase is arguably the most difficult since Soldiers who are trained to fight must coach local leaders to connect with the population as well as

177

institute programs that provide economic growth. The gains of governance and economic development made by STRIKE were starkly contrasted to the hardships of the locals inflicted by the Taliban.

Each phase of COIN, "clear, hold, and build," has some element of offensive, defensive, and stability operations, and transition from one phase to another forces shift in assets and thinking. In military manuals, the clear, hold, build framework is generally drawn in three small rectangles, which are each further divided into offense, defense, and stability, and as a unit shifts from the clear phase to the hold and then the build phase, the proportion of the offense, defense, and stability changes, either increasing or decreasing depending on the phase.

The figures in the military manuals are meant to show the delicate balance of protection, development and offensive operations in order to secure the people, but these figures do not adequately illustrate how to determine that balance of limited assets. Leadership is often described as an art and a science, and there is no greater test of this balance for a leader than during counterinsurgency operations where leaders from the platoon, company, battalion, and brigade must find that equilibrium between force and nation-building.

Increasing the level of difficulty for leaders is that no set framework works in all situations. How one infantry company interacts with the villagers in its area of operations will be necessarily different from how another company a few kilometers away operates.

As Soldiers we are trained to "close with and destroy the enemy," so the notion of developing civilian government and economic institutions is foreign. Hence, the build phase is often seen as the most difficult, and the military tends to rely on both the recommendations of the other government agencies, such as the State Department, as well as Soldiers within the ranks that have special skills in this arena.

Soldiers and Officers come from all different walks of life and education levels, and each brings a unique skill set to a job. When you are living on a small outpost, mechanical skills gained from working on motors as a kid may help in repairing a broken, overstressed generator or carpentry expertise may give way to better living quarters, both of which seem better suited to that soldier than perhaps asking him/her to piece together a PowerPoint presentation. That presentation, however, is extremely useful if you are on a large Division staff and need to portray a concept to a large group of those same diversely skilled people. So in a rural area that lacks running water and electricity, the special skills within the ranks become critical. A Soldier from a farm in the Midwest is indispensable in helping connect with and passing knowledge to the people. The Soldier is capable of helping teach sustainable farming techniques to the local Afghans. This further helps build trust between the people and the unit.

We had a unique example of specialized skills at FOB Wilson. The Afghan battalion in charge of garrison operations had received a fire truck as part of its authorized equipment. Soldiers were assigned as firefighters but had no training. In searching through STRIKE's headquarters staff, I located a senior non-commissioned officer assigned to the operations section as National Guard augmentee. In discussions with him I learned that he was a retired fire chief from Minnesota and was happy to help train the Afghan Soldiers. Within a few weeks, the Afghan Soldiers were racing around the FOB in the fire truck practicing for real fires and even responded to several actual fires on the FOB to include the burning down of the Afghan Army Officers' dining facility.

Reliable institutions, such as a fire department, police force, and local government, are critical. As a counterinsurgent, the Brigade needed to establish institutions that the locals would believe in and would side with, and these were in direct competition with the Taliban's institutions and way of life. Military COIN doctrine, Field Manual 3-24.2, specifically describes the build phase as "programs designed to remove the root causes that led to the insurgency, improve the lives of the inhabitants, and strengthen the Host Nation's ability to provide effective governance."[42] A real-world example is the judicial system of the government of Afghanistan competing with the "shade tree Sharia courts" of the Taliban. During the build phase, the counterinsurgent often pushes institutions that mimic their own, however the court system of the United States would undoubtedly fail in Afghanistan. The successful system in Afghanistan would reflect the character of the locals and enable them to progress as their skills grow.

---

[42] Build. (2009, April). *FM 3-24.2: Tactics in CounterInsurgency*. Headquarters Department of the Army. Page 3-21.

The drastic drop in significant enemy activity can be attributed to a mix of the hard fighting against the Taliban, which vastly reduced their numbers, and the onset of cold weather, stripping the trees of their foliage. Given our new proximity to their historic hiding places, there was no place for the Taliban to hide, so they left the area. This accompanying reduction in kinetic operations assisted the Brigade in helping launch Operation Dragon Wrath, which had two key objectives: prevent the Taliban from returning and build local government and economic institutions that, together, were our hold and build phases of COIN.

Recognizing that the Brigade replacing us in the coming spring would likely have a different troop composition, Colonel Kandarian wanted to set up a feasible mechanism to prevent the Taliban from returning to where the Brigade now resided. So under his direction STRIKE purchased miles upon miles of twelve-foot high concrete barriers called T-Walls. As soon as the local national contractors began delivering the T-walls to FOB Wilson, both ANA and STRIKE Soldiers began the construction of a new road for the people of Zharay. The "security road," as we named it, was an east-to-west running road that paralleled Highway One and was located several kilometers south of the Highway in the green zone.

The security road connected COP Kolk in eastern Zharay to strongpoint in Diwar, Sangsar, Lakokhel, Gundy Ghar, and to Azim Jan Kariz in the west. The strongpoints with the road became mutually supportive, and each was given a section of road to monitor to prevent the Taliban from infiltrating. The south side of the road was lined with the twelve-foot barriers so that to the north, between the road and Highway One, the locals could move easily and function without fear of the Taliban. Meanwhile, the area south of the security road served as a large engagement area to interdict the resurgence of the Taliban and their supply lines.

The local farmers of Zharay could get to their fields on the south side of the wall by passing through ANA-manned checkpoints adjacent to the strong points. In a sense, the security road limited the locals' freedom of maneuver around the district, but at Shuras, the Brigade and our Afghan partners were able to shape their perceptions of the road and the wall. The protection of the people in their homes was STRIKE's greatest priority, and the road provided that protection.

The use of walls and barriers is not a new concept. We were certainly not naive enough to think the wall would serve as a manifestation of the "good fences make good neighbors" concept; rather we viewed it as a means to establish a "protected city" where those beyond the wall would have to pass through security gates to enter. The wall was an obstacle that the Taliban had to contend with if it wanted to reach the people of Zharay. In Iraq, the U.S. lined virtually every road in the Rashid District of Baghdad to separate Sunni and Shia neighborhoods, however our "security road" was the first of its kind in Afghanistan.

One unintended consequences of the security road was a problem we should have readily anticipated in hindsight. The emplacement of the wall ignored the natural flow of the terrain and, subsequently, the natural flow of water that accompanied the heavy winter rains. The wall suddenly produced a submerged and impassable road at several locations. Several combat outposts were now islands. Winter in southern Afghanistan, unlike winter in snowy eastern Afghanistan, features a tremendous amount of rain as the temperature stubbornly hovers just above freezing.

The FOBs and the COPs faired even worse as the high HESCO walls turned many, including FOB Wilson, into something akin to above-ground pools. Tents in low lying areas on the COPs and FOBs were completely washed out, and at one point nearly two feet of water stood in the Battalion's aid stations. The heavy rains quickly saturated the ground, and the water pooled. Soldiers were left with daily drudges through rainwater and mud not only on patrols but also on trips to the latrines.

Simple culverts would have prevented the problem along the security road but these were not emplaced during the rapid road construction. So instead of building the road correctly the first time, STRIKE was forced to repair the road and emplace hasty culverts. These repairs had to be expedited due to the heavy impact the defective engineering was having on the people. It would have been a propaganda victory for the Taliban, if as a Brigade, we did not fix the flooding that we caused.

Beyond the efforts of the security road, the Brigade continued to patrol daily through the winter, using the lack of foliage to locate and eliminate Taliban weapon caches. Lacking global positioning systems and precise maps of the area, the Taliban had resorted to a slew of other markers, as rudimentary as string tied to trees, to identify where their weapons were buried. Many of these sites were booby-trapped, and the Brigade continued to take casualties.

On January 12, 2011, elements of Delta Company, 2-502 Infantry were clearing compounds near Nalgham in search of weapons caches when a dog handler from the 212th Military Police Detachment stepped on an IED. Despite the efforts of Staff Sergeant Jason Heyboer and Specialist William Pickel, who applied multiple tourniquets and dressed several other wounds to stop the bleeding, Sergeant Zainah Creamer died from her injuries. She is the 25th female in the U.S. military to have been killed as a result of combat operations in Operation Enduring Freedom. She received both the Bronze Star and the Purple Heart.

Nearly a month later in central Zharay, elements of 1-75 Cavalry with attached sapper engineer elements were on a mission to destroy multiple Taliban bunkers south of the village of Mollyan. Maneuvering to the first bunker, the patrol identified a possible improvised explosive device, which was subsequently reduced with an explosive charge. The patrol advanced to the target bunker and reduced it to rubble. This blast led to the discovery of an additional bunker to the east. The area was littered with bunkers and caches that were well concealed, once invisible under the thick foliage. Patrols were aggressively pushing harder and harder into the Taliban's support zone and taking away their supplies and capabilities.

As the patrol maneuvered to inspect the bunker, a blast erupted when the last man in the formation, Specialist Nathan Carse, triggered a victim-operated IED. Upon reaching SPC Carse, First Lieutenant Patrick Lavin found Specialist Carse struggling to breathe and so 1LT Lavin removed SPC Carse's gear and ordered him to remain calm as he assessed his injuries. The blast had amputated SPC Carse's left leg and left arm. 1LT Lavin was applying tourniquets to stop the bleeding when Staff Sergeant Patrick Smith and the platoon's medic arrived to assist.

As the medevac helicopter landed, Specialist Carse was raced 150 meters across an open wadi to the landing zone. Despite the horrific wounds it had witnessed, the patrol rallied, collected SPC Carse's gear, and continued the mission to destroy the bunker including two additional IEDs. Sadly, Specialist Nathan Carse died of the wounds he sustained in the IED blast; he was later awarded a Bronze Star and Purple Heart. 1LT Lavins and SSG Smith for their calm, professional demeanor and ability to lead following the loss of one of their men both received an Army Commendation Medal with V device for Valor.

Although the Taliban was not frequently engaging the STRIKE Soldiers in small arms battles as it had done when the foliage was dense and concealing, the indirect attacks using IEDs still proved devastating. The loss of Soldiers posed challenges to the leadership. Losing a friend and comrade in arms is difficult for many to deal with but the mission must continue. In the midst of this, leaders had to redirect the Soldiers to the new mission and to understand the change from heavy kinetic strikes and operations to teaching villagers how to farm and clear overgrowth from canals. It would have been easy to blame a villager who lived nearby for the death of a Soldier, yet blaming that person would not have prevented the next IED strike and death. By building trust between the villager and local government, the Afghan Army and ISAF would prevent the Taliban from returning and operating freely.

Leadership is about finding a balance, only this time the balance was between the emotions of the Soldiers and the mission. The mission is easy to continue when it is action-packed and filled with air assaults, night raids, small arms fire, and air strikes. It is extremely difficult to execute when it involves sitting down and drinking chai with the local elders. That was precisely what the build phase required, though.

As a foreigner in Afghanistan you are naturally distrusted in a land that has been invaded constantly for centuries. As a foreigner in Zharay district, the home of the Taliban and where intense fighting has left people dead, survivors angered, and property destroyed, you are practically hated. But incrementally the Brigade broke down this hatred through local Afghan channels. Putting an Afghan face on solutions was critical for our success.

The build phase of a counterinsurgency operation is not only the most difficult but also the most time-consuming. The STRIKE Brigade was on a 12-month deployment to Zharay so we would not see the results of the build, but we needed to lay the groundwork for our successors from the 10th Mountain Division.

Every leader and military unit has a sphere of influence. The concept of a sphere of influence is exemplified in family, where the parents have direct influence over the children and some influence, depending on the issue, between each other and other relatives. Moving further away from the immediate family to the community, the influence becomes less potent. Finding the correct sphere of influence is critical in terms of winning over a local population.

A company commander would interact with the elders of each village in his area of operation to influence that village. The company commander would listen to their needs, and without promising anything he knew he could not guarantee, he would do his best to help the elders. By the delivering what he promised, especially if it is something that the Taliban could not deliver, the company commander not only won favor with the local elders but also empowered the elders.

To further empower a village elder, a battalion commander or the brigade commander might interact with that individual village leader personally. The Afghans understand the military rank system and know that the higher the rank the greater the deliverables, but the persistent risk is developing oversized egos among the village leaders. Moreover, through too much interaction and empowerment, the perception within the villages could be that the elder is a puppet of the foreign forces. To mitigate this risk, open and public Shuras were necessary. The local Afghan leadership, to include the district governor, police chief and Afghan Army leaders, were at the Shuras, and, as Americans, STRIKE minimized our presence.

I sat through a dozen or so large Shuras at the District Center, Howz-e-Madad, and Nalgham, and watched quietly from the back. This was Afghanistan, and as guests of the government we did not want to be intrusive, but we aimed to help. We supplied rice, beans, and soft drinks for the Afghan Army to cook and feed the guests from all the villages. I tended to laugh to myself watching the Afghan Army Soldiers with their helmets and body armor on and their M-16 rifles strapped to their backs, wander through the large tent serving Chai and soda. I laughed not because they were helping but because they were not comfortable in the gear and it was so evidently a show.

The locals who attended these Shuras knew where all the luxuries were coming from, but the Afghans needed to be in the lead. If the Brigade needed to supply the food and drinks so that the ANA could illustrate its hospitality, or *melmastia* in Pashtun, then so be it.

The large Shuras provided a visible connection to the locals for the varying spheres of influence levels, but the real connection with the people was through the small unit interactions. Works programs for the people evolved through these exchanges, such as improving the water flow to the fields. The Taliban frequently used the thick foliage that grew in and along the canals for cover, undergrowth that hindered the flow of water, and threatened any villager and farmer who sought to clear out the vegetation. As a program to employ locals and assist the farmers, Afghans in several villages were paid to clear out the canals and line them with plastic sheeting.

The plastic sheeting served a two-fold purpose. One, it prevented the bushes that grew thick and menacingly along the canals from returning, and two, it improved water flow to the distant fields. Fights over water usage were common among the locals, and after several weeks of talking with villagers throughout the district, the Brigade began to understand that usually a couple of elders would determine how the water flows, to what fields, and when.

Typical American gardening and farming techniques include watering a garden or crop a little bit everyday once the seeds are planted. The Afghan technique is to flood their fields with nearly a foot of water once the seeds are in the ground and then not to water it again. The Afghan method of farming wastes a tremendous amount of water, but it is their chosen way.

In his Twenty-Seven Articles and in speaking about a different people, T.E. Lawrence in 1917 aptly wrote, "Do not try to do too much with your own hands. Better the Arabs do it tolerably than that you do it perfectly." Nearly 100 years later, the Brigade debated this concept in terms of farming. As a way to improve the lives of the people of Zharay, several civilians from the United States Agency for International Development (USAID) taught farming classes and created a training center at the district center. The concept of farming lessons for villagers seemed bizarre to many of the Soldiers and Officers who had spent months fighting, but it is a clear example of the balance that counterinsurgency operations require. Farming classes were also a means for a better way of life for the villagers especially for those whose fields were far from the major canals and the Arghandab River. These classes not only provided a viable alternative to the Afghan flooding techniques but also demonstrated that other crops that could grow in the rich, dark soil of the green zone.

Education was also another concern of the locals throughout the district. The Taliban had significantly hindered the education system in Afghanistan so that few boys and no girls were educated. Ignorance was a powerful tool of the Taliban, something that we fought constantly. In June 2010, no schools were operating in Zharay. A *Time Magazine* article by Joe Klein entitled, "Afghanistan: A Tale of Soldiers and a School" followed the lack of schools in Zharay and the previous efforts of both Canadian and American units to open a school near Sanjaray.

The Pir Mohammed School was built in 2005 by the Canadians and closed by the Taliban in 2007. Windows were broken, furniture destroyed, and IEDs and booby traps were placed in and around the small building. In the article, Captain Jeremy Ellis, the Commander of Dog Company, 1st Battalion, 12th Infantry Regiment, stated, "from the start, the people here [Sanjaray] said they wanted better security and the school."[43] The thought of securing the school seemed simple and could have been the legacy of CPT Ellis' Company in Zharay; however, achieving this goal proved highly complicated.

Captain Ellis had planned to build a strong point next to the Pir Mohammed School that would eventually become an Afghan Police station. This way, the police could protect the teachers, students, and school, which was located south of Highway One along the edge of the green zone. On February 21, 2010, Soldiers of Captain Ellis's company were patrolling near the school when an IED detonated and killed one Soldier and severely wounded another. CPT Ellis decided to "stop the patrols down there after that, given the rules of engagement, it was just too dangerous to keep going there and getting blown up."[44] As Joe Klein highlights, "in another war—Vietnam, for certain—an American Officer might have cleared the Taliban-controlled area with air strikes. But that sort of indiscriminate bombing doesn't happen in Afghanistan."[45] A year later, Operation Dragon STRIKE had cleared Zharay well enough so that the brigade was able to move beyond the

---

[43] Klein, J., (2010, April 15). Afghanistan: A Tale of Soldiers and a School. Time Magazine.
[44] *Ibid.*
[45] *Ibid.*

minimum level of security. Operation Dragon STRIKE provided the Brigade with the ability to accomplish more and to open schools like Pir Mohammed.

As Lieutenant Reed Peeples of Dog Company's 2nd Platoon stated in the article, "For months, we've been trying to win over the people of this town—and we haven't produced anything tangible. They are sitting on the fence, waiting to see which side is stronger." The efforts of CPT Ellis and Dog Company are commendable and illustrate an important aspect of the "build" phase, but the issue of insecurity and the heavy presence of the Taliban were not addressed prior to their arrival in Sanjaray.

Unlike the STRIKE Brigade, CPT Ellis's company, battalion, and brigade were un-partnered, meaning all operations and conversations with the locals were only with Americans. The Afghan National Army Brigade that was supposed to help them in their fight for Zharay had been re-directed at the last minute to Helmand Province to assist in the clearance of Marja, leaving the battalion ill-equipped to deal with the dynamics of Zharay and to navigate the lack of district leadership and the presence of sudo-warlords.

The reality is that Dog Company understood COIN and what was necessary for success, however security was still an issue. STRIKE's success came through the heavy clearance and the removal of the Taliban as well as the presence of our Afghan Army partners. By late February 2011, through the efforts of the companies and battalions, there were three functioning schools across Zharay district to include the Pir Mohammed School. The other two schools were in Howz-e-Madad, and there was one adjacent to the district center that educated both boys and girls.

Counterinsurgency operations are a delicate balance of combat and connecting with the people while providing their security. The people will side with those who provide security and demonstrate having their best interests at heart. This premise is perhaps best demonstrated in an incident that happened to Dog Company in 2009. A motorcyclist approaching a patrol failed to heed the warning shouts to stop. A warning shot was fired and by sheer bad luck ricocheted off the ground and struck the driver of the motorcycle in the hip, passing through him and striking the two children that were behind him on the bike. None of the wounds were life-threatening—the two children were hit in the legs—but the villagers saw them being aided and medevac'd by helicopter. As Captain Ellis points out, "In a weird way, it turned into a plus for us [Dog Company], after they were released we continued to treat them with antibiotics, painkillers, and new bandages. When the people saw how well we were treating them, they were grateful. The motorcycle driver's brother started helping us with some good information."

The people are the critical link in COIN operations, despite all the heavy-handed efforts required to establish security. If you take care of and listen to the people, then you will win them over to your cause. Operation Dragon Wrath was the counterinsurgency continuation to the highly kinetic operations of Dragon STRIKE. As a Brigade, we had destroyed homes with bombs and razed fields with MICLICs, but then STRIKE made amends with the locals for that destruction. Security was established, and as a team, we sought to emplace methods to hold the Taliban away from the population and to build the economic institutions within Zharay.

Chapter 16
Partners

Nine-tenths of tactics are certain, and taught in books:
but the irrational tenth is like the kingfisher flashing
across the pool, and that is the test of generals.

T.E. Lawrence

The sun was setting earlier and earlier as Operation Dragon STRIKE moved into its sixth week. The nights were growing cool. It was a welcome relief from the constant hundred-degree heat of the day. It was nice to be able to walk to the latrine without breaking into a sweat. It made the heavy loads we carried more bearable. Halloween was just two days away when tragedy struck.

"Shonna Ba Shonna" was the brigade's mantra that was constantly repeated both with encouragement and in disgust. As the first fully partnered brigade in Afghanistan, STRIKE was expected to work shoulder to shoulder with our Afghan Army partners. Patrols were combined. If STRIKE Soldiers were going out on a mission, then their Afghan partners were with them. If a logistics patrol was going to KAF to pick fuel, ammunition, and other supplies, then the ANA were going to Camp Hero next to KAF to do the same. If Soldiers were pulling security in a guard tower, ANA and American Soldiers were sitting next to each other.

Real partnership, however, is tough. Language is a barrier so communication is difficult without an interpreter. The culture and customs are also so vastly different. The actions of a young American Soldier are different than those of a young Afghan Soldier who was raised under strict Islamic sharia and what one Soldier thinks is funny, the other finds offensive.

Late at night, a young American and young Afghan sat in the southwest guard tower of COP Kandalay. Together, they stared out through the camouflage netting, watching the approaches to their outpost while their brothers in arms slept. Each guard tower was partnered and a partnered contingent of Soldiers was at the gate and in the command post monitoring radios. The silence of the night was

189

suddenly broken in the southwest tower when the young American passed gas.

His partner, the Afghan Soldier, suddenly stood up and began yelling at the young American who did not understand the fuss. Offended, the Afghan climbed down the down and abandoned his post. The American Soldier used the tower's radio to notify the command post that his partner had left. The Officer on duty in the command post, a first lieutenant, noted in the duty log that the Afghan Soldier had left the tower and prepared to investigate.

As the Officer prepared to leave the command post, the Afghan Soldier returned to the tower. Instead of alone and returning to his duties, the Afghan brought four other Afghan Soldiers with him. The group climbed into the tower and began attacking the American. The Afghans punched, kicked, and scratched at the young American who attempted to protect himself. Suddenly, the Afghan Soldier who had been on guard duty at the post fell out of the tower. Frustrated and angry, the Afghan raised his M-16 rifle up and toward the tower.

The sound of shots caused the American lieutenant to begin running toward the tower. Racing around a corner, he heard shots continue to ring out, piercing the cool night air and waking everyone in the tiny outpost. Seeing the Afghan Soldier firing at the American in the tower, the Officer raised his M-4 rifle, took aim, and shot the Afghan Soldier.

The Afghan fell to the ground, bleeding into the dust, gravel, and shell casing he had fired. As his life drained out of him, chaos and confusion ensued throughout the outpost. The Afghans who had been asleep woke to the sight of an American standing over their dead comrade. There was no opportunity to defuse the situation. The two armies sharing the same tiny outpost were not enemies, still the Afghans pointed their rifles and RPGs at the Americans who, in turn, pointed theirs back at the Afghans. Both sides moved trucks into position for use of the large caliber crew-served machine guns. The company commander attempted to defuse the tension and determine what was happening, but no one knew. The company commanders notified their respective battalion commanders who notified their respective Brigade commanders.

In an instant, the Shonna Ba Shonna partnership at COP Kandalay was gone. Both ANA and American leaders outside of COP Kandalay scrambled to get on site, to understand the situation, and to end the dangerous standoff. Partnership was paramount for not only the success of Dragon STRIKE, but for the future of Kandahar and Afghanistan as a whole. The Afghan Army Soldiers of 3-205th Corps represented half of the Soldiers in Combined Task Force STRIKE. Partnership, however, is more than just Soldiers physically together on the ground. It includes the intangibles that the Afghans brought to the fight. The contribution of the Afghan Soldier is more than the simple addition of bodies to the battlefield.

I learned simple math at a young age. Addition, subtraction, multiplication, and division came easily. Never could I have suspected how important math would be in combat, in operational planning, and in counterinsurgency. For example, to take and defend a fixed position such as a bunker, the ideal ratio is 3:1. In other words, you aspire to have three offensive soldiers for every one defensive solider. If there is a squad of insurgents in an area, then at least a platoon-size force is needed to overtake the insurgent squad.

The math grows more interesting when examining complex plans since certain assets such as attack aviation are "force multipliers." A platoon that gains aviation support, for example, can expect its mathematical force equivalent to be multiplied by a factor of 12. These calculations are part of military planning doctrine and can seem arbitrary as different assets in the military arsenal are assigned different force equivalent multiples. Still, the most fundamental "number" of military math is the one represented by the individual Soldier on the ground. Aviation assets or artillery rounds are able to destroy a house or a compound but it is the Soldier that needs to be there on the ground. It is the Soldier who directs aviation assets and orders the artillery rounds; without the Soldier on the ground the force multipliers are blind.

In Afghanistan, I learned the math of the counterinsurgent, and I learned the complexity of the "intangibles," those are the skills and knowledge of the host nation forces. I learned that when one U.S. Army Infantry Brigade Combat Team was fully "partnered" with an Afghan National Army (ANA) Brigade, the combat power of Soldiers on the ground was essentially doubled. I say "essentially" because the numbers on paper are doubled but the reality on the ground is always somewhat different than the facts on paper. To effectively double the combat power on the ground, the intangibles must be identified and either limited or exploited.

The success of a counterinsurgency is predicated on the ability of the host nation's legitimate government, which is supported by its people, to provide security and uphold the rule of law. In terms of Afghanistan, the host nation had to build its own internal force, the Afghan National Security Forces (ANSF). The ANSF consists of four different entities: the Afghan National Army, Afghan National Police (ANP), Afghan Border Police (ABP), and the Afghan National Civil Order Police (ANCOP). Two separate ministries in the Afghan government control the ANSF. The ANA is part of the Ministry of Defense while the ANP, ABP, and ANCOP fall under the umbrella of the Ministry of Interior.

Comparatively the ANP is similar to a county sheriff in the United States. The ABP are just as their name indicated, and they man checkpoints along the border looking for smugglers, illegal activity, and unauthorized crossings.

The ANCOP is a paramilitary organization designed to assist the district police as necessary. A battalion of ANCOP rotates through the districts to man checkpoints and patrol areas while the ANP attends training. The ANCOP essentially holds down the fort while the ANP are gone learning how to be a police Officer or patrolman. The ANP fills its ranks with recruits from the districts where they will serve. Just because a local has signed up to be a policeman, however, the Afghan is not a "real" policeman until graduating from the provincial police academy.

The structure of an ANA Brigade is modeled after the United States Army. On paper, an ANA brigade had the same number of Soldiers and equipment, such as radios and vehicles, as a U.S. Brigade. The Afghan MoD has training academies and commissioning sources that, similar to those in the American system, produce a core of educated, competent leaders. The reality, however, is different.

On the ground and in action, there is dysfunction. The number of Soldiers present for duty on paper is not the same as the number of Soldiers on the ground. The Afghans had a habit of counting Soldiers on leave as present for duty. Soldiers who were AWOL were not being properly discharged, were still being paid, and carried on the books preventing new Soldiers from being assigned to the Brigade.

Additionally, not all leaders understood their role and many abused their position, such as withholding goods from the ANA Soldiers. And many Soldiers did not understand how move and operate as a unit.

That is not to say that every aspect of the ANA or a partnered system is flawed; perhaps the greatest force multiplier the ANSF brought to the fight was human intelligence and situational awareness, which often gave us a lethal edge. The benefits between the STRIKE Brigade and our 3rd Brigade, 205th Corps ANA partners were mutual. The ANA provided us with situational awareness and cultural understanding, an ability to engage and talk to the village elders, and a conduit for critical information. STRIKE, on the other hand, provided the ANA with our own intelligence assessments of the Taliban harnessed from our drone and signals intelligence, provided daily training, developed targets, instilled a warrior ethos, and perhaps, most importantly, helped train their non-commissioned Officers.

Ideally, partnered units have advisors who can work with the ANA constantly to help develop these skills however no advisory team existed for the STRIKE Brigade. The task of advising and monitoring our ANA partners was my primary responsibility.

Prior to deployments to Afghanistan, many Brigades were being restructured into "advise and assist" Brigades, which does not mean much except the addition of 45 Officers and Senior Non-Commissioned Officers whose job it is to mentor and advise the ANSF partners. These teams are distributed to the subordinate Battalions at the Brigade Commander's discretion and provide a supplemental conduit for development, planning, and training of the ANSF. As a surge brigade, STRIKE was not restructured. So the tasks of the "advise and assist" section fell to me. Thankfully the top-heavy hierarchy of the ANA made my job much easier.

By focusing on the Brigade staff and Colonel Murtaza, I was able to influence ANA Soldiers at the Battalion, Company, and Platoon levels. I had counterparts at each of our Battalions who worked with their partner battalions to do the same. Some battalions, by nature of the varying personalities that comprise them, worked better with their partners and had greater success. Personalities play a huge role in the ability to coach, teach, and mentor a foreign force as well as to spur them to execute complex missions on time.

Partnering to develop host nation security forces is not always safe either. The tower incident at COP Kandalay on October 29, 2010, showed us how a cultural misunderstanding can escalate. Misunderstandings, however, were not the only threat. The Taliban were proud of their ability to commit insider attacks against coalition and Afghan forces. Insider attacks and misunderstandings build distrust that must be defused to salvage the partnership.

I arrived at COP Kandalay at first light with Colonel Kandarian and Colonel Murtaza. Behind closed doors, they sat with and listened to all parties involved. They questioned the American Soldier in the guard tower, the first lieutenant that fired on the Afghan Soldier, the Afghan Soldiers who went into the tower to attack the American Soldier, and both the ANA and American company commanders. Tensions were high and action needed to be taken.

The two Americans involved were removed from COP Kandalay to prevent any reprisals from the ANA. Both the ANA and STRIKE Brigade as well as RC-South conducted investigations into the "green on blue" incident. The investigations ultimately concluded that the incident was the result of a cultural misunderstanding and did not require further disciplinary actions. Colonel Murtaza removed the involved Afghan company from COP Kandalay and replaced it with another company of Soldiers less than 24 hours later.

The next morning, in a speech to his staff, Colonel Murtaza expounded on the importance of professionalism, partnership, and cultural understanding and that as Afghans they may not understand the behavior of their partners at times but that they needed to remain professional and work through those issues.

Mentoring, like partnering, is not a simple task. Both require tremendous patience and understanding to be effective. The reality is not everyone is meant to teach and mentor the ANA or other militaries.

On December 11, 2010, when Colonel Halim, the 205th Corps Logistics Officer, arrived at FOB Wilson unannounced with two Canadian mentors. The group wanted to meet with Colonel Murtaza and Major Abdullah, the 3-205 Corps Logistics Officer. Following the typical formalities of greetings, it became evident who had orchestrated the meeting when one of the mentors instructed Colonel Halim to use the agenda that he [the mentor] has provided. The agenda was meaningless and a waste of time. The agenda did not address any issues the ANA were having on FOB Wilson or the outlying outposts. Real, meaningful discussions are Afghan-driven and do not come from ISAF conceived meetings.

To help Colonel Halim save face, Colonel Murtaza managed to ask for more HMMWVs instead of Ford Rangers due to their greater resilience against IEDs; more winterization gear for the Soldiers, specifically long-sleeved shirts; more wells for water on the FOB; and the construction of a bigger dining facility for the ANA.

One of my most memorable issues with the Canadian mentors arose during a discussion of maintaining the ANA latrines. In the perspective of the 205th Corps mentors, since ISAF had the contract to build the latrine, the mentors felt it was also ISAF's responsibility to maintain the ANA latrines. I did my best to mask my frustration and respectfully told the Canadian Lieutenant Colonels that "under their logic if I gave the ANA a horse and if the ANA failed to feed and water the horse causing the horse to die it was still my fault despite me giving the ANA the food and water to actually feed the horse." I was flabbergasted when the Canadian mentors said yes, that was pretty much the case. The ANA had mechanisms and systems for their own contracts to repair the latrines. It was not, I felt, our responsibility to walk through the ANA latrines each morning to clean them and ensure the ANA flushed the toilets.

The ANA is an army of adults, and the Afghan culture has been around for centuries. I remember distinctly telling the mentors that "America is not responsible for everything." Ultimately I told the Canadian mentors that we would work with the ANA Brigade to submit more contracts for the maintenance of the latrines, but the ANA needed to do their part. Nothing is free. The ANA needed to step up and ensure maintenance was being done and that they were not trashing the latrines themselves. I knew, for example, that the Afghans were not used to sitting on toilets and would regularly stand on the seats instead, causing them to break.

Next on the Canadians' agenda was centralized parking for the ANA, which became the tipping point for me. It was something Colonel Murtaza and I had previously discussed, and we had come to the consensus that at the time it was not feasible. But the Canadian mentors had decided to meddle in something that did not concern them. I was thoroughly disgusted with the conversation and the meeting as a whole.

Colonels Murtaza and Halim had not been asked there to discuss these issues; rather the Canadians were making a point of bringing the issues up to me in front of them. In personal notes from the meeting, I wrote in utter frustration, "I told the audience once again that this is not Camp Hero. We are 'shonna ba shonna' [shoulder to shoulder] and not capable of creating a giant parking lot. The ANA vehicles are parked throughout the FOB with their partners. Extremely frustrated at this point, I stated that the FOB is full of shared hardships. We all live in tents, walk through dust, and live next to each other. Yes, we will continue to improve the quality of life on the FOB, but it takes time and is not the priority compared to operations." It is easy for those who live on Kandahar Airfield, like the Canadian mentors, who rarely go into combat to nitpick issues at the smaller outposts. The Canadians who came to FOB Wilson brought problems, not solutions.

During my daily notes of ANA activities that I sent to Colonel Kandarian and other leaders across the Brigade, I further voiced my displeasure at the Canadian mentors and what I clearly perceived as a waste of a trip and a missed learning experience for the ANA. "Based on my perspective, the entire meeting was 205th Corps mentor initiated and driven," I concluded. I based this on three facts: One, Major Post had coordinated the flights for the Corps logistics Officer and his mentors. If Colonel Halim needed to speak or see Colonel Murtaza, he would have driven to FOB Wilson. Two, Colonel Murtaza did not receive word of the meeting through ANA channels. And three, the mentors were pulling Colonel Halim's strings like a puppet, telling him to use their agenda for the meeting.

I further detailed my displeasure in my notes. "Events like these need to be ANA-initiated and -driven, otherwise we are doing their work for them. We need to allow the ANA to identify their problems and develop solutions to fix them, not have mentors completely driving the mission. Throughout the majority of the meeting, COL Murtaza completely ignored the conversation and continued to sign paperwork. In the future I recommend that we continue to assist the ANA while remaining in the periphery and stepping in only when necessary. The meeting reminded me of a quote by T.E. Lawrence, *27 Articles*, "Do not try to do too much with your own hands. Better the Arabs do it tolerably than that you do it perfectly. It is their war, and you are to help them, not win it for them.""" (ANA Note from 11DEC10)

To my dismay the next day I received a call from those two Canadian 205th Corps mentors about my notes regarding their actions and the meeting as a whole. Somehow my notes were leaked out of the Brigade and ended up with the Command of RC-S, which shared notes with the 205th Corps mentors. The two logistics mentors did not apologize for the meeting. They were upset that I would write something so strong. My notes forced them to explain their actions to their superior Officers. Certainly the two mentors were well-intentioned but those intentions had, in fact, led to the least desirable results, allowing the ANA to rattle off the things that needed to be done without establishing their own method for completing them. When developing a host nation force, you need them to execute tasks on their own. Encouraging anything less is a mistake. And I did not want to spend the rest of my career rotating back to Afghanistan every other year because we failed to train the Afghans correctly in how to complete tasks themselves.

The ANA is a leader-centric organization. In the U.S. Army, the command structures highly encourage decision-making at all levels as long as it is legal and meets the Commander's intent. The ANA rely on their leaders for constant instruction. If Colonel Murtaza had an issue with conditions, especially the items on the Corps Logistic Officers "Agenda," he would simply talk to one of two people: Colonel Kandarian, his partner, or Major General Hamid, the 205th Corps Commander, his superior. Colonel Murtaza would not have contacted the Corps logistics Officer directly since the ANA believe in the chain of the command and Major General Hamid was his commander.

As the brigade ANA mentor it was my responsibility to submit a monthly assessment for each ANA Battalion and the Brigade as a whole using the Commander's Update Assessment Tool (CUAT). Tools are meant to be useful and the CUAT was a tool that was painful to complete accurately because I was dependent on numbers from the ANA. The CUATs are widely read by the ISAF chain of command so accuracy is a critical. These tools enabled our higher headquarters, RC-S, and ISAF as a whole, to look *objectively* at the personnel, equipment status, training, operational capabilities, and overall leadership of the ANA Battalions, Brigades, and Divisions. I highlight "objectively" because in reality it was subjective. Despite all the quantifiable data available the capabilities of an ANSF unit is based on a person's judgment.

The U.S. Army uses a similar tool called the Unit Status Report (USR), which is filed monthly, but this report is automated and quantifiably examines personnel and equipment that is on hand and operational. With the Afghans, there may be an overage of Soldiers on the books but not in reality. At one point I found there was a surplus of ANA Soldiers in the daily personnel report but the reality at the outposts was that at least 40% of the ANA had gone absent without leave (AWOL). Some ANA would take leave and simply not return, and the ANA Commanders at the company level did not know how to properly report these missing Soldiers. To save face, they just said the Soldier was present for duty but the absences became apparent when a combined patrol would leave a COP with 40 Americans and only 12 Afghans.

Similarly, a piece of equipment might have been on the books but was damaged and not mission-capable. The system could work if everything were completely automated and updated constantly as with the American system, but it was not. So the math of assessing our partners became subjective, and our expectations were mitigated by their actual performance and achievements.

I did not want the ANA to mirror the United States Army or any other western Army; rather I wanted the ANA to become what the forces of Afghanistan needed to be. It would have been presumptuous and foolhardy for a Captain in a tiny district of Afghanistan to pretend that he might be able to shape the future of the entire Afghan Army. But if I failed to help the ANA to progress correctly, then I was negatively shaping the future of the ANA at least within our partnered brigade.

What I saw, though, was that our ANA partners needed to be a force that was not only loyal to the government of Afghanistan but also to the people they protected, regardless of tribal affiliation. Time in a deployment is limited and STRIKE had big goals for the year. I focused on three aspects of the ANA partners: leadership, corruption, and proficiency in tactics. The 3rd Brigade, 205th Corps needed to be a force multiplier by the time our replacement Brigade arrived and capable of not only exercising partnered operations but operations on their own and teaching our replacements about the people and culture of Zharay.

Chapter 17
Partners: Leadership

Character in the long run is the decisive factor in the life of an individual and of nations alike.
President Theodore Roosevelt

After my short liaison stint with the Canadian Battle Group at Kandahar Airfield, I was looking forward to working with the Brigade's ANA partners and doing some real work. Planning was interesting, but I wanted more. I was experienced with working with foreign militaries during my time in Iraq where I had worked with the Iraqi Army and Police and while on staff at Army Europe Headquarters where I worked with militaries from several neighboring countries. I enjoyed my previous opportunities with those militaries, but this opportunity, to work with the Afghans, meant something more to me.

STRIKE was in a horrific fight, and I felt like I could help. Long-term stability for the district was only possible if our ANA partners could fill the vacuum when we left. Despite the wishes of my family who preferred I stayed as safe as possible, working with the ANA provided me with the opportunity to go out on patrols and battlefield circulation nearly everyday. If Colonel Murtaza was going out to see his troops, then I was going with him. I am not one to sit behind a computer all day nor am I an adrenaline junkie, but I don't like making plans and decisions for others without understanding their situation, capabilities, and conditions.

One of David Kilcullen's *28 Articles* of counterinsurgency is simply put: "Be there." Though the concept is meant to apply to the local population it simultaneously applied to the development of our Afghan Army partners. I needed to be there with them to understand their process better. I could tell them how to do things, however. That would only teach them how I would do things and would not be sustainable to the Afghans. If the Afghans do not use their systems and processes, then once I left they would rely on the next unit until there were no more coalition troops. The thought process and solutions needed to be organic to how Afghans operate and conduct business. What we could provide were the additional skill sets that they wanted and needed, but before I could assist I needed to assess.

Concurrent with Operation Dragon STRIKE was the development of our Afghan partners at all levels. And with that partnership came frustration at all levels and on both sides of the aisle. The frustration on the American side was due to our expectations of what a Soldier should be and our misconceptions from Iraq, which had a long-standing Army and formal training. Afghanistan was not Iraq.

Under Taliban rule, Afghanistan did not have standing Army, and any sort of formal training had occurred decades before under Soviet supervision. The training academies in Kabul were very basic in their instruction. STRIKE not only wanted but needed our 3-205 Brigade partners to show up. STRIKE Soldiers were being killed every day and our partners needed to be there with us, not to die with us or in our place but to show the Afghans that there were Afghans there to help, not just a foreign force on their soil. The ANA understood the local dynamics, politics, and terrain far better than we ever could.

The initial frustration on our partner's side stemmed from two issues: one, their leadership and two, their expectation for handouts. The Brigade was initially commanded by Colonel Fatah; I use the word "commanded" generously here. Colonel Kandarian fought with and pushed Colonel Fatah through channels at RC-S and ISAF to get him and his Brigade to leave Camp Hero near KAF and live on FOB Wilson. As the Army COIN manual for tactics points out, "HN [Host Nation] leaders may be appointed and promoted based on family ties or membership in a party or faction, rather than on demonstrated competence or performance."[46] The leadership assessment from the COIN manual was very much true of Colonel Fatah who upon arriving at FOB Wilson refused to leave his office because the air conditioning was better in it despite having his own living quarters with air conditioning. After weeks of failing to do anything, Colonel Fatah was promoted out of his command position and replaced by Colonel Murtaza.

---

[46] Leadership. (2009, April). *FM 3-24.2: Tactics in Counterinsurgency.* Headquarters Department of the Army. Page 8-3.

Being a *jengi*, or a warrior in Pashtu, in the Afghan military means being many different things. Colonel Fatah was far from jengi and cared more about his comfort than his men. He cared more about his social status than ensuring that his men were trained and ready to fight. In the Afghan Army being a leader and jengi encompasses several qualities. A jengi leader in Afghanistan is one that has not only tactical prowess but is also able to make decisions that support their Islamic beliefs, has the capability to motivate others and the ability to support the Afghan government; otherwise the Army units would devolve into militias. Fortunately there were several leaders within our ANA partners that were jengi.

One of the most memorable questions I have ever been asked occurred during my board to gain an appointment to the Army's Officer Candidate School, when the President of the Board asked me, "How would you describe leadership?" I quickly and naively at the time responded that "leadership is about leading by example and not telling your Soldiers to do anything you weren't willing to do yourself or haven't already done." I had seen *Band of Brothers*, watched a plethora of war movies over the years, and read all sorts of books and that was what leadership boiled down to for me. I was disappointed that the President of the Board did not agree with me. He said, "It's easy to take the lead and have people follow you, but a true leader gets his men to do what they don't want to do when they are cold, exhausted, or just plain don't want to do it. Motivating others to do what they think is impossible is real leadership." It took me along time to understand what the President of the Officer Candidate Board meant. Everyone gets tired, exhausted, and cold at some point, and in those moments, it is easy to settle for the wrong thing. Leadership is about getting people to do the right thing all the time, even when no one is looking. It is teaching a Soldier to pick up the trash before it becomes "Colonel trash."

Not every Soldier and Officer of our partnered unit understood what leadership was. On October 13, 2010, the Chief of Staff of the Afghan Military, General Karimi was visiting FOB Wilson to get a brief from the ANA and see how Operations were going. Colonel Murtaza had restricted driving of ANA on FOB Wilson to official business only and had ordered roadblocks set up on the FOB to reduce traffic; however, the intelligence Officer of the 5th Battalion did not believe the rules applied to him. As the Officer approached the roadblock in his tan Afghan Army Ford Ranger, a young ANA sentry informed the Officer that he was not permitted to pass. Frustrated, the ANA intelligence Officer got out of his pick-up and punched the Soldier. The Officer then drove through the roadblock. Upon learning of the incident, Colonel Murtaza had the Officer detained and sent back to Camp Hero to be reassigned.

The actions of the ANA battalion intelligence Officer showed a clear lack of discipline, military bearing, and professionalism, and Colonel Murtaza's actions demonstrated that he was a fair Officer to both his Soldiers and Officers alike. Colonel Murtaza did not tolerate those who disobeyed his orders, and he showed that punishments will fit the crime. If Colonel Murtaza would have let this incident slide because one of the parties involved was an Officer, then word would have spread like wildfire to the other ANA Soldiers in the Brigade and confidence among the Soldiers for their superiors would have eroded.

Critical to discipline and professionalism in the Afghan Army is the ability to make decisions that reflect their society, which is based on Islam and belief in the Prophet Mohammed. As a leader there is fine balance between supporting operations and beliefs. During one of the morning meetings to discuss operations, the Brigade's Religious Officer stood up to complain that hygiene in the dining facility was not to the standards of the Qu'ran and that "inappropriate" things were occurring in the living area. As my interpreter explained to me later that "inappropriate" was a euphemism for homosexual activity between the Afghan Soldiers, but the ANA were embarrassed to discuss such things in front of me.

At the discussion of "inappropriate" behavior, Colonel Murtaza cut in and said, "This meeting is not about praying; it's about operations. Don't waste our time! Talk about praying on Fridays or during religious meetings. That is not now! Soldiers must pray. It is their duty, however they need to do it when they can." Embarrassed, likely due to my presence in the meeting, Colonel Murtaza sought to change the subject and began discussing other subjects with his staff and commanders. At the time, I saw Colonel Murtaza balancing the necessity of being focused on operations as well as the inherent role of Islam in Afghanistan.

Colonel Murtaza always supported his men's beliefs. Colonel Murtaza himself was Sunni but on days like December 16, 2010, he recognized that some of his men were Shia and it was their night of power when the Shia celebrate the life and death of the 4th grandson of the prophet Mohammed near the city of Karbala. For the holiday, Colonel Murtaza gave the day off for his staff and other men not needed for patrols so that they could pray and fast.

December 16, 2010, was also a day that revealed Colonel Murtaza's understanding of the role of counterinsurgency operations in Zharay. During the day, Admiral Michael Mullen, the then-Chairman of the Joint Chiefs of Staff, visited FOB Wilson to ensure that Soldiers on the ground were getting everything they needed. Admiral Mullen asked Colonel Murtaza about his unit's role and function during the Operations and Intelligence (O & I) Brief, and not having been coached, Colonel Murtaza flatly stated that, "There needs to be only one DCoP [District Chief of Police] in the area. The police need to get out and work so that the ANA Soldiers can be used for other operations." Colonel Murtaza went on to discuss the role of Haji Lala and Tooraliya, who were, for lack of a better phrase, mini-warlords within Zharay empowered by the previous ISAF unit and district governor. Colonel Murtaza saw them "operating outside of GIRoA [Government of the Islamic Republic of Afghanistan] and they could become the next Mullah Omar. The police are the law." Colonel Murtaza's words demonstrated not only to the STRIKE Brigade but the Chair of the Joint Chiefs of Staff that there was an end state for Afghanistan, a state governed by laws.

Throughout the coming months, Colonel Murtaza demonstrated his tactical prowess and understanding of how his unit needed to operate and cooperate with the both the district police and government. The ANA's mission was expanding, and as their area of operations grew, Colonel Murtaza knew he did not want to fight continually to reclaim hard-earned terrain. While in Maiwand for a discussion about future operations, Colonel Murtaza put forth an Afghan-derived plan for the ANP and ANCOP to take over a series of checkpoints in order to free up his men to conduct clearing operations.

Interestingly, the ANCOP commander, LTC Sadat, stated he had no issues taking over the checkpoints, however LTC Abdullah, the 6th Battalion Commander who currently ran the checkpoints, did. LTC

Abdullah was one of the most corrupt leaders I have ever met and his issue with leaving the checkpoints likely stemmed from his self-interests and his eagerness to steal from the locals. I worked throughout my deployment to have LTC Abdullah removed. Despite being investigated for stealing fuel from ISAF and against Colonel Murtaza's wishes, LTC Abdullah remained in command. LTC Abdullah had influential friends. The extent of his corruption will be discussed in further detail later.

Colonel Murtaza was also a fan of conducting "health and welfare" inspections on his Soldiers, which are more or less a look into their living quarters. During an inspection on the garrison support unit (GSU), Colonel Murtaza's team found several knives (including butcher knives), ammunition, and a large quantity of uniforms stashed in tents with no Soldiers. Colonel Murtaza was extremely dismayed at the findings and openly stated in a morning meeting in front of the GSU Commander that it "confirmed what he already knew. There are some bad Soldiers in the GSU." He then sent the findings to the 205th Corps Commander along with a request to have the GSU commander removed because the findings demonstrated the "GSU lacks leadership and are a bunch of thieves." Not surprisingly though, the GSU commander remained in command as he was also politically well-connected.

Obeying orders out of fear is one technique that leaders over the century have employed. Machiavelli in *The Prince* highlighted the pros and cons of leaders who are loved versus feared. Colonel Murtaza managed to inspire both emotions deftly among his men. He was feared by his Soldiers due to his rank and ability to accomplish tasks but was also loved for his willingness to be with his Soldiers. Barely a day passed when Colonel Murtaza and Colonel Kandarian were not crisscrossing the battlefield, meeting with their Soldiers.

At times Colonel Murtaza was harsh with his Soldiers, and at other times he provided great encouragement to keep them in the fight. Colonel Murtaza also pushed the partnership between the STRIKE Brigade and his Soldiers and often preached to his Soldiers that they needed to do more. Colonel Murtaza would highlight the elephant in the room that his Soldiers often forgot, reminding them that "we [the Americans] would not always be there and they needed to care about their country more than we did."

I suspect many of the attributes that Colonel Murtaza expressed to his men were lessons he learned from observing Colonel Kandarian and the things he said to his Soldiers and staff. As partner Brigade Commanders, their offices were next to each other so that they could work "Shonna Ba Shonna." The entire tactical operations center complex was set up this way so that the ANA staff office and the STRIKE staff offices were next to each, and on the main TOC floor, the ANA sat next to their American counterparts.

Sadly, in spite of the directives from both Commanders, partnership at times was strained. I remember early on being called in by Major Haas, the STRIKE personnel Officer, who ordered me to go meet with his Afghan counterpart and get information for him. Being outranked, I was in a difficult position. On one hand, I had a responsibility to push partnership. But on the other, I was being ordered by a higher-ranking Officer. I had to be diplomatic and pick the right battles, but at times I would ignore these orders by Major Haas, forcing him to find an interpreter and work with his partner. The ANA personnel Officer was not going to learn anything from me about personnel management and needed to be with his partner.

I was an easy conduit for a lot of staff sections until I learned the trick of arranging meetings between the staff sections and their ANA partners. The Americans would look foolish asking me to ask an Afghan a question when the Afghan was in the room. Over time they got to know each other, and my workload was greatly reduced. Captain Bryan Vaden, the Brigade Signal Officer, after building a connection with his Afghan counterpart, began teaching classes on the use of PowerPoint, Word, and Excel and having slides for these basic classes translated to Dari.

"Rank is nothing; talent is everything," is another one of David Kilcullen's 28 Articles and is meant for leaders to look for talented individuals wherever they maybe and not to discount an idea or concept simply because it comes from a low-ranking individual. This premise also holds true when dealing with a young host nation's Army. Many Afghan Officers and Soldiers are in certain positions because of their connections but that does not necessarily make them right for the job. The trick becomes recognizing those with real talent who are the natural leaders. Other members of Colonel Murtaza's staff who demonstrated this talent were his executive Officer Colonel

Quandahari and his operations Officer LTC Rahim, but those men were not fighting every day. In a testament to his leadership and capabilities, Colonel Quandahari was selected to lead the ANA partners of Gad Zawak in the Horn of Panjwa'i during Operation Dragon STRIKE since they were essentially a conglomerate of different ANA Battalions from around Afghanistan. Not all great leaders in 3-205 ANA were Officers, though.

In early December 2010, Colonel Murtaza and Colonel Kandarian traveled to western Zharay/eastern Maiwand to inspect the progress along Route Dragoon. There, the Soldiers of 3rd Squadron, 2nd Stryker Cavalry Regiment and Colonel Murtaza's 6th Battalion (6-3-205) had sealed off the western edge to prevent the Taliban from escaping and from moving supplies into the area during Operation Dragon STRIKE.

As we moved south off Highway One we saw the construction of two watchtowers and ultimately stopped at strongpoint Iron, which resembled an old medieval castle with four-foot-thick walls that jutted up several stories and circular towers at each corner. Intelligence indicated that the Taliban had used the compound that was now strongpoint Iron for some time due to its remoteness from the population and its thick walls, which provided protection from not only small arms fire but reconnaissance.

Trudging through the deep layer of fine sand, commonly referred to as "moon dust," that covered Iron, Colonel Murtaza walked over to the ANA tents and was dismayed to find few Soldiers around and notably no Officer. One Soldier, Private Nariz, stepped forward, however, and demonstrated that he was a leader, providing Colonel Murtaza with a brief of ongoing patrols and where all the Soldiers were, including those from the company that were manning the watchtower. When pressed, Private Nariz admitted that he did not see his Company Commander, Captain Hayatullah, often. Captain Hayatullah preferred to hide out in comfort at COP Azizullah along Highway One. Recognizing the talent of Private Nariz, Colonel Murtaza later requested that he be promoted to First Sergeant, which instantly increased his rank seven-fold. The reality was that Private Nariz was leading the company so he might as well have the rank.

Expressing his dismay toward CPT Hayatullah and the fact the Soldiers were here fighting while CPT Hayatullah was withholding their hygiene kits and spare clothes that were to be issued in the winter,

Colonel Murtaza got on one of the company's radios to reach LTC Abdullah, the battalion commander. Holding no words back, Colonel Murtaza began berating the battalion commander in front of his men and at one point saying that "he [LTC Abdullah] was giving a bad name to the Army by not giving the Soldiers what is within their rights!" He added that he would call Corps and get new Officers to replace those in the 6th Battalion immediately.

Colonel Murtaza cared about his Soldiers but not to the point where he would be made to look weak. Rather he was a fair and determined leader—a stark contrast to his predecessor, Colonel Fatah, who only cared about himself and his comforts. If a Soldier did not have something such as the correct number of socks, Colonel Murtaza would ask the Soldiers commander why and would fix the problem. Colonel Murtaza and his Soldiers would still be fighting the Taliban when the STRIKE Brigade left.

The Soldiers of 3-205 Corps were running a marathon while STRIKE was just sprinting a mile. Day in and day out, the Soldiers and Officers of 3rd Brigade, 205th Corps needed to be willing to fight. If the ANA Soldiers gave up and quit their posts, then the Taliban were surely going to win because they would be the ones to show up for the fight. The Soldiers knew what life was like under Taliban rule and only a few of them knew what life was like before the Soviet invasion. Our ANA partners were fighting for their future and that was a message Colonel Murtaza used to motivate all of his Soldiers, whether in the tiny outposts in Kandalay, Asoque, Sangsar, Nalgham, Iron, or anywhere on the battlefield.

Chapter 18
Partners: The Ghosts and The Corrupt

Weapons accountability is ground into the heart and mind of every Soldier. In basic training, weapons are issued to Soldiers on their very first day. Soldiers are accountable for securing and maintaining their weapons. Their rifles could mean the difference between life and death in combat. Accountability formation and weapons counts are held constantly, and if a Drill Sergeant finds an unattended weapon, its owner is correspondingly punished. Company commanders have been relieved of command due to lost accountability.

In late January 2011, a container that was used to store excess weapons on FOB Howz-e-Madad for Soldiers on leave was discovered with its lock broken. Following a serial number inventory, two M-4 rifles were determined to be missing. The FOB was immediately locked down. Every weapon in every convoy going on and off the FOB was inspected by serial number in an attempt to locate the weapons and in the hopes that it was an inventory issue rather than stolen weapons.

No convoy was excluded, not even those of Colonel Kanadarian and Lieutenant Colonel Peter Benchoff. At the time of the lockdown, however, LTC Sadiqi had just departed the FOB for Camp Hero, the large Afghan Army base near Kandahar Airfield. No commander's conference was scheduled at Camp Hero. There was no reason for LTC Sadiqi to go to Camp Hero; he just left. Upon returning and for the next few days as the lockdown and inventory continued, LTC Sadiqi loudly protested the searches and inventories. The lockdown was not directed specifically at him, yet he felt the searches were beneath his stature as an Afghan Army battalion commander.

A further investigation was launched, but unfortunately, the weapons were never recovered. American military weapons are extremely valuable, and if there is a means to make a profit, some will always find a way. LTC Sadiqi was never linked to the weapons disappearance but there were suspicions. Lieutenant Colonel Sadiqi was not the only ANA leader viewed as being corrupt.

In an 1887 letter to Bishop Creighton, Lord Acton said, "Power tends to corrupt, and absolute power corrupts absolutely." By western standards, Afghanistan is corrupt. Bribes, random toll stops on the highway run by police, and gifts to politicians are easily unethical situations in the United States, but in Afghanistan such incidents are viewed as a cost of living.

Coming to grips with the different forms of corruption within Afghanistan was difficult. Trying to explain to our ANA Brigade partners the undermining effects of stealing and bribe-taking during counterinsurgency operations was difficult. The American withdrawal from Afghanistan was widely discussed and so was the future of Afghanistan. Withdrawal meant uncertainty for many and the only means to stem the uncertainty for some was to possess financial stability by any means necessary. The crux of the issue was the more the ANA or any other government official demanded bribes or robbed the people, then the more they alienated the people, undermining the Government of Afghanistan and a stable future.

Lieutenant Colonel Abdullah, the commander of the 6th Battalion, was perhaps the most corrupt person in the 3rd Brigade, 205th Corps.

The 6th Battalion was originally part of 1st Brigade and had been assigned to Zharay to provide security along Highway One. Like the 5th Stryker Brigade, 2nd Infantry Division, 6th Battalion's role was strictly limited to the Highway. Its members so often referred to themselves as the "Highway Kandak [Battalion]" that American forces believed the 6th Battalion was actually a special ANA unit designed to operate on the Highway. The reality, however, was that they were an infantry battalion and their personnel and assigned equipment matched identically those of the other battalions within 3-205 ANA. In mission only was the 6th Battalion a "Highway Kandak," but by telling so many people that they were one, LTC Abdullah was able to remain far longer on detail along Highway One than he should have been.

In May and June 2010, the STRIKE Brigade began its partnership with LTC Abdullah and his men. STRIKE immediately became suspicious of the 6th Kandak Soldiers as they ran checkpoints and shook down vehicles as they past through Zharay. The Soldiers of 6th Battalion in checkpoints in Sanjaray would provide security to convoys headed west to Helmand with construction equipment and other supplies. Many of these convoys had private security escorts but still chose to pay for protection from the 6th Kandak because their odds of being attacked were greatly reduced when the ANA was present. Protection was derived not from the 6th Kandak being viewed as *jengi*, or warriors; rather a cut of the protection money went to the Taliban or other local warlords. The fact that convoys without an ANA escort were at greater risk for attack helped perpetuate LTC Abdullah's corruption game and that he was working with local Taliban.

Highway One has long been a source of revenue in Afghanistan and of critical infrastructure, like a sole bridge leading out from an island. Highway One is not only the main thoroughfare in Afghanistan; it is, however, the main road through Zharay. The people of Zharay live close to the road, and LTC Abdullah's greed and antics both alienated the locals and made travel and commerce unsafe. I have no direct evidence that LTC Abdullah stole money himself, however consistent and repeated reports from the villagers of Sanjaray painted a picture of aggressive searches by his Soldiers. A common complaint from the locals was that their wallets were being searched so thoroughly that they were returned empty to their owners. As a military leader, LTC Abdullah was responsible for the actions of his Soldiers.

STRIKE Brigade's priority was reducing impediments along Highway One, whether they originated from Taliban attacks or from corrupt ANA brigades. As soon as our ANA partners began moving onto FOB Wilson, Colonel Kandarian began the discussion with Colonel Fatah to move the 6th Battalion further west to Howz-e-Madad and Azizullah and away from the major population centers in eastern Zharay. Colonel Fatah was not moved and made the same argument that LTC Abdullah continued to make: the 6th Battalion was the "Highway Kandak."

Being diplomatic is difficult, stressful, and time-consuming, especially when you know your partner is wrong. We did our best. Little did Colonel Fatah know that at that same moment, Colonel Kandarian and I were working to have him removed from command of 3-205 ANA. Colonel Fatah demonstrated an unprecedented ability to consistently do nothing. Surprisingly, only after he got word that he was being removed did Colonel Fatah actually do something. In a desperate attempt to salvage his job, he decided to threaten the STRIKE Brigade with "insider attacks." Not only was it too little too late but Colonel Kandarian was not going to be intimidated by a man who could barely stand under his own weight.

Colonel Fatah's departure was swift, and Colonel Qandahari quickly provided the leadership the ANA needed until Colonel Murtaza's arrival. New brigade leadership would be critical for getting the Brigade out and conducting partnered missions, but moving the 6th Battalion remained an intractable issue.

Despite being ordered by Colonel Murtaza to leave Highway One and move west to FOB Azizullah, LTC Abdullah played the game of suffering from divorced parents. The 6th Kandak originally belonged to 1st Brigade, 205th Corps, and despite being ordered by Major General Hamid, the 205th Corps commander under Colonel Murtaza's operational control, LTC Abdullah refused to listen to him. Under the Afghan military structure orders come from the Ministry of Defense, and LTC Abdullah had not received the order from reflagging his battalion as the 6th Battalion of 1st Brigade to 3rd Brigade.

For the next few months, I emailed and called the ANSF group at Regional Command South working them to get an order to reflag LTC Abdullah's Battalion to 3rd Brigade and under Colonel Murtaza's control. Simultaneously, both Colonels Kandarian and Murtaza asked every ISAF and ANA dignitary to visit the area of operation. LTC Abdullah, either because of naivety, gall, stupidity, or some combination of the three, continued his heavy-handed antics on Highway One, though on a greatly reduced scale. He further antagonized Colonel Murtaza by not showing up for commander's meetings, citing Murtaza's affiliation for 1st Brigade.

Frustrated with LTC Abdullah's antics, I constantly searched the ISAF network for ANA orders dealing with 3rd Brigade. Finally, late one evening in October while scanning the ANA orders on the ISAF ANSF portal, I found the reflagging order. Both the Dari version and a translated copy of the newly published order (cipher) reflagging the 6th Battalion had just been posted on the site. Finally! With ciphers in hand I presented a copy to both Brigade Commanders who were delighted to get LTC Abdullah away from the people of Zharay.

Still, the antics and corruption from LTC Abdullah did not cease, even after his Battalion became partnered with 3rd Squadron, 2nd Stryker Cavalry Regiment. I regularly received reports from CPT Adam Cucchairra about LTC Abdullah taking fuel off the outpost and selling it in the bazaars of Howz-e-Madad. These reports would ultimately find their way to the Ministry of Defense, which, in turn, sent a team down to Azizullah to investigate LTC Abdullah. After three days of questioning, LTC Abdullah remained in command but with a clear warning, one even stressed to him by Brigadier General Hamid, the 205th Corps Commander: one more report, and he would be arrested.

LTC Abdullah was not the only problem Battalion Commander. Lieutenant Colonel Sadiqi, the commander of 1st Battalion and mentioned earlier in this chapter, was also corrupt, though not as overtly as LTC Abdullah. Based out of the outpost in Howz-e-Madad, LTC Sadiqi and his Soldiers were partnered with LTC Peter Benchoff and the Soldiers of 2nd Battalion, 502nd Infantry Regiment.

In an effort to generate a strong partnership, LTC Benchoff immediately reached out to LTC Sadiqi and insisted on many partnered operations and functions. Over time, however, the corruption grew more and more apparent. LTC Sadiqi would invite prospective contractors to his office, and according to these contractors, he would promise contracts from American troops in return for a bribe. Sometimes the bribes were money; other times the bribes were gifts in the form of nice dishes or a chai set for his office. LTC Benchoff would eventually hear the complaints from contractors about LTC Sadiqi. The contractors were upset that LTC Sadiqi was not fulfilling his end of the agreement and delivering the contracts. The sad thing was that LTC Sadiqi's attempts at bribery for contracts were futile and he did not even know it.

The American contracting system is set up so that bids have to be presented from multiple parties and the American contracting Officer has to justify the selection of a contractor. LTC Sadiqi could not influence our ranks.

LTC Sadiqi argued that such visits with contractors and gifts were the cost of doing business in Afghanistan and was a common staple of Afghan culture. LTC Sadiqi, however, was a representative of the Afghan government. LTC Sadiqi promised influence over American Officers and the contracting system. He presented himself as a necessary intermediary for local contracts. The reality is that LTC Sadiqi was no different from the warlords who roamed Highway One prior to the rise of the Taliban.

In an effort to stem the corruption and the local perception that the government of Afghanistan was corrupt, we learned a tremendous amount about the command structure. Within the Afghan Army structure is a dependence on the hierarchy of rank and position. Action required permission from higher. The concept of delegating authority was foreign since that meant delegating power. Frustrated by the system, we had to teach the ANA how to delegate down to lower levels.

When we first arrived, before a partner patrol could be planned, the ANA platoon leader needed permission from his company commander, who needed permission to send out a partnered patrol from his battalion commander, who needed the brigade commander to give his blessing for a partnered patrol. Under Colonel Murtaza, the standing orders for such patrols and many others like them were delegated down, but what makes natural sense to us, Americans, was not necessarily instinctive to the Afghans.

Due to the highly dependent hierarchy, it was easy to trace back the origins of the corruption. This easy tracking does not apply to insider attacks since those acts generally have ideological roots and usually stem from a single disenfranchised Soldier, not a command directive. From my experience with the ANA, greed comes from the top. The power of the position corrupts, and both LTC Sadiqi and LTC Abdullah used their position to better themselves solely.

Day in and day out, STRIKE needed its ANA partners on patrols and missions so our ability to isolate corrupt leaders completely was hampered. Without our Afghan partners, the Brigade was at risk of being viewed as a foreign occupier. The people of Zharay also needed to be comfortable with not only the ANA but all of the ANSF in the district. One of the most difficult aspects of my job was getting the ANA out on combined patrols so that we could achieve a one-to-one ratio of Americans to Afghans on every patrol. Everything the Brigade did needed to have an Afghan face on it. But implementation of this requirement was easier to achieve on paper than in reality. The ranks of the ANA were filled with ghosts, Soldiers who were assigned to the unit but had disappeared.

In mid-September 2010, when I become the lead mentor of our Afghan partners, nearly 1,200 Soldiers in the 3-205 ANA Brigade were absent without leave (AWOL), which was close to 45% of the Brigade. Traveling to the distant outposts, I learned that combined patrols sometimes consisted of 30 American Soldiers and 3 Afghans. This was a far cry from the one-to-one ratio. In fact, ideally, there would be more Afghans than Americans on the patrols.

I heard all sorts of excuses from the ANA Company Commanders as to why there were so few Soldiers on patrols. One reason the ANA

Commander at COP Nalgham gave me for the dearth of Afghan soldiers was that the Americans had only asked for three Soldiers. The interpreters had likely mistaken the message of "we need a few Soldiers to go on a combined patrol" to mean "*only* a few," which translated to three. Notwithstanding the excuses, there were still too few ANA at some of the outposts.

The origin of the missing Soldiers stemmed from when the ANA Battalions moved from the training center near Kabul to Camp Hero in Kandahar. Many of the Soldiers from the north had thought they would be fighting near their homes and in turn, wanted little to do with the heavy fighting in the south. Others had spent months in training and missed their families, so as the convoys left Kabul, they simply walked away to take leave. Other Soldiers did not like sitting and training at Camp Hero, and since Colonel Fatah had refused to leave the comfort of Camp Hero to get his men into the fight in Zharay district, many frustrated or bored Soldiers left in the middle of the night. Soldiers from 1-75 CAV had been at Camp Hero to train the ANA in counter-IED techniques and first aid, so from one day to the next, as accountability formations were held, attendance was dwindling.

The American military has a well-established system for getting rid of AWOL Soldiers: after 30 days the Soldier is dropped from the rolls so that the slot on the roster can be filled by another Soldier. The Afghan Army has similar rules but there is a lot of discretion in how the rules are implemented. Even more significant for the 3-205 ANA was that the lower level Officers did not know what the rules were or frankly what to do with AWOLs. I had to research through translated field manuals for the ANA method of getting rid of AWOL Soldiers and how to request new ones.

What I learned was that after an ANA Soldier is marked absent for 60 days, his name may be dropped from the rolls and the personnel Officer can then submit that name to Corps Headquarters to request a new Soldier who would in turn submit a request from Kabul. All told, the process should take 90 to 120 days from the time a Soldier went AWOL to the arrival of his replacement. But if the AWOL Soldier returned, he was generally sent back to his unit to fight without repercussion.

As word spread around Afghanistan of the heavy fighting in the south, some of the Soldiers who left Camp Hero, when Colonel Fatah stagnated the Brigade there, returned. The rumor was that the returning Soldiers had heard there was an opportunity to kill the Taliban and wanted to get into the fight. Daily, I requested and got copies of the ANA personnel status report that was radio-sent to the Brigade headquarters. I sent a copy of the ANA personnel report out daily to all of our battalions to compare with the numbers they showed on-hand. Each night during our combined battle update briefs, Colonel Kandarian would address the personnel numbers on the screen so that Colonel Murtaza could force his subordinate commanders to explain where their Soldiers were and why they weren't out with their partners. We were forcing the ANA to address the AWOL issue.

During the ANA staff meeting on October 21st, Colonel Murtaza finally let his frustration show over the AWOL numbers and number of Soldiers present for duty. Calling on his personnel Officer, Colonel Murtaza asked him if the numbers were correct, and the personnel Officer responded, "That the number of 1,186 Soldiers was incorrect." Curious about the number Colonel Murtaza asked why his partner [Colonel Kandarian] had different numbers. And the personnel Officer said that he had not received the numbers from two of the battalions so he did not know the total number of AWOLs from those units. Colonel Murtaza was embarrassed. He was embarrassed that this dialogue occurred in my presence and even asked my interpreter to stop translating as he berated his staff and commanders in Dari. After the fact my interpreter explained how frustrated he was, yet despite his embarrassment, fixing the AWOL issue became important to Colonel Murtaza. He began counting Soldiers present for duty every time we visited a combat outpost.

Slowly with our ANA partners, we made progress. Colonel Murtaza requested that Brigadier General Hamid send out his personnel Officer to teach his staff and the battalions how to remove the AWOL Soldiers from the personnel roster. Steadily Soldiers began flowing to 3-205 with coming-in groups of 60 to 100, and by December 2010 the AWOL numbers hovered around 600 and had dipped even further to 400 by April. The ANA Soldiers, however, knew that fighting was going to intensify as the foliage returned and especially as our replacement Brigade began taking over operations. Ultimately Colonel Murtaza began implementing a leave rotation program to ensure his Soldiers would not randomly go AWOL, rather they would all have an equal opportunity to go home and visit their families.

Working with the ANA was always a fine balance between pushing them to do better within their own systems and alienating them. Corruption as well as the ANA's physical absence had detrimental effects on our ability to conduct counterinsurgency operations. The STRIKE Brigade needed its Afghan partners to be reliable: that meant present and incorruptible. And so with corruption minimized to the best of our ability and the ANA present and accounted for, we focused on making them better Soldiers. The Afghans were fighters; we needed to focus them and train them to fight as a team so that the Taliban would not be able to resurge in the area.

Chapter 19
Partners: Tactical and Technical Proficiency

Helping others to help themselves is critical to winning the long war.

Quadrennial Defense Review Report
2006

Snap...Snap...Snap. Snap. Snap. A bullet suddenly flies by as the world erupts into a hornets nest of incoming small arms fire. In an instant the calm, silent, methodical movement of a combined patrol becomes chaos. Soldiers instinctively seek cover. While American Soldiers attempt to determine the distance and direction of the incoming fire, the ANA become a wall of death. The ANA fearlessly and often uncontrollably fire every weapon they possess. I witnessed the ANA fire RPGs and M203 grenade launchers, while expending rounds from their M16s at such a rate that their weapons overheated. Un-oiled bolts jammed in their receivers as the heat of so many rounds being continuously fired cause them to expand and swell.

The ANA loved to shoot, and when the opportunity arose they would put so much fire on the Taliban that I am surprised the Taliban are still around. While in the Arghandab, I saw the ANA jumping up from behind cover to fire their RPGs, 40mm grenades, and their M16s at a distant and invisible enemy that was randomly firing mortars at us. Unfortunately, the ANA's enthusiasm came with two profound deficiencies. One, the ANA were not very accurate. And two, the ANA often ran out of ammunition. The ANA, in their basic training, are taught the fundamentals of how to shoot, but their application of these skills in a meaningful way (i.e. to shoot accurately) was often lacking. Showing the ANA how to apply the fundamentals they were taught became a priority.

The Afghan National Security Forces were the exit strategy for NATO from Afghanistan. The ability to defend oneself is critical for long-term success for a variety of obvious reasons, including defending against external influences and internal uprisings. Afghanistan shares borders with Pakistan, Iran, Russia, China, and India. Consequently, out of sheer necessity the Afghans must be able to defend their own borders or face a perpetual threat to their sovereignty. Internally, Afghanistan is vulnerable to influential and powerful warlords as well as a resurgent Taliban movement. Critical to a successful withdrawal of the U.S. and NATO from a stable Afghanistan was a strong and capable Afghan National Security Force.

In the Army's Field Manual (FM 3-24) on counterinsurgency Operations, the description of a host nation's security force is extremely detailed. The full establishment of one in Afghanistan would not be achievable in our short time in-country. As the lead mentor for the ANA within the STRIKE Brigade, I had no intention of pushing our doctrine onto the ANA Soldiers and Officers either. Instead, I pushed them to learn and follow the systems that the Afghan government and Ministry of Defense had developed. In many cases their solutions mimic those of the American military, but there were also Afghan solutions to be implemented for Afghan problems.

I constantly assessed our ANA partners. I questioned whether Afghan Soldiers were going on patrols? Were the Afghans resupplying themselves? Or were the Afghans dependent on their partners for food, water, and ammunition? Was the ANA Brigade staff planning operations independently? At the end of our deployment, STRIKE wanted our ANA partners to be able to plan, prepare, and execute combined operations to secure the people of Zharay. An independent ANA was STRIKE's end state for our Afghan Army partners, but to achieve such a goal I was often finding years of bad habits.

Since the establishment of the ANSF, the typical method of getting the Afghan Army ready to fight was just to give them everything. ISAF units would provide food, water, ammunition, and sometimes money through a program called the "Commanders Emergency Relief Fund." I recall, in July 2010 in the Arghandab prior to the start of Operation Dragon STRIKE, talking to several Canadian mentors attached to one of the battalions from 1st Brigade, 205th Corps when one mentors remarked that the Afghan supply system was broken so they just gave the ANA money to buy food. When they ran out, he explained, they would have to rely on the American partners. I was dumbfounded. This was not fixing the supply and training problem; it was simply doing the minimum so that Afghans would at least fight.

By partnering with a new unit, STRIKE had an opportunity to avoid the trappings that has plagued other ISAF units for years. Colonel

Kandarian, from the start, stressed that STRIKE would teach the ANA the right way, not the easy wrong way. STRIKE needed its Afghan partners on patrols and on missions, but more importantly it needed its partners to be independent when STRIKE redeployed back to Fort Campbell.

At no point would STRIKE allow its partners to fail or the mission to fail so we constantly possessed contingency plans. Units carried extra ammunition, food, water, and other supplies as necessary to keep the ANA in the fight, but it was never a first choice. Platoon leaders talked to their partner platoon leaders to ensure the ANA was bringing the supplies it needed for patrols. Company Commanders and Battalion Commanders did the same with the partners at their level.

For the ANA it was easiest to ask their partners for something instead of attempting to use their own systems and supply channels to get the equipment. As a brigade, we said "no" a lot. Specifically we said "no" when the ANA would come and ask for computers, internet lines, and fuel without even attempting their own channels. I told several ANA staff members that if I got them a computer, then they would have to get me six camels. No camels, no computer. I often received a puzzled and dumbfounded look from the ANA. My interpreter would tell me that they thought she was interpreting incorrectly. And so I would explain that while "they [ANA] never owned a computer, I never owned a camel and I really wanted one." Exasperated with my sarcasm, the ANA would walk off, but eventually they learned that they could fill out a form and get dozens of computers and other supplies from the 205th Corps supply depot.

Still, I needed more than jokes to get the ANA where they needed to be. And so we developed a system. If the ANA Brigade had submitted a request to their higher headquarters for supplies and it was denied, and if the ANA had the "denied" form, then I could work to get a contract submitted to fulfill that shortcoming. Colonel Kandarian had wisely assigned a liaison to the RC-S mentors to 205th Corps so I knew what the ANA had in warehouses at Camp Hero as well as in the Afghan Army warehouses in Kabul. Every time the ANA logistics Officer would show me a copy of a denied request form, I would scan them and email a copy to the liaison who would present it to the 205th Corps logistics Officer and see if the denial was warranted. Once this process was in place, supplies began to flow to the ANA. The Soldiers had stoves, firewood, winter clothes, extra boots, socks, toothbrushes, and just about everything else that the ANA could imagine. The ANA were learning to sustain themselves.

Forcing the ANA to use their own supply channels and methods was critical for the long-term success of the 3-205 Corps and greatly developed their confidence in their own systems. Colonel Murtaza and his staff quickly recognized this need for independent systems, and they began holding their own logistics meetings. The first meeting occurred in November and quickly devolved into Colonel Murtaza berating his battalion commanders and their logistics Officers. The logistics Officers claimed that they were not submitting forms for "quality of life goods" such as toothpaste, shampoo, soap, and so forth because the forms were being denied. Colonel Murtaza called them liars and told them, "to show me a form that I disapproved and I will approve all requests to improve the Soldiers quality of life."

The Afghans are very proud, and being called a liar was a severe insult. The ANA were also overly sensitive to accountability. If an ANA Soldier signed for a hundred toothbrushes or weapons, then that Soldier would hide them thinking it was his responsibility to keep them safe. The Soldiers did not realize they were supposed to distribute them to others or have others sign for them so that they were no longer accountable for the good. Paradoxically, this demand for accountability encouraged the ANA to be hoarders. When supplies come in to the Brigade it is necessary that the subordinate units demand what is theirs.

At first I thought this was due to possible corruption as the quartermaster might have been stealing equipment meant for the Soldiers, but the reality was that he and his men signed for everything out of an anxiety over losing track of items. Breaking them of this fear was difficult as it permeated not only the transportation of supplies but their use of them.

The ANA would pile into just a few vehicles and leave the remaining locked up in the motor pool for fear that a vehicle would break down and it would be their fault. It was shameful for them to have to report a damaged vehicle, even though accidents happen. If a vehicle was damaged due to poor driving, which was often the case, the ANA would shoot the vehicle with an RPG, fire a bunch of rounds into it, and blame the accident on a Taliban attack. Colonel Murtaza was well aware of such acts through his own channels and could identify

221

when such incidents occurred because the stories of the involved Soldiers rarely matched. One such incident occurred on March 16, 2011, when an ANA HMWVV rolled over, severely wounding four Afghan Soldiers and killing another. The platoon leader from the 1st Battalion involved in the accident fled to Kandahar City. However, based on the initial reports from the ANA, it was believed that he had been captured by the Taliban. It took several hours to straighten out the facts and for the ANA to track the platoon leader down in Kandahar City and return him to Zharay.

With the logistics of the ANA Brigade a constant work in progress, it was necessary to focus on the aspects of survival and being a Soldier. STRIKE subsequently concerned itself with ensuring the ANA knew the mantra "shoot, move, communication, and a little first aid."

Teaching the ANA to move tactically was relatively easy. The high threat of IEDs inspired the ANA to learn out of the sheer necessity for survival. Safely moving through the green zone meant following the path of *most* resistance. If there is a series of grape walls and a trail that runs along it, then you choose the more arduous path. You climb over the grape walls and clear the ground of IEDs as you move. Trails are too easy. When a Soldier is tired and undisciplined, they move to the trail, which is littered with IEDs. Similarly if there is stream or canal nearby, then you choose the water. You get wet to stay alive. The Taliban struggled make their IEDs waterproof, so the canals were safer than the hard ground.

The ANA also learned how to detect IEDs and operate the mine detectors. But as the combined force STRIKE adapted to the terrain of Zharay, the Taliban adapted to our techniques. Soldiers began finding IEDs on rooftops and in houses. There was no safe place in Zharay, so we taught the ANA to adapt and be disciplined. The ANA and STRIKE Soldiers shared risks everyday so to survive the ANA themselves began assessing situations and where the threat could be.

Accepting the fact that there were IEDs throughout the district and the tenacity of the Taliban to emplace ambushes in the dense foliage, the ANA needed a basic understanding of first aid. The STRIKE's medical company set up a training program for the ANA medics. The ANA medics received a basic course in Kabul but needed more knowledge and techniques to be useful in the field. The ANA medics were also given room in the aid station at FOB Wilson to run clinic hours. Working Shonna Ba Shonna with American doctors and medics, the ANA were able to learn more life-saving techniques as well as treat more mundane illnesses such as the flu and sometimes the sexually transmitted diseases that plagued the local population. The ANA throughout Zharay were taught how to apply tourniquets. Due to the often catastrophic damage inflicted by an IED, medics and doctors are not always able to save a limb, but a simple tourniquet applied correctly often saves a Soldier's life.

The United States Army and military as a whole is the best equipped and most technologically advance armed forces on the planet. In Afghanistan, like Iraq, I had both secret and unclassified internet connections, encrypted radios on both my vehicles as well as attached to my body armor that was no bigger than a walkie-talkie. I had handheld and vehicle mounted global positioning systems. I, like all American Soldiers, had the ability to stare at a screen and track other units traversing the battlespace.

Our Afghan partners, on the other hand, lacked modern and reliant communication equipment. The ANA used man-pack radios with giant whip antennas reminiscent of the Vietnam War and unsecured personal cell phones, which were spotty at best. The few cell phone towers that did exist in the districts were shut off at nightfall. The Taliban would threaten the tower operators to ensure power was turned off when darkness fell. The Taliban feared being tracked by their cell phones late at night, and so they wanted the towers off.

The ANA were highly efficient in talking on the radio, but their ability to provide an accurate picture of events remained limited. Brevity is a deeply ingrained virtue among American Soldiers, but the ANA often attempted to relay complex descriptions that were lost over the network. I could always just imagine the private in some distant operations center attempting to scribble down the longwinded message.

Literacy had not been a priority under the Taliban, so many of the ANA Soldiers who could read and write had only learned to do so relatively recently. Still, they tried. The ANA's Religious Officer doubled as the education Officer, and he pushed literacy programs throughout the Battalions, traveling to the small outposts to teach classes. Additionally, Colonel Murtaza sent a three-man team from

Camp Hero to FOB Wilson to teach literacy classes so that at the very least the Soldiers could read the Qu'ran.

Over the course of the deployment the communication skills of the ANA evolved. Their capabilities did not mimic ours so their skills did not need to meet ours; all the ANA needed was to be capable of getting their message out, whether it was a situational report or the daily personnel report to the leaders who made the decisions.

Firing a weapon was never an issue with the ANA. Firing a weapon accurately and in a controlled manner was the real issue. At ANA basic training the emphasis is on familiarization, not qualification.

Every American Soldier is taught basic rifle marksmanship during basic combat training, and when you arrive at your unit, you are assigned a weapon, which remains your weapon during your entire assignment with the unit. This process enables Soldiers to adjust the sights on the weapon to their position so that they will consistently hit a target at 300 meters. The ANA did not follow this process. Once again, out of fear of lost accountability or shame of a potential insider attack, the weapons were collected and locked up when the ANA were not on patrols. When the ANA prepared for patrols, the weapons were merely handed back out without concern for assignment.

Through several long discussions with Colonel Murtaza about the pros and cons of their weapon accountability method, I convinced him that they could still lock up the weapons upon completion of a patrol but also have them assigned to each Soldier according to their serial number. I explained to Colonel Murtaza that when we [the Americans] are not deployed, this is how we keep track of the weapons so that every time an Army unit goes to a range to practice, every Soldier has the same weapon every time. To me it was common sense, but in terms of overcoming the ANA's mindset, it proved to be a huge victory.

The American military consists of individuals who are not only fantastic war fighters but also trainers and instructors. The military system is designed so that Soldiers are taught and trained by other Soldiers. The Drill Sergeants at basic training are Soldiers. At the United States Military Academy, the future Officers are trained and instructed by Soldiers not only in combat skills but also English, chemistry, history, math, and so forth. At every unit in the Army, Soldiers are trained and prepared for war by other Soldiers. Consequently, the responsibility to teach others also sharpens the

Soldier instructor's level of expertise. With our ANA partners we struggled because the primary mission was always to destroy the enemies of the United States. But training our ANA partners was a close and competing second.

To that end, the STRIKE Legion Academy - Maiwand (SLA-M) was a program implemented by 3rd Squadron, 2nd Stryker Cavalry Regiment at COP Azizullah. The idea originated from our predecessor unit (5th Stryker Brigade, 2nd Infantry Division) in Zharay and Maiwand. The plan was for the unit to use its own non-commissioned Officers to train some of the non-commissioned Officers in the ANA and some of the Afghan National Police. There were Ministry of Defense training programs for the ANA and ANP alike, however, these schools were away from the district and limited in their number of available slots. Our SLA-M program allowed the Soldiers to stay near to the district and to further hone their skills in marksmanship, communication, and first aid. But more importantly, the program taught the ANA and the ANP how to lead themselves.

The Soldiers learned how to march others around, lead physical training sessions, and teach classes. Ten ANA Soldiers from 6th Battalion graduated on November 20, 2010, and were able to return to their platoons to teach their fellow Soldiers. Certificates were printed and presented to the Soldiers in a ceremony during which Colonel Murtaza praised them for their efforts and their desire to become better Soldiers. This served as a point of pride from the soldiers, and the presence of their leaders at the ceremony helped to build esprit de corps within the unit. Soon, more Soldiers in 6th Battalion were lining up to attend the course. Later SLA-M courses focused on maintenance of equipment like weapons and vehicles. Slowly the ANA Soldiers were gaining the skills that were required for long-term independence from ISAF partners.

Generating and maintaining a common operating picture is critical for military leaders so that decisions can be made quickly. The combined tactical operating center with its digital maps and instant updates is ideal for a fast and accurate depiction of the battlefield, but for our partners it was overwhelming. The U.S. Army trains using these tools so we are accustomed to how things look and where the information is. To our ANA partners the information meant little. To generate a common picture that could transcend not only technological limitations but also language barriers, our maps and graphics necessarily became cartoon sketches.

A simple sketch of Zharay could and did save countless hours of conversation via interpreters as we worked to ensure both the ANA and our own soldiers understood the plans. Then the ANA would draw and write out its operations order based on the sketch, and the STRIKE Brigade staff would do the same. The sketch concept worked to help diffuse other issues. For instance, at one point, the ANA staff had no clue which combat outpost had water wells to support their Soldiers. As such, Colonel Murtaza could not request wells for the other outposts. When asked about this by the ANA, I quickly rattled off a list of those outposts with wells, only to be met with confused looks. Sketches, once again, came in handy to overcome the language barrier and to develop a common operating picture we could all understand.

Consistently and constantly our ANA partners improved. Their ability to support themselves minimized the strain on American assets as well as gave them the confidence to operate on their own. The goal had been to develop our ANA partners so that they could "plan, prepare, and execute" operations on their own. By early April 2011, the ANA systems were working. The ANA were receiving orders from their higher headquarters and executing missions ranging from transporting Soldiers and goods from Camp Hero to FOB Wilson to conducting their own combat operations. The staff of 3-205 ANA was receiving orders to provide quick reaction forces and basic clearing operations and the ANA were able to execute them without seeking our assistance. Ideally, the ANA would have taken the lead in all operations and our combined patrols would have shifted from a 3-to-1 U.S./ANA ratio to a 1-to-3 U.S./ANA ratio. When the STRIKE Brigade left Afghanistan in May 2011, the ANA still had a long way to go to achieve complete independence but had improved drastically from the fledgling Brigade they had been just 10 months prior.

Chapter 20
Partners: Sons of the Shura

*A man may die, nations may rise and fall, but an idea
lives on.*

President John F. Kennedy

"Good idea fairy" is a military phrase that refers to that mythical
creature who whispers ideas and advice into our leaders' ears. The term
is not a favorable one and describes one of the most loathed
phenomena in the military, one in which subordinate Soldiers are stuck
making the often impossible or seemingly ridiculous "good ideas" a
reality. To be fair, not all ideas from the good idea fairy are bad. In fact,
many that appear inappropriate, out of place, or without context are by
design from higher-level leaders who have a different perspective on
the fight. Still, ideas from battalion, brigade, and division leadership
regularly seem inexplicable to the Soldier on the ground.

In Iraq, the explosive formed projectile (EFP) was an extremely
deadly type of IED that easily pierced vehicles' armor, even that
protecting our tanks. An EFP is a cylindrical tube generally six inches
or so wide that is packed with explosives and capped with a convex
copper top. When the explosives detonated, the pressure from the gas
and heat melted the copper as it exploded outward in the direction of
the cylinder like a cannon. The copper forms a molten slug. The slug,
like a bullet, travels with such velocity that it easily destroys everything
in its path. As the copper slowly cools in the air it is traveling through,
it hardens into copper shrapnel that tears through gear and people at
will until the projectile runs out of kinetic energy.

Everyone wanted to stop the deadly EFPs. The only true way to do
so, however, would have been to eliminate EPFs entirely by halting
their production and movement into our battlespace. This was not
possible so a lot of interim solutions were proposed. In other words,
the good idea fairy made its appearance.

In my battalion, I heard one solution of mounting water cans full of
sand on the sides of our Stryker vehicles to augment current armor.
The vehicles already had steel plates and RPG cages, which made them
look like dark, rumbling birdcages. This idea was quickly rejected when

I mentioned that by heating sand up to molten temperatures as the EFP passes through, glass would be formed, which is just as destructive to flesh as metal but does not show up on x-rays, making it even more difficult to find the shards.

Another similar proposal was to just use a bunch of water cans filled with water instead of sand, the concept being analogous to firing a bullet into a bucket of water. I calculated that two water cans would fit between the vehicle and the RPG cage, making one row, and you could fit six rows per side. There would then be 24 water cans on the vehicle each weighing forty pounds. In other words, we would adding nearly 1,000 pounds on an overtaxed vehicle without ever knowing if a foot of water would be enough, not to mention dealing with the containers bursting when penetrated by shrapnel.

Having a science background, I did some rough calculations and showed that this idea too was horribly flawed. Each vehicle would need nearly five feet worth of water surrounding the vehicle to dissipate the energy of an EFP enough to stop from entering the personnel area. The additional 5,000 pounds of water would destroy just about everything on the vehicle from the struts to the hydraulic systems. These critical systems give the vehicle its height and the engine would strain to move the vehicle now with additional 10 feet of girth around the battlefield.

With no easy solution in sight to stop EFPs, the hard and best solution was being good counterinsurgents. By gaining the support of the local population, we were able to harness the population's knowledge to stop production and employment of EFPs in our area through pinpoint raids.

In Afghanistan, the good idea fairy that I constantly grappled with was called the "Sons of the Shura." The concept of the Sons of the Shura (SoS) was based on the Afghan Local Police model that was being employed by Special Forces units in a few select villages. At the time there were only 13 ALP locations in Afghanistan, two of which were in our battlespace. One was in the Arghandab District and the other was out west in Maiwand District.

The ALP were meant to be a village initiative whereby the villagers could stand up and defend themselves against the Taliban. In many of the remote villages, conventional ISAF forces were unable to sustain their presence and keep the Taliban at bay, but with training and support from American Special Forces, the villagers would be able to defend themselves. The militias are a purely defensive force consisting of individuals who were vetted by both the Special Forces teams on the ground and the village elders. The individuals selected to be part of that force are then given uniforms, a small salary, and training by the SF teams. The ALP were given implicit instructions to conduct small patrols only around their village and to run checkpoints. If there was trouble with the Taliban attempting to gain access to the village, the ALP were backed up by their Special Forces Team that was only a phone call away and could bring tremendous fire power to any problem.

The crux of the ALP resides in arming the villagers to defend themselves. At least initially funded the ALP were funded and equipped by United States Special Forces, under their mandate for developing foreign internal defense forces. Under this mandate, Special Forces units were legally allowed to arm the villagers. The villages that had ALP were remarkably stable and secure whereas the surrounding villages were not. Many of the villagers that the STRIKE Brigade met with wanted ALP implemented in their communities. The villagers wanted to be responsible for their own security because the locals did not have reason to trust their government. Unsurprisingly, the Government of Afghanistan was hesitant to allow the ALP to spread throughout the country. The leadership in Afghanistan understood that the United States and NATO would eventually leave, and by arming so many villagers, they feared the U.S. ultimately could be creating militias and warlords that might challenge the Afghan Government.

Wanting to expand the STRIKE Brigade's ability to control Zharay and the surrounding districts, Colonel Kandarian proposed the concept of the "Sons of the Shura," which like the ALP would provide village stability and defense but would be run by the Brigade instead of Special Forces. For the STRIKE Brigade to execute such a concept, three hurdles needed to be overcome: one, support of the local Afghan government and Afghan security forces; two, a means to pay the villagers; and three, a means to arm the Afghans villagers.

In early October 2010, I flew with a small team to FOB Maholic, which was once Mullah Omar's house when he led the Taliban in the 1990s. At the small outpost on the northern edge of Kandahar City, I met with the Special Forces head of the village stability operations for southern Afghanistan and his men. The SF Lieutenant Colonel and his team of three walked us through their process of selecting villages, the pay scale for the villages, and the equipment needed for the villages before fielding a plethora of questions from us.

As I sat there listening and discussing village stability, I had grandiose visions of T.E. Lawrence. I did not foresee myself riding across the Registan desert on camel to lead the Afghans in open charges against the Taliban bases near the Pakistan border, rather I firmly believed that the only victory in Afghanistan would stem from the villages. Lawrence understood this. All security, like politics, is local.

By establishing stability and security in individual villages and then showing each village how it was interconnected to its neighboring villages, a security network and bubble would develop. Ultimately, through economic development, the villages would band together to form higher level government and provide common services such as education and justice. In time, the villages would connect to form a district, which would lead to the inception of a province and then ultimately a unified Afghan government. In many ways, the current Government of Afghanistan functions in the opposite manner. It was developed under international direction following the fall of the Taliban in 2001. The central government held Shuras to meet with distant villages of the country but was not formed by and is not empowered by the people.

The concept I developed for the Sons of the Shura would help bridge the gap between the Government of Afghanistan and the villages through the Afghan National Police. Through a multi-step process, the SoS would be created. The process would be deliberately and painstakingly slow to vet properly the individuals that the Brigade would be arming. Then under the guidance of the village elders, the SoS would swear an oath on the Qu'ran to defend their village and follow the instructions of their village leaders and the ANSF.

Importantly, the SoS would be accountable to the ANSF, and within a year of signing up for and pledging to the SoS, the individual was required to begin the process of becoming an Afghan National Police. The SoS was not touted as a long-term solution. The SoS concept was a program for immediate security within the villages that would lead to recruitment into the ANP under the Ministry of Interior's control.

In order to harness the local support necessary for the SoS to move forward, Colonel Kandarian reviewed the idea with Colonel Murtaza. He was initially hesitant but ultimately saw the SoS as an opportunity to free up his men from remote outposts and to consolidate them and their efforts. Colonel Murtaza's main concern was how to best control the SoS so that if his men had to conduct an operation, the SoS would not shoot at them and vice versa. There was no easy answer other than oversight, training, and communication.

On October 17, 2010, Colonel Murtaza and Colonel Kandarian together proposed the idea of the Sons of the Shura to the local leadership in Zharay including Karim Jan, the then-District Governor; Bismullah Jan, the District Chief of Police; and the other Bismullah Jan, the District's NDS Chief. As my notes from the meeting indicate, the SoS discussion was far from productive. The focal point for Karim Jan was on the need for village elders to be involved. Karim Jan's idea of village elders was the wealthy landowners who did not live in the district. These landowners only returned to Zharay from Kandahar City to collect rent from their tenant farmers and were not involved in day-to-day life in the villages. Karim Jan's "village elders" were his political and financial backers, swaying his allegiance to them and not the good of the local population that was struggling to survive. The district leaders also failed to grasp the concept of the village defense. Karim Jan instantly nominated Haji Lala to be the first individual to have an ISAF-backed militia, and they thought he should have 300 guards as well as vehicles and heavy weapons, all provided by STRIKE.

One problem with this idea among many was that Haji Lala lived in Sanjaray, which was the one heavily populated area within Zharay. Sanjaray was saturated by nearly two battalions worth of American and Afghan Soldiers. The SoS were needed in the remote villages further south, the villages deep in the green zone that we could access but not easily. The ideal villages consisted of a couple hundred people not the thousands living in Sanjary. So as the meeting with the district leadership disintegrated, Colonel Kandarian worked to defuse the notion of giving Haji Lala a militia and stressed that the individuals who made up the SoS had to be vetted by a village Shura, not one individual.

The meeting accomplished little beyond seeding the SoS concept into the minds of the district leadership. The concept still needed to be directed and focused, however. Karim Jan saw the SoS more as a means to consolidate power and make money than to shore up security.

In order to tout his works and efforts, Karim Jan invited Governor Wesa, Kandahar's provincial governor, to come talk to the people and hold Shuras in Zharay. Karim Jan believed that through these Shuras and trips along Highway One with the provincial governor, he could demonstrate his efforts toward bettering Zharay. The few trips he took with Governor Wesa, however, had the opposite effect. Karim Jan was removed as District Governor. Talking with the people, Governor Wesa realized that Karim Jan was not part of the district. The people never saw him, never heard from him. It is difficult to rebuild a district when the district governor does not live in the district. Karim Jan choose to spend his nights in the relative safety of Kandahar City.

So in a matter of a few short weeks, the SoS concept had been pitched to the district leadership and then the leadership was fired. The turnover temporarily shelved the SoS concept, but if it were still to be implemented, work remained to be done. So the STRIKE's staff continued working through two more difficult legal issues: paying the SoS and arming them.

A typical Army Brigade or military unit does not have the charter to raise a militia. Foreign Internal Defense (FID), as it is called, is, however, part of the Special Forces' mission and what a Green Beret spends years learning to do. A Special Forces unit simply requests funds, receives a bunch of cash, and then makes payouts as needed. For a typical Army unit, funds are more difficult to come by and are typically associated with a contract for services. In Iraq, stability was developed during the surge by paying the locals to guard their own streets and towns. The program was part of the "awakening movement" there, but in Afghanistan the rules were different. The Government of Afghanistan did not like the idea of Special Forces creating militias, let alone any and every conventional American unit doing the same. Contracts, in turn, needed to be creative so that when the time was right for the STRIKE Brigade to initiate the Sons of the Shura, the villagers would be paid to protect the critical infrastructure such as a much-needed water well. It was semantics, but it was just legal enough to work.

The last obstacle to be addressed was how to arm the SoS. Similar to the funding issue, Special Forces units have the mandate and ability to arm local villagers while a regular Army unit does not. The Brigade sought to get a legal exception through ISAF and the Afghan government in Kabul that would enable the Brigade to arm the SoS when we were ready to move forward with the project. That legal exception never materialized, however, forcing us to find alternatives that would circumvent our restrictions. Working with our ANA partners, I attempted to learn how they got rid of weapons found in caches and how we might redirect them to the people.

While working through the ANA's process, I learned that the ANA were upset that our Brigade was holding on to weapons found in Taliban caches. Their complaint was that STRIKE did not trust our ANA partners with the weapons, which was potentially a valid interpretation. For the ANA, having the weapons, even temporarily, was a point of pride. The ANA wanted to have their pictures taken with the weapons and have media releases to show the people of Zharay what they were doing for them and their security. I was delighted to hear that and explained to Colonels Murtaza and Quandahari that STRIKE Soldiers were not holding onto weapons to keep them away from the ANA rather they were treating them as evidence. Embedded law enforcement personnel were extracting fingerprints off the weapons, among other intelligence from the cache. Furthermore, the weapons were at times needed to prosecute an individual in the Afghan court systems and could not be destroyed.

The ANA really wanted any potential press conference to be held at Camp Hero so that they could be praised by General Hamid, but Colonel Kandarian and I suggested why would we not invite General Hamid out to Zharay. Let General Hamid come out and see the Soldiers of 3rd Brigade. Together with our ANA partners, a system was worked out in which once a month the weapons would be consolidated at FOB Wilson and then the ANA could hold a press conference in Zharay's district center.

As the discussion returned to the Sons of the Shura and possible using the captured weapons to arm the villagers, I began to understand the Afghan level of distrust. I learned that the Afghan Army was supposed to possess a detailed inventory of all captured weapons. And all weapons on the inventory were supposed to be destroyed. The inventory was to be sent ahead to Camp Hero so when the weapons arrived later, another inventory would occur. This process was designed to ensure that no weapons went "missing" during transportation. Hence, the ANA did not and, according to them, could not surrender weapons to the SoS program or give them to the villagers themselves. In the eyes of the ANA, it would have been rearming the enemy.

The ANA also did not trust the ANP to be in charge of the weapons. The ANP was recruiting new Officers and did not have enough weapons for everyone in its ranks. Despite the perception that the Afghans are laid back in terms their operations compared to NATO forces, the Afghans were extremely strict regarding accountability, especially when it involved sharing resources with their fellow ANSF. Since the ANP are under the Ministry of Interior and the ANA are under the Ministry of Defense, there was no legal way for the ANA to simply give the weapons to the ANP. Colonel Murtaza insisted that the only way he could give weapons to the ANP let alone the SoS would be if he had an order authorizing him to do so, which meant that General Hamid at 205th Corps would need permission from the Ministry of Defense, which would require permission from President Hamid Karzai.

As the path to arming potential Sons of the Shura volunteers stalled, the broader concept began to take hold when Karim Jan's replacement District Governor Sahardi engaged the people. He was an actual leader who listened to the people and their desires for the ALP concept. The people wanted better security in the remote villages.

Alternative ideas to arming the SoS began to float around the STRIKE plans cell. One idea from a colleague was to create a neighborhood watch. So instead of armed villagers who would be capable of keeping the Taliban at bay until ISAF and the ANA arrived, he wanted to give the villagers road guard vests, whistles, and cell phones to report Taliban movements.

Personally, I thought the neighborhood watch was a horrible idea on several levels. One, if the Taliban ever wondered who in the remote villages was supporting ISAF, all they would need to do was shoot the guys running around in bright orange and green fluorescent vests and blowing their whistles. Two, why give the villagers cell phones to report tips? Most villagers already had cell phones and were not reporting Taliban movements as it was anyway. And three, what happened at night when the Taliban turn off the cell towers and the villagers were left out on their own? By giving the villagers cell phones and guard vests, the Brigade would simply be making targets for the Taliban without any means for the villagers to defend themselves. If the SoS had weapons, in theory, they could fend off the Taliban long enough for the ANP, ANA, and/or ISAF to arrive. Without weapons, phones would do nothing.

The improved concept of the SoS as a "neighborhood watch" was briefed to Colonel Kandarian during a future plans update brief and not only did he scoff at it, he destroyed the notion. I was thankful that I was not the one briefing the idea. The bottom line remained that the Sons of the Shura needed to be armed.

There was a limited time frame that made the creation of the Sons of the Shura permissible in Zharay and that was during the winter. With both the thick foliage and Taliban gone from Zharay, the time to emplace the SoS in any village was before the green leaves and the Taliban returned for another fighting season. Ideally, one of the first villages to possess the SoS would have been on or just south of the security so that its location expanded ISAF's already developed security bubble. Such a village would also enable ISAF to respond rapidly to any incidents, further enhancing the villagers' trust in both ISAF and the ANSF.

Despite the growing support among the District's Leaders and ANSF as well as a potential means of funding, the SoS did not evolve off the drawing table and into the villages during the STRIKE Brigade's tenure in Afghanistan. No one was able to arm the Sons of the Shura. I understood the ANA's hesitance over providing weapons from a cache to the Sons of the Shura or even the ANP because as an American Soldier, I am bound by similar legal restrictions and accountability for my own assigned weapon. In the United States, the U.S. military does not give weapons to local police departments nor should an Afghan Army unit do the same. There are proper channels for a reason, and both the Ministry of Defense and Interior did not want to encourage the development of warlords, and maintaining strict control on available weapons was critical to that end.

The concept of the Sons of the Shura was a good idea, albeit a difficult one. I believed in local security, however the Brigade ran into several obstacles, and before we could overcome these legal impediments and employ the concept, time ran out. The green began returning in mid-March 2011, forcing STRIKE's focus to shift from the build phase of Economic Corridors to ensuring that our security road and new tactical infrastructure held. The returning Taliban needed to send a message following their defeat during Operation Dragon STRIKE, and we began receiving our replacement Brigade. Training and preparing our replacements became a priority to ensure their Soldiers could survive the rapidly approaching fighting season.

Chapter 21
Incoming and Outgoing

We few, we happy few, we band of brothers;
For he to-day that sheds his blood with me
Shall be my brother

Henry V
William Shakespeare

Time to go home. Soldiers were ready to go home. The heat, humidity, and the Taliban had taken a toll on the STRIKE Soldiers. Thoughts frequently drifted to home and to waiting families. As much as I and every other Soldier in the Brigade wanted to go home, the mission was not over yet. Like the dangers of a unit initially deploying, the complacency of redeploying is just as dangerous.

A relief in place, commonly referred to as a "RIP," describes the often-dangerous time of the transition of authority (TOA) from one unit to another. It's a precarious time because one unit is itching to get into the fight and one is itching to leave.

Toward the end of March 2011, elements of our replacement unit, 3rd Brigade ("Spartans"), 10th Mountain Division began arriving at Kandahar Airfield and moving onward to FOB Wilson and the surrounding combat outposts to relieve the STRIKE Brigade. The process would take nearly four tedious weeks as a lot of tasks needed to be completed.

There is generally a sense of complacency at all levels in the unit that is preparing to leave as the outgoing Soldiers have months (in our case, almost a year) of hard fighting under their belts and are ready to be back home with their families. Leaders try to fight the lack of enthusiasm, but it is difficult. Patrols and operations still continue, but Soldiers are distracted with packing their gear and equipment while simultaneously making room for the next unit. It is a ballet of logistics and operational needs. Soldiers are in a rush to get the job done so that they can leave, but these same veteran soldiers also need to show the new Soldiers the ropes on everything from heat acclimation to enemy tactics.

Patrolling with a new unit generally starts off slow with just the leaders of the new unit (a platoon leader, platoon sergeant, and squad leaders) going on patrols with the old unit to visualize and understand conditions and terrain. One could argue that the old platoon should just take the entire new platoon out with it as soon as possible so that all of the Soldiers of the new platoon learn together at once. The problem with that is there are too many people. A smaller force is often easier to control. So the leaders, returning from patrol, train their Soldiers on what they saw and experienced. As the days progress, more and more Soldiers of the new platoon are integrated into the daily patrols. The patrols tend to be a one for one swap. So as the new unit incorporates its Soldiers, the same number of Soldiers is left back at the patrol bases and forward operating bases to work packing equipment.

Ultimately a 50-50 mixture of new unit and old unit Soldiers are patrolling so that a fulcrum is reached. Progress beyond that point puts the new unit in the lead and the old unit in a limited and supportive role. This process occurs at all levels in the military, including staff sections, so that units entering a battle space are prepared as best as possible and can learn as much as possible from the old unit.

Depending on the conditions, the RIP can last for as long as a couple of weeks. In our case, the Spartans wanted an extended RIP to ensure their Soldiers were ready for the fighting season, which was mere days away. During the RIP with the Spartans, signal intelligence had pick up radio chatter from Taliban operating in the area, telling other fighters in the area to "shoot at the Soldiers with the swords on their patch and not the birds because the birds will fire back." The patch comments refer to the 10th Mountain Division's crossed bayonets, which form the roman numerals "10," while the bird refers to "Old Abe," the screaming eagle on the 101st Airborne Division's insignia. The STRIKE Brigade was the only 101st Division Unit in Kandahar Province and the comments, despite their ominous foreboding of future attacks, were a point of pride with STRIKE that the Taliban feared us.

My RIP was difficult to say the least. Major Travares had left the plans cell a month prior and moved to the 1-75 CAV to serve as their Operations Officer, which left Major Lancia in charge, who was the Brigade's Provost Marshall. She had spent the majority of the deployment working on governance at the Arghandab District Center, military police issues and coordinating the role of the Brigade's Tactical Explosive Detection Dogs (TEDDs) so her knowledge of the future plans was limited. The STRIKE Brigade was the first Brigade in the military to train its own Soldiers to handle military working dogs, and 60 Soldiers had been sent for training early in the deployment and returned a few weeks later with dogs capable of detecting explosives. With approximately four dogs per company, not a single combat patrol was conducted without a dog to help detect IEDs, vastly reducing the risk of IED-related injuries and death.

Major Lancia provided a tremendous life-saving asset to the Brigade with the TEDDs, and consequently she had not been through much of STRIKE's planning process. Major Cox had also moved on and passed his duties as the Brigade's Operations Officer to Major White. So between Majors Lancia and White, and in terms of knowledge in the operations and plans shop, I was the continuity.

In many ways, I had constantly and consistently been involved in the majority of the planning the entire time but my main priority and concern was turning over the handling of our Afghan National Army partners. I understood that the Spartans would come in with their own plans for operations and means of doing everything. Telling them our process would be irrelevant, so instead I sat down with their plans Officer and gave him a digital copy of all our plans and a brief history of the area, Economic Corridors, Dragon STRIKE, and other smaller operations. I knew Majors White and Lancia would also answer most of their questions regarding assets requests and plan submissions for higher level support such as drones, so I backed away from transferring the plans section over and focused on the ANA.

Once STRIKE left Zharay, the ANA were the only true continuity for the district. Through their actions on patrols and as partners to ISAF, the ANA could save lives, and the Spartans needed to know how to work with them and to continue their development throughout the Brigade.

The Spartan Brigade was coming in more aptly organized than the STRIKE Brigade had been. The Spartans had an organic Stability and Transition Team (STT) in addition to its infantry battalions to liaise with the ANA. The STT consisted of nearly 50 Soldiers and Officers, including an additional Colonel, a couple of Lieutenant Colonels, several Majors and Captains, plus a slew of senior non-commissioned

Officers. This nearly 50-man team would be doing what I had done for almost the entire deployment.

Ideally, the STT, a group of problem-solvers, could help train the Afghan security forces as well as push the partnership between the Afghans and an ISAF unit. The STT were intended to push the ANA's independence and sustainability. I, however, instantly saw issues develop, not in how the STT was task organized but more in their functionality as a unit. For each battalion, the Spartans designated four- to five-Soldier teams from the STT to embed with the battalions with their Afghan partners. However, the Spartans, including their subordinate Battalions, had not developed a personal relationship with their ANA partners yet. So instead of the ANA and the Spartans working side by side, they were simply standing side-by-side and talking and functioning through the STT Soldiers. No trust or relationship between leaders had been built.

During the RIP process, I attempted to instruct a Major and a Lieutenant Colonel in the STT that the embedded teams should be seen but not heard or perceived as a separate entity. My recommendations fell on deaf ears as the personalities of the STT leadership tended to be stronger than voices on the ground. It's easy to get involved in the day-to-day activities between partners but that does not necessarily or automatically build trust between partners. Instead the STTs were becoming intermediaries for conversations.

During the RIP process, I began to see the issues arise. In one instance, the STT Major came to me saying he had heard one of the STTs asking about buying gear for the ANA and about the ANA not wanting to go on certain missions. I equated the ANA request to the STT as a little kid asking one parent for something after the other parent has already said no. STRIKE was leaving and ANA had already received a "no" answer from us and were pushed to go on all missions. Now, the Spartans were there and so the ANA had a different partner from whom to make demands. The STT, however, was not helping itself recognize the partnership games.

To me, if a team of advisors is supposed to help the Afghan Army, then they need to be with the Afghans all the time. Instead, the STT sequestered itself away from the ANA Brigade Headquarters. The STT took over a small old brick building that had been the old 1-502 Infantry Battalion TOC and concerned itself with converting several of the rooms into a gym and movie room. I was disgusted with the thought and knew then that the STT would be completely ineffective in helping Colonel Murtaza and his staff.

Colonel Murtaza and his staff worked in and around the shared TOC complex with not only the STRIKE Brigade but now the Spartans, yet his "mentor" was in a small distant building. He would not be around for the constant little discussions that always arise or to be there when things needed to happen. The Afghan culture is not one where you simply show up for a meeting and leave. One need look no further than the *Pashtun-wali* tenant about hospitality. When working with the ANA, communication is through direct conversation not via email or phone. If the mentor is not present when a situation arises, he would likely only learn about the issue long after it has become irrelevant.

During the process, I felt my complacency and edginess toward the process growing. I was frustrated watching the STT move into an irrelevant role. Colonel Murtaza also seemed displeased at the process and the fact that he was going to have to start over with the Spartans.

From my perspective, I expected to see some appreciation not toward me but for the hard-earned knowledge that STRIKE was attempting to impart. Many Soldiers had died and lost limbs during the deployment, and the Spartans seemed to care little about learning from their sacrifices. I heard Soldiers from 3rd Brigade, 10th Mountain talk about not understanding why they had to climb over grape walls and move through canals. The Soldiers did not understand the IED threat.

I feared a resurgence of the Taliban upon our departure. I feared that the Spartans would suffer heavy losses and then cower on the outposts, giving the Taliban control again over the local population in Zharay. I feared that the partnership and trust built between the STRIKE Brigade and the ANA would disappear. It is not easy to build and develop relationships with a host nation's military, but STRIKE Soldiers at all levels and of every military occupational specialty had contributed to achieving that relationship. The relationship was not just built by leaders at the Brigade level but by the Soldiers who lived and patrolled with the ANA, with the cooks who helped initially feed the ANA in June 2010, to the welders and maintenance Soldiers who taught the ANA how to repair the Afghan equipment and vehicles, and to the medics who not only kept the wounded ANA alive in the heat of the battle but also taught their medics how to care for their fellow ANA Soldiers themselves.

Out with the old and in with the new is a constant in the current Army deployment cycle. The first flights back to Fort Campbell began on April 2, 2011, but would be stretched out for the next two months. The majority of the STRIKE Brigade would be back by the end of April but the Soldiers of 2nd Battalion, 502nd Infantry Regiment would stay a little longer. The Battalion moved to FOB Ramrod in Maiwand to conduct a series of air assaults with the Spartans to help shape conditions for the fight in Western Zharay and eastern Maiwand during the long, hot, and impending fighting season mere weeks away.

The clearing operations by 2-502 and its partners led to the reduction of IED belts around Nalgham, destruction of weapons caches and the interdiction of nearly half a million dollars worth of drugs. I had asked Major White if I could stay for a few more months but my request was ignored and I ended up leaving Afghanistan on April 16, 2011, two days before the Transition of Authority from the STRIKE Brigade to the Spartan Brigade. The area of operation for nearly a year for Combined Task Force STRIKE was now the responsibility of the Spartans who fought under a motto of "with my shield or on it."

From Kandahar Airfield, I flew to Manas Airbase in Kyrgyzstan where I had spent only a few hours transiting into Afghanistan nearly 10 months prior. Here I waited for nearly three horrifically boring days as a backlog of Soldiers, due to previous weather delays, was processed and sent to their destinations. I am not sure if I would have rather been there in Manas with the cool air and rains or back in the heavy heat and humidity of Kandahar Airfield where still others waited to leave.

At Manas we slept on bunk beds in large gymnasium-type buildings. I had gotten so used to my tiny cot, which was extremely hard and squeaked with every breath I took out on FOB Wilson, that the springs and softness of the mattress at Manas irritated me. I was used to being ultra-busy, constantly having something to do and now I had nothing. It was a waiting game. At Manas there was at least hot water, movies to watch, fresh coffee, and time to talk. I was on the same flight as one of my friends from the STRIKE Brigade staff, Major Gerry Nunziato who was STRIKE's Civil Affairs Officer.

With nothing but time on our hands, we talked about the future and where we were going. He was waiting for orders to return to Fort

Bragg, North Carolina, the home of Civil Affairs, while I could only wonder what would be next for me. I constantly asked myself whether I want to stay in or get out of the Army. I had already received orders for another permanent change of station and would not being staying at Fort Campbell. But my PCS would not be immediate. I had rapidly deployed and wondered about returning to my life. I wondered if my car worked since it sat in storage for a year, I wondered where my household goods and clothes were and when I would get them back again.

Finally after three days it was my turn to fly out, but as it turned out, that is not so simple. There would be several hundred other STRIKE Soldiers on the flight, and a Soldier simply does not walk onto a plane and leave as you do when you are deploying. To re-enter the United States, Soldiers returning from combat are required to go through customs inspections, metal detectors, and a complete head-to-toe search. Soldiers, despite having the best training in the world, sometimes have moral lapses and make mistakes. The process is designed to allow the Soldiers to go through an amnesty period to rid themselves of any potential contraband such as ammunition, grenades, war trophies like AK-47s, and anything else that is not personal property or had been assigned to them. Soldiers are given the opportunity to rid themselves of the items properly or face prosecution under the Uniformed Code of Military Justice. Nobody is perfect and sometimes rounds get stuck in pouches or brass ends up in the lining of body armor. Going through the same process in Kuwait when I was redeploying from Iraq, I found a smoke grenade that had been buried in a pouch. I had been injured on my final patrol in Iraq and broken my arm and had somehow missed the grenade until that point. Soldiers generally do the right thing and put the found items in the amnesty boxes for disposal.

Moving an entire flight's worth of Soldiers through the inspection process, though, takes several hours and upon completion everyone is in lock down in a small waiting area while all the large duffle bags and tough boxes filled with sensitive equipment are packed up, placed on pallets, and strapped down for the flight. Everything and everyone is weighed. Only then, when the plane is ready, could we finally begin the boarding process by filing in true Soldierly fashion onto the plane.

I had expected to fly through Leipzig, Germany, as I had on the way to Afghanistan but this time the plane stopped for fuel in Cork, Ireland. After deplaning while the plane was refueled, Soldiers wandered through the airport, taunted by the Guinness and whiskey advertisements everywhere. Unfortunately, as Soldiers still in transit from combat, we were not allowed to imbibe.

Taking off again for the final leg back to Fort Campbell, I remember staring out the window and the beautiful green fields of Ireland and thinking how far we'd come. Days prior I had been covered in dust and dripping sweat in Zharay and now I was one final leg from the United States. In Afghanistan like many other STRIKE Soldiers and other deployed Soldiers, I would go days without being able to shower due to a lack of water or find myself suddenly being shot at or near an exploding rocket. Then a flight changed everything. It would be a sudden transition back to civilization: driving cars while obeying speed limits, ordering whatever you want at a restaurant, and using a cell phone. During deployment whenever I went to the DFAC, I got whatever was being served, and you don't get it your way. You get the food however it is prepared. I would need to get used to making choices again.

Hours later the plane descended from the dark sky to land at the Fort Campbell Army Airfield, and sitting there while the plane taxied to the passenger terminal, the excitement was palpable. Young or old, Officer or Soldier, it did not matter as STRIKE Soldiers stared out of the windows looking at the large crowd, no one was immune from the excitement. It was our homecoming. Husbands, wives, children, parents, all waited for that plane with signs, tears, and roaring applause. Like my previous deployment, I had no one waiting for me and after the long flight had accepted that fact.

I lingered on the plane to allow the younger Soldiers off first to see their families. I had no arms to rush into and figured that I would probably get run over as the Soldiers raced to their families. When I finally got off the plane, sitting at the base of the stairs was Specialist David Bixler and several other wounded warriors from the Brigade. Specialist Bixler had earned the Silver Star and Purple Heart for running off a cleared path to save the life of a fellow Soldier on September 30, 2010. The Soldier that SPC Bixler saved was not an

American but his Afghan partner. During his efforts SPC Bixler stepped on a pressure-plated IED and lost both of his legs.

Seeing SPC Bixler and the other wounded warriors I realized that I could not feel sorry for myself that no family was there to meet me because in reality I was surrounded by my family. Soldiers like SPC Bixler did not feel sorry for themselves. SPC Bixler chose to come out to welcome his friends and fellow Soldiers back home. Shaking his hand as I passed by, I thanked him for all he had done for STRIKE and moved to my place with the other Soldiers from my flight so that we could all be released into the care of our families.

On that tarmac I was both sad and happy to be home. I was happy to be home, to hold my son and see how big he had gotten. I was sad that others would not be able to do the same. My fellow STRIKE Soldiers had given so much over the past year to defeat the Taliban in their historic home. The STRIKE Brigade had fought valiantly with our Afghan Army partners in the districts of Arghandab, Zharay, and Maiwand, and in the Horn of Panjwa'i. Staff Sergeant James Hunter would be the first STRIKE Soldier to be killed in Afghanistan on June 18, 2010, near the village of Pashmul, and Corporal Brandon Kirton would be the last to die during the Brigade's fight in Afghanistan on May 18, 2011.

Together, Hunter, Kirton, and the rest of STRIKE had conducted the largest combined clearing operation to date in Afghanistan. All Soldiers in the Brigade strove everyday to not only destroy the enemy but to also build a better Afghanistan. Some Soldiers, in their efforts, made the ultimate sacrifice. In total, 65 American Soldiers were killed fighting for the STRIKE Brigade in the environs around Kandahar City from June 2010 to May 2011.

Many STRIKE Soldiers would return home heroes: 111 Soldiers earned the Army Commendation Medal with V-device for Valor, 38 earned a Bronze Star with V-device for Valor, five Soldiers earned Silver Stars, and one Soldier would earn the Distinguished Service Cross, the second highest medal for Valor in the United States military.

For extraordinary heroism during Operation Dragon STRIKE between September 16, 2010, and December 06, 2010, the brigade would be awarded the Presidential Unit Citation, which is the highest military honor a unit can receive. For extraordinary heroism for operations in Kandahar Province from June 29, 2010, to April 18, 2011, the STRIKE would also be awarded the Valorous Unit Award.

For the majority, however, simply returning home would be enough considering the nearly 600 earned Purple Hearts for wounds sustained in combat.

Leaving the hangar at Fort Campbell's Airfield, I was thankful to be back in the States and wondered when I would return to Afghanistan again. Despite STRIKE's best efforts, I knew that the Taliban were not defeated. The Taliban would slip through the porous border of Pakistan and back into southern Afghanistan.

The Taliban would test the Spartans' resolve and their ability to hold Zharay. Mullah Mohammad Omar and his Taliban followers could not and would not let their previous defeat go unanswered. Only time would tell if what my fellow STRIKE Soldiers and I did was successful, meaningful, and contributed to the long-term stability of the people of the districts of Arghandab, Zharay, and Maiwand, of the people of Afghanistan.

Epilogue

June 2014
West Point, NY

It has been over three years since leaving FOB Wilson. During that time, a lot has changed and much has not. Both the United States Army and Afghanistan are transitioning. No one knows what the future will hold for either.

The future of the Army is slightly more predictable. The Army, which has fought continuously for the last 13 years, is on its way to becoming the smallest it has been since before World War II, yet the fighting is not over. The constant threat of global instability ensures the Army will continue to deploy. There are NATO obligations to rebuff Russia in Ukraine, Africa remains a constant topic, and recently Iraq continues to devolve into a potential civil war. Deployments will not necessarily be as a combat force but as advisors, trainers, and operators in multi-national training exercises.

Afghanistan is more complicated. I constantly follow the news to see what is happening with both the STRIKE Brigade and with Kandahar. STRIKE is back in Afghanistan for its third deployment since 2010. The past two deployments, the Brigade served as advisors and trainers to the Afghan Army.

As STRIKE fights on elsewhere, Zharay remains a troubled spot. On October 7, 2013, a group of 40 U.S. Army Rangers infiltrated Zharay late at night to extract a high-value individual. The group was moving from the landing zone into the compound of the target when an improvised explosive device detonated. The blast instantly killed four while seriously wounding fourteen. Among those killed was First Lieutenant Jennifer Moreno who was commissioned as an Army Nurse but volunteered to serve with the Rangers as part of a cultural support team. Such teams are designed to help the Army become more effective and improve the Army's ability to engage and interact with local women.

About 10 weeks later, Forward Operating Base Wilson, now named Pasab, was heinously attacked. A group of insurgents attacked the base wearing suicide improvised explosive vests as well as a vehicle-borne IED on January 20, 2014. The attack was initiated with the detonation of the vehicle rapidly followed by the arrival of the eight additional suicide bombers who attempted to storm the gate and gain entry into the base. The initial blast killed one American Soldier and looking at pictures of the damage, I was reminded of my time at FOB Wilson. I remember watching our Soldiers build the gates and walls. HESCO baskets were connected and filled to create an impenetrable barrier. I remember the HESCOs next to the TOC absorbing 82mm recoilless rifle rounds during my first day. I remember sleeping next to the HESCOs along the landing zone because there were no cots or tents available. Seeing the pictures of the aftermath, I was saddened by the loss of life and wondered what STRIKE would do. I felt I should have been there.

Such horrific attacks and loss of life could be seen as ISAF failure, however I see it as desperation by the Taliban. Afghanistan is at a pivotal point. The Taliban is floundering in its attempt to connect to the people, to solidify a power base in their historical home before the transition occurs.

Shortly after returning from Afghanistan, I was visiting family in New York City when the news broke that Osama bin Laden had been killed. The daring raid by a team of Navy Seals, CIA operatives, and members of the Army's 160th Special Operations Aviation Regiment (Nightstalkers) into Pakistan is the stuff of movies and Tom Clancy novels. Yet the United States military did it, demonstrating an unrelenting resolve to complete the mission.

I was staying at an apartment near Manhattan's financial district the night of May 1, 2011, and staring out the window, I could see that hollowed space that is ground zero. From the window, I stared in awe at the construction site whose lights never dimmed. Twenty-four hours a day, the site grew. In the streets, New Yorkers whose lives had been shattered nearly a decade prior were celebrating.

The landscape of New York and indeed the world itself was changed forever on that horrific day in 2001. It was that day that pushed me to want to serve, and it was the continued fight that took me to Afghanistan. Serendipitously ten years later, I learned of Osama Bin Laden's death at the site of the attack in New York City.

A few days later, I was back at Fort Campbell when President Obama addressed the Soldiers of the 101st Airborne Division in person after having just met with the members of Seal Team 6 and the 160th

Nightstalkers, the team that conducted that daring raid. Still I understood that the mission was not over. Osama bin Laden might be dead, but the Taliban lived on.

I had seen the devastation that the STRIKE Brigade had inflicted on the Taliban in the Arghandab, Zharay, Maiwand, and the Horn of Panjwa'i. Just as the U.S. had remained resilient in its search for Osama bin Laden, the insurgents were also resilient. In the summer of 2011 the Taliban needed to come back to Zharay and the environs of Kandahar. The Taliban needed to make a statement, but it was not my turn to fight. The Soldiers of the 3rd Brigade, 10th Mountain Division had to stand its ground, the ground STRIKE fought hard to gain. The new Soldiers had to continue to make strides in connecting the people to the government.

Sadly, I was leaving the brigade and the 101st Airborne Division. As fast as I had arrived, I was once again leaving. I had orders, and while President Obama was speaking to Soldiers from my brigade, I was clearing Fort Campbell to move to Fort Jackson, South Carolina. Within a month I would become a company commander. And despite my duties as a company commander and in other positions over the past few years I have kept an eye on the security, stability, and events as they occur in Zharay and around Kandahar City. I have remained curious about STRIKE Brigade's legacy and if our efforts have truly made a lasting difference.

I am not so sure though. There is a tradition, though not written, to blame the other guy. As a new unit comes into an area, it will blame the departing unit for the situation it inherited. Right or wrong, it is always easier to pass blame, and I am pretty sure the Spartans of 3rd Brigade, 10th Mountain Division did. Though both Brigades are Infantry Brigades in the United States Army, we both had different leaders and different ways of fighting.

Reading the news about Kandahar, I was happy to see the Afghan National Army in the lead at times and at others dismayed in my perception of how the Afghans were fighting. Like all Soldiers, I have opinions about how things should be done and how to fight, but I had my chance and it was now someone else's turn.

I was saddened to see young Soldiers killed due to inaction. I suspected that the Spartans took a more cautious approach to counterinsurgency operations. The paradox of COIN is you must be with the local population to gain their trust and improve, safety and security. If a unit separates themselves from the local population too much and thereby alienates the local security forces, then the risk to the unit increases. Risks are continual in combat, but the goal is to minimize them in the long term, not abide them. The more action and involvement a unit has, the safer the unit becomes.

In February 2012 I had the honor of being on a flight and sitting next to LTC (retired) Alfred Rascon and SSG (retired) Salvatore Giunta, both Medal for Honor recipients from the 173rd Infantry Brigade for actions in Vietnam and Afghanistan, respectively. As I talked with SSG Sal Giunta, he described with complete humility that the he was just doing his job. He earned the nation's highest medal for valor doing what he was trained to do and trying to save his friend and battle buddy. His words reminded me of Specialist Bixler who ran into an IED-laden field to save his ANA counterpart and SSG Rivadeneira who placed himself between a suicide bomber and his men, even managing to fire two rounds into the chest of the bomber before the man detonated the bomb strapped to him. SSG Rivadeneira sacrificed himself for his men. Those are the heroes and the memories that are etched in my mind. Those who fought day in and day out against the entrenched Taliban are the heroes and legacy of STRIKE.

Sadly, the actions of a few individuals despite all great successes can tarnish a unit and be detrimental to the counterinsurgents progress. On March 11, 2012, 16 civilians including men, women, and children, near the village of Zangabad in the Horn of Panjwa'i were murdered. Zangabad was one of the three objects for Gad Zawak during Operation Dragon STRIKE and our success left a NATO presence in the Horn.

Former Army Staff Sergeant Robert Bales pled guilty to murder and is currently serving a life sentence for the murders. Combined with the "kill squad" from 5th Brigade, 2nd Infantry Division that was based at FOB Ramrod in Maiwand District prior to the STRIKE Brigade's arrival in 2010, it is no wonder the people of southern Afghanistan possess a deep distrust of foreign troops. Before we arrived and after we left, the locals endured tragedy and crime.

For every inch of progress made in the fight against the Taliban, it only takes a single individual to erode that momentum. Counterinsurgencies' success is dependent on the critical thinking and hard decisions made by individuals in the fight and on the ground. And when those decisions are wrong and not immediately corrected, the enemy wins.

The "kill squads" and Robert Bales of the world are recruiting tools for the Taliban and other jihadists groups. Insurgents gain strength when the counterinsurgent flounders, forcing the counterinsurgent to attempt to regain the initiative. Regaining lost trust from the population is never easy.

Insider attacks and distrust in 2012 were on the rise. Some could argue that the actions of individuals like Robert Bales and the "kill squad" have no correlation with the increased number of insider attacks, rather such attacks are just the Taliban implementing a new tactic. The counter argument to such statements is that insider attacks are an indicator of individuals being swayed to a cause by extrinsic actions.

The individuals willing to conduct such acts are those who sit on the fence, those who are unsure of their beliefs and are easily swayed by current events and propaganda. These young men joined the Afghan Army and Police to defend their country but something changed in them. Something, whether a person or event, caused them to lash out against their partners. These events might be the heinous killings of Afghan citizens who died while sleeping in their homes in Panjwa'i or the act of an unhinged pastor in Florida who decides he must burn the Qur'an.

There will likely always exist three populations of people in Afghanistan. The first two are resolute in their beliefs and side either with the Government of Afghanistan or with the Taliban. Both resolute groups will also constantly fight over the third group, the undecided, because whoever controls the on-the-fence population will control Afghanistan.

Insider attacks make headlines and erode trust between ISAF and the Afghan security forces, but it does not sway the population like the senseless killing of civilians does. ISAF has the capabilities to build massive walls and compounds to protect ourselves but that does not help the people nor our Afghan counterparts who lack that luxury. Afghanistan is the home of the ANSF and the Afghans simply do not have the ability to hide. The risk of insider attacks is high for both ANSF and ISAF and should be a mutually shared issue. The risk, if shared, could be minimized and inspire trust. Solving insider attacks is a process that is easier said than done, but it is an inherent risk of combat.

General Curtis LeMay, a World War II pilot and later head of Strategic Air Command, once said, "I'll tell you what war is about. You've got to kill people, and when you kill enough of them, they stop fighting." The combat that General LeMay, spoke of, however, is not the combat of Afghanistan. The Taliban does not have an Army like the Nazis or the Japanese. The Taliban has fighters who believe in the cause and are recruited into the ranks by that cause. Counterinsurgency is about breaking the cycle, about showing the local population that another way exists.

Counterinsurgency operations are expensive, time consuming, and dangerous regardless of whether the counterinsurgents are working in Afghanistan, Iraq, Vietnam, Africa or any other area in the world. There is no simple or easy fix; only through long-term commitment is the counterinsurgent able to create a stable and secure environment. Afghanistan is referred to as the "Graveyard of Empires." Afghanistan has endured Alexander The Great, the British, the Soviet Union, and the Taliban. Breaking the invasion trend in Afghanistan means ensuring that the people believe in the Afghan Government and its representative institutions such as the Army and Police.

The commitment necessary for success as a counterinsurgent does not mean increased numbers of Soldiers and troops on the ground but through commitment of financial support, trainers, and as an opportunity to legitimize the Afghan government at all levels once security is established and maintained.

Thirty-four months since redeploying, I still have hope for Afghanistan and the Afghan people. The people of Afghanistan need to care more about their future than NATO or any other extrinsic organization does. I am optimistic but my optimism is fading. Setbacks are mounting and the initiative is diminishing. The STRIKE Brigade gave the districts of Arghandab, Zharay, and Maiwand an opportunity for success. The Soldiers of STRIKE gave the people of those districts their best efforts and set the conditions for success. The Taliban was cleared, a plan was implemented to hold the Taliban at bay away from the local population, and governance and economic development began. STRIKE turned over the districts in a better condition than we had found it.

With its over 8,000 Soldiers involved, Operation Dragon STRIKE still remains the largest combined operation to have occurred in Afghanistan. The sacrifices for success are worn in the heavy Black Hearts of those that were there and the 65 families that will be forever without their loved ones. For its actions and valor during Operation Dragon STRIKE and the deployment to Afghanistan, the Brigade was awarded the President Unit Citation and the Valorous Unit Award. Over the course of the deployment, the Soldiers of STRIKE would collective earn one Distinguished Service Cross, five Silver Stars, 38 Bronze Stars with V device, and 111 Army Commendation Medals with V device.

Only time will tell if what we as the STRIKE Brigade and as a nation have done is enough. Afghanistan will transition, hopefully into something new and not return to the grips of the Taliban. I will forever by proud of my fellow STRIKE Soldiers and our efforts. I continue to use what I learned under the great leaders and Soldiers of STRIKE.

I am a STRIKE Soldier! I fight where I am told and I win where I fight!

Index

About the Author

Captain Hummel was raised in Fort Myers, Florida. He is a graduate of Boston College and joined the Army in 2005 after completing graduate school at the University of Iowa. Following completion of Basic Combat Training, Captain Hummel attended Officer Candidate School and was commissioned a Second Lieutenant in December 2005. He has served in a variety of leadership and staff roles. He deployed to Iraq in 2007 with 2nd Cavalry (Stryker) Regiment from Vilseck, Germany, as part of the surge working both as a Squadron Battle Captain and Platoon Leader. Following the deployment, Captain Hummel worked on the United States Army Europe Staff as a CBRN Operations and Plans Officer.

After completing the Captains Career Course in 2010, Captain Hummel joined the 2nd Brigade (STRIKE), 101st Airborne (Air Assault) Division from Fort Campbell, Kentucky, for its deployment to Afghanistan for OEF 10-11.

Captain Hummel continues to serve in the Army, having recently completed graduate school at Vanderbilt University. Captain Hummel is currently an instructor in the Department of Chemistry and Life Science at the United States Military Academy at West Point.

Made in the USA
Charleston, SC
04 March 2017